The Three Minute Meditator
Fifth Completely Revised Edition

© David Harp and Nina Smiley, 2007

mind's i press   ISBN 978 - 0 - 918321 - 43 - 5

To purchase additional copies, please visit

www.thethreeminutemeditator.com

or Call 1 - (800) MOJO - IS - I (665 - 6474)

We'd like to hear from you!
Please contact David Harp at
david@davidharp.com
or Nina Smiley at
nsmiley@mohonk.com
with any suggestions.

First Edition	Second Edition	Third Edition	Fourth Edition

Also Available in a
Variety of Foreign
Language Editions

Important

We believe that meditation is one of the healthiest habits that you can cultivate. But if you are currently under the care of a physician or undergoing psychotherapy, please discuss this program with your doctor or therapist before you begin. We would also like to stress (if you'll pardon our use of that word) that this program is explicitly not meant to be used in lieu of either medical or psychological help. Should meditation raise your awareness of physical or emotional issues that you feel uncomfortable with, or that need to be dealt with, please seek the help of a competent professional.

Acknowledgements: David

I would like to thank two groups of people for their help and inspiration:

They are, firstly, my teachers and mentors. Some, like Stephen and Ondrea Levine and Jack Kornfield, have gifted me with their spriritual guidance. Others, like Charles Garfield, Matthew McKay (whom I must also thank effusively for allowing me to use portions from our book Neural Path Therapy), and Stephen Bank, have furnished me with role models and training in my role as a counselor. Others yet, such as Karl Scheibe, the late Robert Knapp, Nina Menrath, Art Warmoth, and Larry Horowitz, have helped to provide me with the academic background necessary to produce even a simple book like this.

They are, secondly, my clients. From the Shanti Project in the late 1970's to the Haight Ashbury Free Clinic in the early 1980's to the Marin County Grief Project and other organizations for whom I now do some volunteer counseling — my clients have taught me the value of opening my heart. From its bottom, I thank them today.

I must also thank my partner, Rita Ricketson, for her indispensable help and support (and for Katie and Lily, too).

And of course my beloved twin, Nina.

—David

Acknowledgements: Nina

With love to Frieda and Fred, who gave us our start.
To Bert, for being such a remarkable partner in all aspects of my life.
To David, my remarkable twin, whose sharing goes so deep.
And to all whose hearts I've touched along the way, and who have touched mine — you know who you are.
With delight in discovery, one moment at a time…

— Nina

READ THIS FIRST...

Welcome to the fifth (and completely revised) edition of *The Three Minute Meditator*.

In the first pages of our book, we — David and Nina — want to introduce ourselves and offer some general information about the life-enhancing practice of meditation and mindfulness (which we'll define in a moment, if these terms are new to you).

We know that some of you will want to get working, right away, on the "how tos" of the book — the actual exercises. So we'll begin by describing how you can use the "Box Method" if you want to get started with the substance of this book as quickly as possible.

For now, all you need to know is that Step One, Understanding The Mind has basic building blocks that provide a larger context for Step Two, Clearing The Mind, which contains the bulk of the actual Three Minute Meditator exercises.

As you'll see on the next page, we make it easy for you to read only as much as you like, while still getting the most important information in a convenient format.

Quick Start: The Box Method

In a rush to get started? The most important elements of each page or section of the book are "boxed." Readers who want to quickly reach the first Three Minute Meditation Exercises in Chapter Four can use the "Box Method" to start doing the work right away rather than reading about it. You can still get the gist of the theory sections in Chapters One, Two, and Three just by reading each boxed section of the text as it appears.

So if you can't wait, just skim through the pages. Look at each boldface heading and feel free to read as much as you'd like of any section that particularly appeals to you. If the heading doesn't grab you, just skip from one box to the next. This will get you to the first meditation exercise and through Step One, in no time at all!

Then, after you've gotten a few of the Three Minute Meditations from Step Two under your mental belt, you can always come back and read the whole rest of Step One at your leisure!

If you're not in that much of a hurry, you're welcome to read every word of text — including, of course, all the boxes.

In the pages that follow, we'll talk about who we are and offer you some simple definitions that may come in handy. We'll discuss how this book is organized (and include two very different ways of describing that organization). We'll talk about why many meditation books and methods are not beginner-friendly, and end by looking at why you probably need to meditate...and why we definitely did!

> **Please read the entire section that precedes this box.**
>
> **Then, if you're in a big rush to begin meditating, you can read only the "Boxed" sections.**
>
> **Simply scan and skim and skip your way down to the next box, making sure to check out all headings and diagrams!**

It's Not All About Us, But...

Some of you may want to know our story before you begin to use *The Three Minute Meditator* program. Others may not. With the Box Method, it's your choice!

> Want some biographical info on us? Then read on. If not, skim and skip your way down to the next box!

Twins...

From college on, we may have looked reasonably successful and popular to other people, especially those who didn't know us intimately. But inside David was vain, insecure, and prone to anger, compulsively macho, and a hypochondriac to boot. Nina, on the other hand, tended towards depression, was overwhelmed by clutter, and had a difficult time being direct about her feelings. Our thoughts and emotions seemed to control us, rather than the other way around.

It's no exaggeration to say that learning to meditate has transformed our lives. Although life is still far from perfect, every time we meditate, our ability to handle old fears and desires (or new ones) grows stronger. Relationships with friends and family become more loving and less judgmental. We like ourselves better. And we're even beginning — as our practice continues — to feel some minimal control over that mysterious, mutinous creature called the mind.

Using the exercises and concepts in this book for only minutes each day, you can let go of fear, anger, and stress. *The Three Minute Meditator* techniques have enhanced our abilities to live fully and joyfully, one moment at a time. They can do the same for you.

...and Teachers!

Although we've taken very different career paths, we are both teachers. And whenever we learn to do something, we like to teach it, in the simplest way possible, so as to offer "immediate gratification" to our students.

In addition to his work on meditation and mindfulness, David has taught close to a million people to play the blues harmonica (he holds the undisputed world's record for "Most People Taught to Play Harmonica at One Time") and has created two dozen instructional books, CDs, and videos. Their topics range from harmonica (of course!) and a variety of other musical instruments to music theory, back pain, and how to fight the common cold. He is also the creator of Harmonica-Based Mindfulness™, Harmonica-Based Stress Reduction™, and HarmonicaYoga™!

In the process of teaching many hundreds of workshops, he's learned a lot about how people learn. And he's drawn upon Nina's background in psychology as well. But perhaps his most important finding is that most people, when learning something new, are more successful if they learn to perform the skill "a little bit" right away, rather than taking a long time to learn to do it perfectly. Big surprise!

Nina discovered another aspect of the same phenomenon, when, after receiving her Ph.D. in psychology from Princeton, she taught at the University of Maryland. Some students would become very anxious at the start of a difficult course. "Fear of failure" would lead to heightened stress that would hamper their ability to concentrate. As David did, she realized that simplified basic instruction and early success are important components of an effective teaching method.

Nina now teaches mindfulness and Three Minute Meditation techniques at Mohonk Mountain House, a Victorian castle resort in New Paltz, New York. She has also developed a program, Never Diet Again: Welcoming Weight Loss and Wellness, that combines mindfulness and small successes into simple life-changing techniques.

Out of our personal and teaching experiences, the concept of *The Three Minute Meditator* was born — It is better to do three minutes, two minutes, or even 30 seconds of meditation and feel some benefit, than to say "I can't..." and never even try.

Many tens of thousands of people have used *The Three Minute Meditator* method to develop the clear, serene, compassionate mental state that is known as "mindfulness."

It works, *if* you use it. The choice is yours!

Definitions: "Meditation" "Mindfulness" and "Exercise"

The following definitions are important so we've "boxed" them.

> **Meditation** is the art of mental self-control. Each of the Three Minute Meditations in this book is an **exercise** that will help you understand and gain control over your mind and your thoughts.
>
> **Mindfulness** is a mental state characterized by clarity, insight, compassion, and serenity, no matter what is going on around you. For thousands of years, meditation has been considered the most effective method for developing mindfulness.
>
> So meditation is the type of exercise that will bring you to the state of mindfulness. Just like weight-lifting is the type of exercise that will bring you to the state of being strong...

How This Book Is Organized

The Three Minute Meditator is divided into seven steps. Each step consists of a number of chapters.

Usually, the first chapters of each step will offer lots of general instruction and some personal anecdotes, as well as hints, examples, and metaphors. Then, in later chapters of the step, we'll give you a variety of exercises to choose from.

Each chapter ends with an "...In a Nutshell" page (which provides you with a quick bottom line account of what you need to know, remember, or continue to work on from that chapter).

Each step ends with a "What You Need to Know" section that briefly describes the most important elements or lessons of that entire step. If you happen to put the book down for a while, this makes it easy to review only the "What You Need to Know" pages for each step, before starting a new step.

The Seven Steps

Although this book is action-oriented, we believe that understanding the human mind is the first step towards working more skillfully with it. Thus we include a certain amount of the theory and philosophy of meditation, as well as the cognitive (brain function) science that lies beneath it. We've arranged the book so that most of the basic theoretical material is in *Step One: Understanding the Mind,* which is composed of Chapters One through Six.

Step Two (Chapters Seven through Fourteen) is the heart of the book — the most basic Three Minute Meditation exercises. We call these *"Clearing the Mind"* meditations. They can be learned almost instantly, and practiced, with great benefits, for a lifetime. Each of these is an exercise for building the "Mental Muscle™" (more on this, later). Mental Muscle™ allows us to reduce stress and enhance well-being, by working more skillfully with thoughts, words, events, and emotions.

In *Step Three: Watching the Mind* (Chapters Fifteen through Eighteen), we'll present a series of analogies and exercises that will help us focus our mental attention onto the mind itself. You'll learn to look at your thoughts as though you were watching a movie or DVD, and learn to "map" your own neural paths as they criss-cross through your "neural neighborhood."

In *Step Four* (Chapters Nineteen and Twenty), you'll learn the Visualization techniques that will supercharge your mindfulness practice, the attention splitting" Progressive Neural Desensitization technique that will allow you to work more easily with painful thoughts or events, and the Relaxation Exercises which will help you both to relax your body, and to handle physical pain in a more skillful manner.

After you've spent some time with the exercises in Step Two, Step Three, and Step Four — you'll be ready for Chapters Twenty-One and Twenty-Two, which make up *Step Five: Softening Around Pain*. In this part of the book, we will provide you with simple and effective exercises that will help you begin to deal more skillfully with both physical and mental pain.

In *Step Six: Great States* (Chapters Twenty-Three through Twenty-Five) , you'll learn how to cultivate three essential mental states — "Compassion," "Don't Know," and "Non-Judging" — that will further help you to gain control of that often mutinous entity known as the human mind!

Step Seven: Living in the Now (and The Master Skill) will introduce you to a way of being in the world which creates a sense of spaciousness, clarity, and grace. Some people would call this the "mindful lifestyle." Regardless of the label, we think it's just the most satisfying and practical way to be.

The Appendices: Spiritual and Specific

We'll begin the Appendix part of the book with a section entitled *Further On Down the Road: The Meaning of Life and the Life of Meaning*. It consists of dogma-free material which can be used either to enhance the practice of any religious tradition that you may already be involved with, or used on its own. This may or may not be of interest to you at all. Or you may decide to work with the Seven Steps for now, to get the down-to-earth, real-world benefits, and come back to the "bigger picture" later on.

Additional Appendices demonstrate how mindfulness and the Three Minute Meditation techniques can be applied to a few specific problem areas, such as issues around food and issues around aging.

> This method is divided into seven "Steps" plus appendices. Once you've read the first two or three steps, you'll have plenty of exercises to work on for a while, while you (eventually) read the rest of the book.

Different Folks, Different Strokes

No two people are the same. Our likes and dislikes, our strengths and weaknesses, our needs and wants vary. These differences affect the ways in which we like to learn, and they will affect the way in which we can best learn to meditate, as well.

> People like to receive information in different ways. For some, a picture is worth thousands of words. Others might prefer to listen to an audio presentation. Yet others are more attuned to the printed page, and find metaphors and analogies constructed of words to be most useful.
>
> We'll talk about how these different preferences can help or hinder a meditation practice, a bit later on. And we'll try to use a variety of information "formats" — including lots of diagrams and metaphors — to get our message across in the most effective way, as demonstrated in the following visual and metaphoric examples. Please keep reading if this subject interests you, or just head on down to the next box.

For Visual Learners: How We "See" *The Three Minute Meditator* Method

If you like to "see" what you're getting into, here's a image of how we picture *The Three Minute Meditator* method, as a pyramid, or short, stubby, arrowhead shooting us to the stars!

For Sports Fans: Meditation, Metaphor, and Baseball

Did the previous explanation of the Seven Steps, plus the Appendix, seem complicated? Did our arrowhead picture leave you cold? If so — especially if you're both a sports fan and a person who likes information in the form of words — you may be entertained by our analogy comparing baseball to *The Three Minute Meditator* method. Football fans? Soccer fans? With a few substitutions (like "tackling" for "batting,") you too can make this metaphor work for you!

Imagine someone who's never participated in any kind of athletics or physical activity, and knows nothing about baseball (maybe he or she is from Mars, where there are no sports), but wants to play — and think about this:

Step One: Understanding the Mind is like our complete rookie learning the basic general way that competitive sports work, i.e., two teams, referees, coaches, special places to play called "fields." Really bottom-line stuff. Similar to learning that neurons transmit information and form neural paths, or of the existence of the Fight or Flight Response.

Then our rookie learns more specific information about baseball: a batter tries to hit a ball that the pitcher throws, and then has to run around the bases. Fouls and strikes, umpires and coaches. Lots of new words and concepts — just like learning how thoughts trigger the Fight or Flight Response in humans, or how focus on the breath triggers the Relax and Release Response — but without understanding these concepts, you just can't play the game.

Step Two: Clearing the Mind is like the exercise program that our absolutely unathletic would-be ballplayer might undertake before it's time to even grab a bat, throw a ball, or round the bases: running, weight-lifting, agility training, and so on. Just as we meditators need to build Mental Muscle™ before we can do much, our total baseball beginner needs to build up his or her arms and legs before doing anything else.

Step Three: Watching the Mind is like our player studying baseball strategy, including his or her own strengths and weaknesses, and those of teammates. Learning to observe the other teams in the league, studying famous game situations that are likely to re-occur. Important stuff to work on, but without the next steps, only an academic exercise.

Step Four: Visualization and *Step Five: Softening Around Pain* are like the very specific actions — batting, throwing, and catching — that a baseball player must practice until they become automatic.

Step Six: Great States offers three more specific (and slightly more advanced) tools that meditators need, just as our rookie will eventually need to learn a few of the more important and more advanced ballplaying skills, such as stealing bases, or walking a batter.

More Than the Sum of Its Steps...

Obviously, without the running and strength-training exercises of Step Two, the wanna-be player would not have the muscle — or the beginning meditator the Mental Muscle™ — to do the more advanced techniques of Steps Four, Five, and Six. Without the underlying understanding of the game from Step One, and the strategic knowledge of Step Three, they wouldn't know what to do with either that muscle or technical skill.

The steps are summed up in Step Seven, Living in the Now. After working with the first Six Steps, the stories, fears, angers, and desires of the mind are less important, and we have more enjoyment, spontaneity, and creativity in our day-to-day existence, with reduced stress and pain. We can do much of our living without thinking, and certainly without worrying or obsessing. Perhaps this state of Living in the Now is what Baseball Hall of Famer Carl Yastrzemski of the Red Sox meant by the very last part of his comment (italics ours):

"I think about baseball when I wake up in the morning. I think about it all day and I dream about it at night. *The only time I don't think about it is when I'm playing it.*"

Finally, meditation and the practice of mindfulness may eventually prove to be, for some of us, steps on the path to a deep spiritual connection with all of creation. But many roads lead to Rome, as the expression goes: traditional religion, a practice of compassion or service, or even a total absorption in the underlying meaning of baseball may be a route to spirituality. To close with a quote from Super Umpire and Yaz's fellow Hall of Famer Bill Klem:

"Baseball is more than a game to me, it's a religion."

To paraphrase Mr. Klem, "…meditation is more than a way of improving the quality of daily life, it's a spiritual path." And that's what the Further On Down the Road Appendix is all about…

> If you like words, metaphors, and analogies (or if you are a sports fan), our "Baseball Metaphor" may help you to conceptualize the way in which *The Three Minute Meditator* method is organized. If not, this box should suffice.

Why Many Meditation Books Are Not Really for Beginners

We realize that there are thousands of psychologists, philosophers, and metaphysicians who have already written books on the subject of meditation. But most of these are not for the beginning, would-be meditator. *After* you've learned to meditate, you'll find many of these books to be fascinating reading, and a few of our favorite titles are listed in the bibliography. But for those just starting to investigate meditation, they can be downright counterproductive…

Jargon, Complexity, and Dogma

Some meditation books are unbelievably complex — full of long words and torturous, tortuous concepts. When we began to study meditation, phrases and concepts like "manifestation of the unpotentiated noumenon" or "*nididhyasana sadhana*" were daunting, if not a complete deterrent.

But fortunately we realized that you don't need to know lots of big words to meditate. That's like asking someone to learn Chinese so that they can play Chinese checkers!

Once you understand the basic concepts, meditation is a simple thing to do — though not always easy. There's no need to complicate a beginner's book with strange and esoteric jargon or terminology.

Also a problem for many readers, some meditation books are dogmatic. According to them, there is just one "right" way to meditate. Not surprisingly, the "right" way is usually tied to a particular religious, social, or business organization with which the writer is affiliated. Any other method is considered ineffective at best, if not downright sinful.

Not All Meditation Methods Are Alike—But Many Are Similar

While studying many of the available meditation methods, we found that most share certain characteristics. We'll try to present these ideas, exercises, and techniques to you as clearly as possible, drawing the concepts together and elaborating on important themes. After all, why should you, as a beginning meditator, have to wade through piles of jargon and dogmatic writings, if we're willing to act as interpreters for you? Of course, you can (and should) always go back to the metaphysical literature, and explore your areas of special interest, *after* you've learned to meditate. You'll be better prepared to do it then, and our bibliography will help you to do so.

The Most Natural Thing in the World

Contrary to popular belief, the study of meditation does not have to be difficult, painful, or other-worldly. You don't have to "pay your dues" by struggling to obtain a full lotus position before you can begin to explore a state of mindfulness. Struggling is not what this book is about, because we believe that meditation should be an exciting new skill to learn, a skill that has a satisfying flow of its own. In fact, it's the most natural thing in the world to do!

Here's what's most important from the preceding paragraphs:

Over the years, we've read many meditation books that were too complex and/or too "orthodox" to suit many beginners. And we've learned a great deal by doing this. Two things seem most crucial:

• There are just a few underlying themes that run through almost all mindfulness methods. These underlying themes are based — whether the originators of the method knew it or not — on the way that the human brain functions.

• And we've learned, both from studying meditation ourselves and from teaching others, that most beginners prefer their meditation straight: no jargon or cults, and hold the dogma, please!

• Best of all, meditation is natural and easy to do — although figuring out how to get started is the hardest part!

Why You Probably Need To Meditate

Are you ever bothered by anger or fear? Distracted by desires? Depressed, bored, or restless? Does life sometimes seem meaningless? Are you only able to feel happy when everything is going right?

If you never have problems with feelings like these, then you probably don't need this book. You're probably not human, either, since just about everybody manages to make themselves unhappy at least once in a while.

"Make themselves unhappy?" What a strange notion! Why would anybody want to make themselves unhappy?

Of course, it's much easier to believe that circumstances, or other people, make us unhappy. But that's a load of baloney! Because we've all met, or at least read and heard about, those few rare people who are able to be happy no matter what adversity shows up in their life. And we can all name a dozen rich, famous, talented, people whose lives were made miserable by themselves, from Marilyn Monroe to Michael Jackson to the latest professional athlete or actor, whose career has crashed and burned due to drugs, alcohol, or violence. Can't think of anyone like that? Then skim the tabloid newspapers next time you're on a slow checkout line at the supermarket — you'll find a dozen, easy. Make ourselves unhappy? *You bet we do!*

It's not really what happens in the outside world that makes a person happy or unhappy, satisfied or unsatisfied. What matters is how you feel inside your own mind. During the 1929 Stock Market Crash, many of the brokers who dove to their deaths from Wall Street windows had more than enough money left to maintain a modest lifestyle. The stock market didn't kill them, and the window didn't kill them. Their own minds did.

You see, for most of us, the mind can be a cruel and demanding master, constantly criticizing and making judgments. It churns out a storm of contradictory, confusing thoughts. Makes you buy that new sports car on credit, and then worry about the monthly payments. Makes you eat that extra helping, and then obsess about being overweight. Lets you forget about an anniversary date, but reminds you of the time you accidentally wore a pajama top to class in second grade. Makes you complain and feel angry about demands from your child or parent, and then feel guilty for not being the "perfect" father or mother, daughter or son. Jobs, sex, money, health — the list of potentially disturbing thoughts that your mind is just aching to throw at you goes on and on. But it doesn't need to be that way.

> Your mind doesn't have to be a weight around (or, rather, on top of) your neck. Unfortunately, for many of us (ourselves most certainly included), the mind can be more a tyrannical boss than a helpful servant.
>
> Meditation, the art of mental self-control, can quite literally "change your mind" – from a pain-in-the-butt boss to a useful and lively companion! Why let your mind continue to work against you, when you can train it to work *for* you?

Why We Needed To Meditate: David and Nina Speak

The way in which we each became a "Three Minute Meditator" illustrates the way in which you can use meditation to shift from an "embattled" relationship with your own mind to a peaceful and productive coexistence.

14

Please remember that you can just skip down to the box at the end of this section — right now — if you don't want all the gory details of our lives before we started to meditate and mindfulness kicked in!

As David recounts:

"My mind used to be a judgmental, nit-picking boss, and my life generally felt great when absolutely every little thing was going my way, or when something especially satisfying had just happened, and awful the rest of the time. I spent a lot of time feeling depressed, for no obvious cause. But that was how it had always been for me, and I had no reason to think that things should, or even could, be different.

"Things changed as I was about to publish the first nationally marketable edition of my "Instant Blues Harmonica for the 'Musical Idiot'!" package, of which I was enormously proud. While my book was at the printers, a larger publisher (whom I had trusted, and taught to play harmonica) came out with his own version, with a distressingly similar title! My own brainchild, I felt, had been kidnapped, and I was terribly angry, hurt, scared, and depressed.

"But, in my acute misery, a single healthy thought kept recurring: The idea that if I could somehow learn the "master skill" of *coping* with a situation like this, that skill would ultimately be worth more to me than a dozen successfully-published harmonica books.

"That thought persevered. I bought psychology, philosophy, and metaphysical books, and read and re-read them slowly and carefully. Previously, I had read these books for entertainment, or to learn the newest (and hippest) theories. Now, it felt like I was reading for my very life.

"Virtually all of my favorite books strongly recommended some sort of daily meditation practice, so I began, after a twelve-year hiatus, to experiment again with the Transcendental Meditation™ technique that I'd learned but never really practiced in college. I also signed up for a 10-day meditation retreat with psychologist/poet Stephen Levine and Buddhist teacher Jack Kornfield, where I learned that a

15

tremendous diversity of meditation techniques exist. On the fifth day of the retreat, I got a short glimpse of the nature of the mind — and how even a single moment of mindfulness could radically alter my relationship to fear and anger. It changed my life.

"I began to study meditation, and to make it a part of my daily life. As I gained some "Mental Muscle™", my own thought processes became clearer to me. I found myself slightly less dominated by the usual old feelings of fear and desire. Hypochondria, my favorite bugaboo, would still surface occasionally, but I would generally recognize it quickly and let go of it. My previous day-long or week-long depressions began to disappear in seconds or minutes, hours at most. And even the insecurities that had obsessed me since grammar school started to fade quietly into the background noise of my mind.

"I surely don't mean to imply that I'm really together now. I'd better not! First, because it's not true, and second, because if I did, and my friends ever read this, I'd face a barrage of well-deserved ridicule, just as I did when a TV segment filmed to profile me was called (their idea, *not* mine) "The Harmonica Guru"!

"But I am more together than before I began meditating. Today, outside events affect me less, and I can understand and deal with my thoughts and feelings much more easily."

As Nina tells her story:

"David was generally the difficult twin. I was raised to be a good little girl and a good little student. Vassar. Princeton. Teaching at University of Maryland, then associate director of research for a large marketing firm in Washington, DC.

"After that, I joined my husband, Bert Smiley, 90 miles north of New York City to help run his family's business. Mohonk Mountain House, founded in 1869 by Bert's great-grand-uncle, is a unique "Victorian castle" resort set on 2200 acres of spectacular grounds, with 800 employees and a fascinating history. Things were great! Yet...no matter how "good" my life looked "on paper," and regardless of how happy I could feel at times, I still felt stressed, and could be painfully moody (especially for those around me).

"David's interest in mindfulness, and *The Three Minute Meditator* project, were the immediate causes of my beginning to meditate in a way that would eventually change my life. I'd had several opportunities to begin meditating in years past. I now regret letting them slip through my fingers, but I simply wasn't ready, and the time required seemed too onerous. For instance, I trained in Transcendental Meditation^{tm} , only to drop it after several weeks. *Twenty* minutes *twice* a day? Not me!

"Although I had felt much more centered and relaxed when I was meditating, my life was just too busy! Similarly, a few years later, when a friend was living in an ashram, I was fortunate to obtain an interview with a well-known guru who gave me a mantra, which I regret to say I barely used.

"Meditation — in the form of *The Three Minute Meditator* — came into my life 'for real' at a point when my work stress in DC was reaching an all-time high and something had to change. Feeling overwhelmed, frustrated, insecure and put-upon (a great combination!), I began to meditate and learned how to clear my mind and watch my mind. I realized that a drive towards "being perfect" (ha!) was creating stress around almost everything I did, since it was somehow never "enough."

"As I began to work more skillfully with my mind and feel some compassion for myself, I remembered how good it felt not to be stressed all the time. Oddly enough, as I stopped trying to be perfect, I seemed to have more psychic space. Things were getting done more easily and even more quickly. The same things that would have driven me crazy before, now were no big deal. The *issues* were the same, but *I* was different!

"Over the years, meditation has helped me tremendously in understanding and alleviating the stresses of my worklife — *and my life*. I've done weekend and week-long retreats… I've also had *lapses* of days, if not weeks, when meditation had simply gotten away from me. But now I always come back to the simple concepts of *The Three Minute Meditator*, integrating mindfulness throughout my waking hours.

"The reason I keep coming back to meditation *is because it works*. I'm more compassionate towards myself and others, and life simply feels better when I'm meditating. I feel more real to myself, and can *be* more real to others. So why argue with success? I never expected to see such subtle – or dramatic – changes. I've come a long way and there's still a long way to go. What an incredible journey!"

> If you'd like to know more about us, and why we need to meditate, you can read the previous sections. But here's the important point:
>
> We believe in meditation, even though our first efforts at it were unsuccessful. We believe that it's been good for us, and believe that it will help you too. And that's why we wrote this book.

That's "all" there is to it, friends. We believe that if you give meditation a sincere try, you'll find it as helpful and satisfying as we do, and it will become a lifelong practice.

Introduction: In a Nutshell...

• For thousands of years, **meditation** (the art of mental self-control) has been considered the most effective method for developing **mindfulness** (a mental state characterized by clarity, insight, compassion, and serenity, no matter what is going on around you).

• We've tried to make this mindfulness method as simple to use as possible, without excess jargon or dogma.

• Just about everyone can use more mindfulness in their life. We sure did, as we've already explained. You probably do, too.

• The Seven Steps of this method need to be read in order, but you do not have to "complete" or "master" each step before reading about the next. Our Baseball Analogy may help explain this (page 9) if you have not already read it.

> If you want to get to the exercises quickly, you can read all of the "Boxed" material in Step One and skim the rest, until you get to Step Two (which'll have plenty of exercises). Make sure that you look at the diagrams whenever you find one.

STEP ONE:
UNDERSTANDING
THE MIND

In this step, composed of Chapters One through Six, we will cover most of the theoretical information that you'll need to understand how and why meditation works. The topics will range from brain function to metaphysics to the main excuses that people use to avoid beginning or continuing a mindfulness practice.

> Remember: If you're in a hurry to start meditating, please feel free to skim from box to box, while glancing at the diagrams. That'll give you all the theoretical information you need, in the shortest possible time.

Chapter One:
The Greatest Tool
in the World

For thousands of years, the Buddhist psychology (known as the *abhidharma*) has provided tremendous insight into the human mind. But it's only recently — in fact, only since the first edition of this book was written — that more powerful computers and tools such as MRI's and PET scans have allowed cognitive scientists to look directly into the microscopic workings of the human brain. What they see only reinforces, to us, that ancient knowledge of the mind.

> **What's the difference between *brain* and *mind*?** In our definition, the brain is composed of three pounds of grey matter and neurons inside the head. The thoughts and emotions produced by the brain are an important part of a non-physical entity commonly known as the human mind. There may be more — even much more — to the mind (as we'll consider later on), but this definition will work just fine for now.

As David —with Nina's advice and input — has studied this new research, he has integrated it into the applied mindfulness training that he teaches to groups of all kinds, from CEOs to forensic scientists to yoga practitioners. We've included a brief description of his new material in this first chapter of this new edition of *The Three Minute Meditator*, since it provides a simple way to understand how meditation affects the brain and thus influences human behavior. We believe that even a cursory understanding of why meditation works from a scientific perspective — as gleaned from perusing just the boxes of Chapter One — will help you, our readers, to use this method.

Whether we choose to look through the lens of the cognitive scientist or the Buddhist psychologist, we can see that mindfulness is only possible when we can understand (and have some control over) our minds, and the thoughts that fill them. As defined earlier, meditation is the set of techniques which allow us to gain this mental control — which David likes to call "Mental Muscle™" —and to achieve mindfulness (at least some of the time).

You don't need to know how the brain itself works in order to meditate or be mindful. Certainly, some of us just want to know *what* to do, and care little for the *hows* and *whys* of the matter. But for those of us who like to know *why* things work as they do, here's a bit of information about the "underpinnings" of meditation and mindfulness. For those who are more experientially oriented, reading the boxes and looking at the diagrams will get you through this section in only a few moments.

> As David likes to say in his workshops and corporate presentations:
>
> **"The better you understand a tool, the better you can use it. And your brain is the greatest tool you'll ever have."**
>
> To gain a very quick understanding of how meditation affects the brain, please look at each of the following **diagrams** and read the **boxes**. The "scientific" perspective presented is based on a great deal of current research that supports the 2500 year old Buddhist Psychology (known as the "Abhidharma") to a remarkable degree.

Building Blocks of the Brain

The basic structure of your brain goes back hundreds of millions of years, when the first primitive creatures began to develop specialized nerve cells called **neurons.**

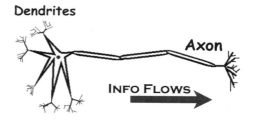

> A nerve cell, or **neuron**, is a tiny transmitter. It receives chemical, electrical, or hormonal information at the "dendrite" end, and sends it through the "axon" end. Your brain is composed of about one hundred billion neurons!

Neural Chains, Paths, or Networks

Neurons attach together to form what we call **"neural paths"** (some scientists call them neural chains, or neural networks). The axon of one neuron connects to the dendrite of the next neuron, just like elephants: the trunk of one elephant grabs onto the tail of the next. Information flows from one neuron to another, and from one end of the path to the other.

Neural Path

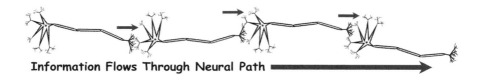

Information Flows Through Neural Path ⟹

Why Neural Paths are Important

Neural paths are the basis of *all* behavior. Consider an animal having a "hard-wired" response to a situation — that is, an instinctual or "built-in" response (like a frog flicking its tongue at a mosquito flying by). Or consider yourself having developed a habitual response of getting angry or depressed whenever a thought of your least favorite co-worker or politician flashes through your mind. No matter what the behavior, animal or human, on the physical or mental level — you can bet that a neural chain is at the bottom of it all!

> Neurons connect end-to-end to form paths or chains, as in the picture preceding this box. These neural paths are what control behavior in all creatures — including us. See something scary, that makes you jump? Simply stated, a neural path has given the command to flood your body with adrenaline and other "fight or flight" hormones!

Two Types of Neural Paths, and the Perceive ➜ Process ➜ Output Formula

There are two main types of neural paths — instinctual paths and learned paths — which we'll discuss in a moment. But one thing that most neural paths have in common is what we might call a "formula" composed of three parts: perception, process, and output.

Perception (seeing, feeling, smelling, or otherwise sensing something) triggers a **Process** that results in some kind of **Output** (often an action or an emotion).

There are a few different types of neural paths. Most share a common pattern:

- A **Perception** (seeing, feeling, smelling, or otherwise sensing or noticing something)

- **Triggers a Process** that results in some kind of

- **Output** (often an action or an emotion).

Instinctual ("Hard-Wired") Paths

The oldest type of neural path – found in even very simple living creatures — provides its owner with what are often called "instincts." These are neural paths that are hard-wired right into the brain. When a certain type of event is perceived, this triggers an automatic process. Information flows instantly from neuron to neuron, and an action (output) results. Here's an example.

One Basic Frog Neural Path

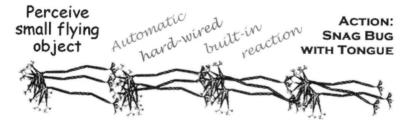

Perceive small flying object — *Automatic hard-wired built-in reaction* — ACTION: SNAG BUG WITH TONGUE

Perception → Triggers Process → The Output is an Action

The frog doesn't "think" about the bug. His reaction is automatic. He perceives the bug, the process of activating muscles and nerves takes place, and his tongue shoots out to snag dinner, in one smooth, instinctual, action.

The "Fight or Flight" Response

Had our frog perceived the shadow of a tall bird-like creature with a long, sharp bill, a similarly automatic process would have triggered a reaction known as the "Fight or Flight Response." This would have instantly activated the various bodily processes needed to jump to safety if that were possible, or struggle with the stork if not.

Another Basic Frog Neural Path

Perception ➔ Triggers Process ➔ The Output is an Action

> Some neural paths are "instinctual" or "built-in" or "hard-wired," as in the two frog examples above. No thinking is required — the neural path is triggered *automatically* once a certain event is perceived.
>
> The **"Fight or Flight Response"** is one of the most common and important components of these hard-wired neural paths.

Learned Neural Paths

Truly primitive creatures have only hard-wired neural paths. But those of us with larger clumps of neurons on top of our necks (aka "brains") can create a neural path through learned behavior, the second main type of neural path.

Want to try an experiment to demonstrate this? Write out the name of this book in longhand, something that you've probably never done before. As you do it, you are creating a brand new neural path in your brain: *The Three Minute Meditator*

Do it five or ten more times. It gets easier, and you find that you can do it more quickly, without needing to think about each word. Do it often enough, and it would eventually become as automatic as writing your own signature.

> Some neural paths are "learned" — we create them on purpose (try the little writing experiment, above, to demonstrate this). We could even say that *all* learning is the result of creating new neural paths in the brain.

Neural Paths, From Weak to Strong

Why is your own signature easier to write than the title of a book that you've just started to read? And why does that title get easier to scribble swiftly, the more you do it? On the surface, the answer is clearly "because you do it a lot" or "practice makes perfect." But on the level of brain function, it's because *each time a neural path is used — it gets stronger.* More neurons join the path, and it gets thicker and stronger and easier to use.

New Weak Neural Path

More Neurons Join In, Creating a Strong Neural Path

Like Cutting Across an Empty Lot

Imagine an empty lot next to your house. By cutting across it, you can reach the corner store more quickly. The first time you do this, you have to thrash your way through waist-high weeds. But walking back from the store, it's a bit easier — you've started to stomp out a path. After a week of daily treks to the store, the path is well-defined, and you could just about follow it with your eyes shut. Neural paths are strengthened by traveling them, in the same way.

> The more we use a learned neural path, the stronger it gets. Just like a path we create to cross a field of weeds gets wider and more tramped down — and easier to travel — the more often we use it.

More Than Times Tables and Riding Bicycles

Learning times tables. Recognizing words in an exotic foreign language. Knowing how to hit a baseball with a bat, or ride a bicycle — learned neural paths are great! But learned neural paths are not just about memorizing information, or creating complex sequences of muscle action which become automatic after many repetitions.

> Learned neural paths are responsible for the way we think and act, for our beliefs and our emotions, our words and our behavior.

Learning Important Neural Paths "By Accident"

The crucial role of neural paths in every part of our lives would be fine, if we always made rational and noble choices about what neural paths to create, and then strengthened them with diligent practice.

> Unfortunately, many of us develop learned neural paths by accident rather than by choice, and we then reinforce them by habit.

A young boy sees that Dad get mad whenever Mom criticizes him. Assuming that Dad is an important role model, the boy tries the behavior for himself. Before long, a neural path that may last a lifetime is forming.

A young girl is discouraged from climbing on a big rock. "You'll fall and hurt yourself." She is frequently discouraged from doing any physical things that are the least bit dangerous. Over time, a neural path is developed that may affect her for the rest of her life. We'll go into detail on neural path formation later. For now, it's just important to understand that:

> Experiences we have as children can often lead us to form neural paths that last a lifetime — especially if we are not even aware of them.

Not Just for Frogs: More on the Fight or Flight Response

When a taxi jumps the curb and heads straight for you, it's no time for analytical thought. No time to wonder if the recent taxi strike has caused this crisis, or if the driver has been driven mad with rage by your "Surrounded by Idiots" T-shirt. No, an ancient and essential neural path kicks in, that same Fight or Flight Response that made our frog leap to safety when he perceived the stalking stork!

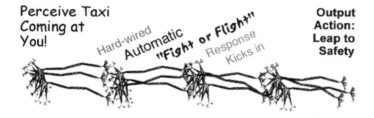

Perception ➜ Triggers Process ➜ The Output is an Action

> We humans share the Fight or Flight Response Neural Path with frogs (and most other creatures). This instinctual, or hard-wired, neural path has been developing over many millions of years — and it can be a lifesaver, as in the out-of-control taxi example above. But it has costs, as well as benefits...

Fight or Flight Response: The Down Side

Like a fire extinguisher placed inside closed glass box, the Fight or Flight Response Neural Path was created for use in emergencies only. Its effects on the body are profound:

• A flood of adrenaline and other hormones rush through our body.

• Blood is rushed from the extremities (feet and hands) into the center of our body, so that if a saber-toothed tiger is gnawing on our left arm, we can still hack at it with our right, without massive blood loss. This, naturally, raises our blood pressure way up!

• The digestive system stops completely, so that all the energy normally used for digestion can go into the muscles of the body for fighting or fleeing purposes.

• Muscles tense in antipation of action, putting tension on the tendons and bones to which they are attached.

The Fight or Flight Response puts your body on an emergency footing. It floods the body with adrenaline and other hormones, which instantly:

• Increases Blood Pressure

• Stops Digestion

• and Tightens all your Muscles!

By Thought Alone

All of these emergency actions caused by the Fight or Fight Response are fine, and a small price to pay for a lifesaving reaction…if they are necessary. Unfortunately, most of the time they are not.

A frog never tortures himself with the question "What if there's a stork behind those trees?" He either perceives a stork (or a stork-type creature like a human, or a crow), then he jumps. If the frog does not perceive a threat, he has no Fight or Flight Response. Human beings are the only creatures who can trigger a Fight or

Flight Response by perceiving something as insubstantial as a thought in their own mind...

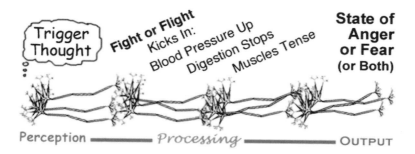

Thus the thought of our least favorite politician or of a terrorist attack, the memory of an auto accident or an abusive ex-spouse, the mental image of having to speak in front of an audience or of facing a meeting with boss and colleagues when not well-prepared — or any other emotionally negative thought or memory — all of these can cause our body to react with the classic Fight or Flight Response. No wonder many of us therefore spend a large part of each day in a state of chronic readiness for escape or battle. A useful state when a real physical threat is present or approaching, but otherwise an unproductive, and even unhealthy, state to live in.

Certain types of thoughts can trigger a full-fledged Fight or Flight Response. Many of us suffer from repetitive thoughts that do exactly this — sometimes dozens of times a day.

So it's no wonder that high blood pressure, poor digestion, and back or neck pain is so common. Why is that? Because those are the very same effects that the Fight or Flight Response is hard-wired to produce, as described in the previous box...

This type of thought can be very difficult to avoid, very difficult not to pay attention to. It's almost as though they have grabbed hold of us — which is why we sometimes call them "Grabby Thoughts." And we'll offer effective ways, in later steps, for dealing with them...

The Emotion Equation™

Perhaps you noticed that the last diagram ended with "A State of Anger or Fear." Anger and fear are, of course, what we call "emotions." Everyone knows that term. But exactly what "emotions" are and how they arise has been the subject of some controversy for a while.

It's a big oversimplification, but we might say that for nearly a century, psychologists have argued whether the physical effects of the Fight or Flight Response cause the emotion to occur, or whether an "emotional thought" causes the Fight or Flight Response. We believe that both statements are true, and that it's a chicken and egg type of process, as the previous diagram and the following box explain.

The Emotion Equation™: A Trigger Thought (or an actual Perception) ➔ triggers the Fight or Flight Response ➔ this causes a variety of bodily sensations ➔ which the brain then interprets as an "Emotion" such as anger or fear.

Thought + Fight or Flight Response = Emotion

This all happens so fast that it may seem as though your thought of the most-despised person in your world instantly results in a Fear or Anger Response...

...and it just about does! When a neural path is used often enough, it becomes automatic (or "achieves automaticity," as a cognitive scientist might say).

Thus a neural path triggered by a thought which pops up in your head — and which results in anger or fear — has been traveled so often that it now has become a deep **rut**.

A rut which is so *very easy to follow* that it takes no thought, no time, no energy, or no will for you to travel it, from that first perception of a negative thought (the thought of your least favorite person), to that ending outcome of anger or fear!

How Can We Solve the Emotion Equation™?

The Emotion Equation™ may sound like a knee-jerk reaction — a neural path that begins with a thought, triggers a Fight or Flight Response, and inevitably results in an Emotion.

Imagine this: you're working on a project in the office, and it must be done by 5 pm. Suddenly, a thought pops into your head — a thought that you've had before, many times — and triggers a neural path.

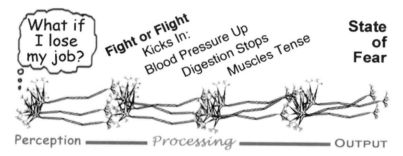

Perhaps, like many of us, you would follow this old, familiar, rutted path of fear thought to Fight or Flight Response to state of fear — even though being in an agitated, fearful state is not likely to help you meet your deadline. You don't want to feel that way, but it's almost as though that thought has "grabbed" or "hijacked" your brain for a while.

Fortunately, there is a simple, although not always easy, way to solve the Emotion Equation™. Here's how it works.

The Fight or Flight Response is an essential part of the Emotion Equation™ — *if it is not triggered, the thought remains just a thought.* For example, think about the nonsense word:

amthagor.

Unless your worst enemy is Joe Amthagor, or your most dangerous business rival is Amthagor, Inc — the thought of this word will not trigger a Fight or Flight Response. Therefore, thinking of amthagor does not result in an emotion.

It's as simple as this:

Thought *plus* Fight or Flight Response = Emotion

Thought *without* Fight or Flight Response = No Emotion

If we can learn to stop or short-circuit the Fight or Flight Response, we can prevent a trigger thought, no matter how scary or anger-producing, from resulting in an emotion.

And there is a hard-wired neural path — called the Relax and Release Response — that can do this, once we learn to control it at will. Which we will. Soon.

Please take a moment and re-read this box. This is an essential concept!

Fight OR Flight, Anger OR Fear

We've been lumping them together as the Fight or Flight Response, but the Fight Response and the Flight Response are slightly different from each other, especially in how they affect us humans.

In the Fight Response, we tend to tighten and clench. Our hands become fists as we prepare to hit, our jaw muscles and teeth clench as we prepare to bite. Often we want to shout, and we say that we "see red." We may breathe rapidly, almost like panting. When thrown into the Emotion Equation™, the Fight Response leads us down a neural path to the emotion that we call anger.

The Flight Response has a "shakier" feel. Butterflies in the stomach, heart palpitations, shallow breathing, perhaps a raising of the hair at the back of the neck. The Flight Response takes us down the neural path to fear.

Symptoms of Anger; Symptoms of Fear

Being able to recognize your anger or fear "symptoms" *as soon as they arise* will be of great use to your mindfulness practice. Consider a cold. If you notice the scratchy throat or just slightly stuffed up nose as early as possible, you can — with the judicious early use of vitamin C, rest, and perhaps Grandma's chicken soup — avoid or at least shorten the cold, or reduce its intensity. You're less likely to infect your family, friends, co-workers, since you'll be careful about hugging or shaking hands or sharing food.

Similarly, once you learn to identify the earliest possible "symptoms" of anger or fear, before the Fight or Flight Response really kicks in, you'll be able to deal with it more skillfully. And less likely to take out your anger or fear on others. But that's another step on the path. For now, just think about how you feel when you begin to notice that you're getting angry or frightened, and we'll use that information later on to good effect.

> The Fight or Flight Response is actually two related responses, not one. We can say that the Fight Response brings us to anger, and the Flight Response brings us to fear. Sometimes both happen together, and we are both angry and afraid. Lucky us.
>
> But there's something we can do about this, especially if we learn to identify the very first "symptoms" of anger or fear, as described above and summarized below:
>
> Anger: Clenching (fists, teeth, jaw). "See red." Rapid breath.
>
> Fear: Butterflies in stomach. Shallow breath. Skin crawls at back of neck or other places.

The Relax and Release Response

Let's return to the taxi scenario. The taxi, for reasons unknown, has jumped the curb and veered straight for you. Your ancient, instinctual Fight or Flight Response has kicked in, enabling you to leap to safety. Now what?

For a while, as you sit by the side of the road, your heart pounds, your blood pressure stays elevated, your digestion is stopped, and your muscles are tense. But eventually, all these functions return to normal. "Phew!" You exhale with a sigh. "That was a close one." And your shoulders drop, the butterflies leave your stomach. What happened?

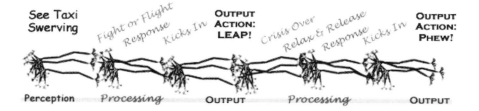

| See Taxi Swerving | *Fight or Flight Response Kicks In* | OUTPUT ACTION: LEAP! | *Crisis Over Relax & Release Response Kicks In* | OUTPUT ACTION: PHEW! |

| Perception | *Processing* | OUTPUT | *Processing* | OUTPUT |

> After a Fight or a Flight Response has been triggered but is no longer necessary, an equal but opposite reaction takes place.
>
> We call this the **Relax and Release Response.** When the crisis is past, your body automatically relaxes, and simultaneously releases the emotion of fear or anger that the Fight or Flight Response has triggered.

But don't worry about "meditation making you so mellow that you just let the taxi run you over." When you have a real **need** for the Fight or Flight Response to kick in, it will — automatically — no matter how mindful you may become!

Instead, it's those unnecessary Fight or Flight Responses — the ones that raise our blood pressure, ruin our digestion, and give us tight muscles and pains in the neck — that we will learn to use the Relax and Release Response to avoid!

> **IMPORTANT:** Focusing mental attention onto the breath is the easiest way to consciously produce the R & R Response. That's why so many of the Three Minute Meditation exercises emphasize focus on breathing.

Meditation, Mental Muscle™, and the Path of Mindfulness

As we said when defining meditation, each of the Three Minute Meditations in this book is an exercise. An exercise that builds Mental Muscle™, which is the ability to keep your mind focused on whatever you chose, whenever you want.

One of the reasons we like to use neural paths as a way to understand how meditation works is that a path — by its very nature — is composed of many steps. When walking down a path in the park, at any point we can decide to stop and rest, if we like. We can decide to turn around and go back the same way. We can decide to change direction, and take a new path. *Every step is an opportunity to choose a new direction, or at least to stop and think, if we want to do so.*

Each Step of the Path Can Be a Choice

Many of us (ourselves sometimes included, unfortunately) live life by rote, or by rut. We follow the same old (neural) paths, whether they are useful or not, forgetting that we have the power, with each step, to change direction. To paraphrase an old saying, "Every saint is just a step away from being a sinner, and every sinner is just a step away from being a saint." (Although it's usually quicker and easier, alas, to change from saint to sinner than vice versa — the former can often be accomplished by just a few bad choices, while the latter is likely to take years of hard work!)

When we can be confronted by a fear thought, or an angry thought, and instead of becoming frightened and running away, or getting angry and striking out, choose to travel the following path…

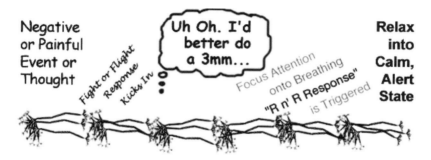

Negative or Painful Event or Thought — Fight or Flight Response Kicks In — "Uh Oh. I'd better do a 3mm…" — Focus Attention onto Breathing — "R n' R Response" is Triggered — Relax into Calm, Alert State

...we become a person of greater mindfulness, of greater personal power.

To put it in words, rather than in diagram form:

Whenever events or thoughts begin to trigger a Fight or Flight Response, we notice what's happening ("Uh-oh. Shoulders rising, fists and teeth clenching — why, the fight part of my Fight or Flight Response is kicking in, and I'm starting to get angry...").

We then turn our attention to whichever of the Three Minute Meditations seems to be most appropriate for the situation.

In Step Two, we'll provide you with a variety of Three Minute Meditator exercises, along with suggestions on when and how to use them. So if you're in a hurry to start using this amazingly effective and time-honored way to short-circuit the Fight or Flight Response (and avoid unnecessary negative emotions), just keep reading the boxes...

Chapter One, In a Nutshell...

In a nutshell, the rest of this book is intended to help us make mindful choices. Because:

Each and every time we decide to practice the meditations and build Mental Muscle™ we reap benefits of great value.

This is especially true — though admittedly harder to do — when we choose to practice a moment of meditation **instead** of following an old, unskillful, rutted path of fear, anger, or desire.

By meditating, during either tranquil or stressful times, we develop the ability to short-circuit unnecessary Fight or Flight Responses caused by repetitive or otherwise unuseful thoughts.

We do this by triggering the Relax and Release Response, often by focusing our mental attention onto the breathing process.

This lowers physical stress, and allows us more control over our emotions.

We reduce the future likelihood of being "hijacked" by our own thoughts, and learn to catch ourselves sooner if it does begin to happen.

We spend more time in a state of mindfulness, becoming more effective, relaxed, and loving human beings. And this is the purpose of meditation.

Chapter Two: Excuses, Excuses, Excuses!

Meditation: The Benefits

If you know enough about meditation to even pick up a book with a title like this one, chances are that you already know that meditation is just full of benefits. It will calm you down and help you to deal with the stresses of daily life, by teaching you to observe and then control your thoughts and feelings.

It will probably allow you to sleep less, while increasing your available energy. It can be used to lower blood pressure and heart rate. Meditation will help you to appreciate life more. It will enable you to face change or loss with greater acceptance and compassion.

> Meditation has been proven to provide great physical and emotional benefits. Knowing about all these benefits, how could anybody *not* meditate? There are three simple answers: excuses, excuses, excuses!

Excuses, Excuses, Excuses!

Yes, there are reasons not to meditate. But not *good* reasons. Unfortunately, many who have developed a "not me" orientation towards meditation are those who could benefit from it the most. But feelings of resistance may prevent them from doing so.

Other people who could benefit from a daily meditation practice just can't quite find the energy or motivation to begin. The hardest part of beginning your meditation practice is just that — beginning!

> Overcoming the excuses which may have prevented you from exploring your own meditation potential is easier when you understand them. Most people who are would-be meditators will find that at least a few of these erroneous beliefs about meditation are blocking their progress.

The Myth Of Innate Ability

Many people who foreclose on their own meditative potential share the mistaken belief that "Successful meditators are born with an innate ability to clear their minds, to focus their attention wherever they please, and to concentrate on their inner lives."

The truth is that *meditators are made, not born.* The ability to meditate is a characteristic that every human being has — an ability that must be nurtured and encouraged in order for it to bear fruit. No matter how tense or unspiritual you may now think yourself to be, rewards await you, but only if you try.

Once you begin to believe this, you can turn your wistful *would-be* meditator self-image into a *beginning* meditator self-image, and thus start to enhance your own life with these tremendously useful techniques. Vividly visualizing yourself meditating will help you begin taking the steps to unblock your meditative potential. Not all of us will have the time or the inclination to spend hours each day meditating. But *anyone* with a sincere desire to meditate can begin to learn and use these techniques *immediately.*

It Won't Work, Anyway

Some people believe in the aggressive tenet that "the best defense is a good offense." Attacking the usefulness of meditation is a way that many who have considered meditating are able to assure themselves that they are not really missing anything by not meditating.

Much of this attack may be based on a pre-programmed sense of failure. People who suffer from this blockage often are asking themselves, "Why even try meditating, since it obviously doesn't work?" Another element of this attack consists of denigrating meditation because not everyone who tries it, continues. Yet this fact may be more a reflection on ineffective teaching techniques and the unrealistic demands that many disciplines try to impose on busy Westerners, than a reflection on the value of meditation itself.

Meditation techniques are identifiable in every major religion since the beginning of recorded history. Meditation has clearly stood the test of time, so if you are using *this* excuse, it's long out of date! Time to give up your excessive skepticism, and become a Three Minute Meditator.

"I Already Meditate (Kind of...)"

Some of us enjoy relaxing moments in which we just let our mind wander, where it will. This may be pleasant. But as you learn more about the discipline of meditation, you'll see that just "spacing out and watching the clouds roll by" is more like daydreaming than like meditation, and can't be expected to provide the tremendous benefits that come with the latter. This is because daydreaming or watching the clouds does not build Mental Muscle™, which is a basic requirement of a meditative practice.

To amplify on this point (since so many of us have at some time confused "going fishing and letting my mind wander" with meditation), David likes to make an analogy with training a dog.

"No one says, with pride in their voice, that they've trained their dog to knock over the neighbor's garbage to look for chicken bones. Or that they've trained their dog to roll in foul-smelling muck. Dogs are perfectly happy to do those things on their own. We teach our dogs to heel, or to fetch, or to come when called — that's what makes a well-trained pet.

"Your mind can wander just fine, or space out all by itself. But teaching it to stay focused on the breath? That's what builds Mental Muscle™, and allows us to follow the path of mindfulness…"

"I Just Don't Have Time"

When you view meditation as an exercise which requires clearing a large time slot each day before you can begin, chances are that you will never get started. Today will not seem right and tomorrow will seem even worse. Life is so hectic for many of us that clearing half an hour or so daily may seem like an impossible task. And to think of doing so repeatedly, perhaps even twice a day, may be enough to leave most of us thinking, "Maybe *next* year, when things ease up!"

For those of us who feel pressured by lack of time, meditation is likely always to remain in our vague and distant future. Ironically, the time spent meditating, even three minutes worth, is often enough to help clear and re-focus the mind. The rest of the day then seems to flow more smoothly, as if time has somehow expanded to meet the needs that arise. This erroneous belief in the time demands of meditation has blocked many a would-be meditator (including, for many years, both David and Nina!).

Introducing... Mindful Multitasking

Many of us feel too busy to sit down for a relaxed meal, let alone set aside a daily period for meditation. Yet meditation need not take time *from* anything else in your schedule. Multitaskers take note!

Consider the act of talking on the phone while you do the dishes, the act of reading a book while flying on the airplane, or thinking about a business meeting while you drive to it. In each situation, you're doing "something extra" without adding time to the original task. Similarly, many of the meditation exercises that we'll provide can be practiced while you walk or work, cook or commute, pump iron or practice piano!

Anything done with complete focus and awareness is a meditation, and will eventually take us in the direction of mindfulness, no matter how mundane (dish-washing meditation? teeth-brushing mindfulness?) it may seem. Once we've learned to meditate, to be mindful — every action and every thought can become the momentary focus of a meditation. In this way, meditation, quite literally, takes no time at all.

Chapter Two, In a Nutshell...

Let's briefly consider (or reconsider, if you've read the above sections) the obstacles or excuses that keep some of us from starting to meditate. In our opinion, none of them, although convenient ways to avoid the work of mindfulness, have much real validity, since:

> • The excuse of "No Innate Ability" is just a myth, because everybody has the ability to meditate.
>
> • The "Meditation Doesn't Work" justification is strictly sour grapes — meditation doesn't work only if you don't do it.
>
> • And though "Kinda Meditating — just spacing out and fishing (or knitting)" may be pleasant, it won't provide the benefits of actual meditation.
>
> • Most importantly, "Lack of Time" is no longer an excuse — because *The Three Minute Meditator* method demonstrates how meditation can be effectively accomplished in small chunks of time.
>
> • Meditation can even be practiced, as described in the full text above — as mindful multitasking — *while* doing something else that doesn't require mental attention. And even in small doses, meditation is remarkably effective in improving the quality of one's life.

Chapter Three: What Is A Three Minute Meditation?

Each Three Minute Meditation is a specific exercise to build Mental Muscle™, which:

• Increases our ability to focus our mental attention, to become mindful.

• Gives us the ability to short-circuit an unnecessary Fight or Flight Response.

To put this in the language of cognitive science, each time we do a Three Minute Meditation, we create a neural path like this:

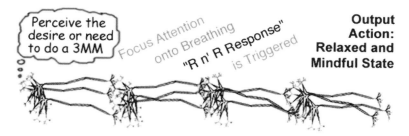

The Three Minute Meditation program is unique. Most other meditation methods advise you to set aside a certain time or times each day for meditation. Some require that a shrine of some sort be built and that meditation only take place there. The most extreme programs demand that you live in a monastery, far from the distractions of the world.

But limiting meditation to specific times or places can have two negative consequences. Firstly, such demands can be hard to adhere to, especially for the beginning meditator who has not yet felt the positive results of a daily meditative practice, and thus is not yet heavily committed to it. Secondly, a time-and-place-specific meditation program somehow sets meditation aside from "normal" existence. Practicing the Three Minute Meditation way avoids both of these problems. Of course, once you begin meditating, you can then explore and pursue *any* style of practice that appeals to *you*.

It's obviously easier to find time to do a number of short meditations during a day than to set aside one or two chunks of twenty or thirty minutes every day. Many of the Three Minute Meditations can be done while walking, or eating, or even stopped at a red light. Others can be practiced during a quick visit to the bathroom! As we said, many can be accomplished through "Mindful Multitasking" — without taking any extra time at all.

Once you get the hang of Three Minute Meditating, you'll find yourself doing many "mini-meditations" that will be amazingly effective in calming or centering you — even though they only take a few seconds!

Once you develop a meditation practice — and experience the benefits of mindfulness — you may find yourself wanting to do some longer meditations, of five or ten minutes or more, in a favorite place. There's no right or wrong way to do this. David likes to do at least one longer meditation, most mornings, while sitting in his favorite chair. Nina enjoys doing a longer meditation while walking to and from work.

Home or the Himalayas?

Both of us have attended retreats in the Vipassana monastic tradition. No talking, no eye contact, no reading or writing, for a week or so. Approximately sixteen hours a day of alternating walking and breathing meditation, with eating meditations strongly advised during mealtimes. We think that retreats are great, and they make us feel very high and clear. But eventually they end, and we have to come home.

Long retreats, and esoteric disciplines, can be of great value — monastic traditions exist in nearly every culture. But sooner or later, unless you're a monk, you'll have to come home — that is, you'll have to make your experience apply to daily life. With Three Minute Meditation, you're already home.

Chapter Three, In a Nutshell...

We'll end this chapter as we began it, with definitions.

Each Three Minute Meditation is a specific exercise to build Mental Muscle™, which:

• Increases our ability to focus our mental attention, to become mindful.

• Gives us the ability to short-circuit an unnecessary Fight or Flight Response.

And add a little quiz...

Q: What's the difference between a meditating monk and a Three Minute Meditator?

A: Monks live in order to meditate better... and Three Minute Meditators meditate in order to live better...

We, and many others, find that integrating our meditation practice throughout the day helps us to use meditation skills in daily life. Ideally, meditation and mindfulness become a way of life, a way of relating to the world, rather than "something that you do for a little while every day".

To quote an old chestnut, "Even the longest journey begins with but a single step". A single Three Minute Meditation may be only a small step, but it will start you on the road to a more mindful life, if you'll only try it.

Speaking of which, please turn to the next page and spend a minute or so — not even three, just yet — with our first two meditation exercises...

Chapter Four: Bringing Meditation Into Your Life: Right Now!

Once you understand the barriers that would-be meditators face, we hope you'll agree with our final analysis, which is: The only thing that now stands between you and meditation is the willingness to begin *right now!*

If your goal is realistic ("I will begin learning to be present with my thoughts and my mind") rather than perfectionistic ("I must achieve 'Enlightenment' right away"), then your progress towards this goal is virtually guaranteed from the outset. All that is necessary is to take a few deep breaths, relax — and continue reading! And breathing, and meditating, as well.

There's an old joke about an intellectual fellow who loved to read. He read all that there was to read about philosophy and became a philosopher. He read all that there was to read about mathematics and became a mathematician. Then he read all that there was to read about swimming... and he drowned.

> There are some subjects that you just have to do more than *read* about. Meditating is one of them. So even though you may feel that you're not yet very well-informed about the subject, right now may be a good time to take three minutes, two minutes, or even one minute, and do the two very simple meditations that follow.

The Favorite Animal "Meditation"

This one is so simple and natural that we put the word "meditation" in quotes. But simple as this exercise may be, doing it will demonstrate some very profound concepts, which we will enlarge upon throughout the book.

Sit comfortably. Now imagine your favorite type of animal — try to see it as a visual image inside your mind. What is it like? Furry or scaly? Big or Small? Does it make a sound? Does it have a smell? Can you imagine what it would feel like to touch?

Please take another half a minute or so to follow these boxed instruction, silly though you may think them to be, before reading on…

As far as we know, humans are the only creatures that can decide to bring an image into their mind and do so, as you just did. It takes a certain amount of Mental Muscle™ to do this, and the entire act can be described as a neural path.

Read instructions about doing Favorite Animal "Meditation"

Create mental image of animal

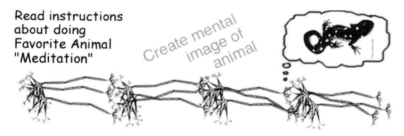

Simple as this exercise is, it proves that you, dear reader, are able to create a mental image inside your brain, and then observe it.

By doing so, you've demonstrated two crucial abilities:

• To be able to bring an "image" into your mind in the form of a thought, and

• To be able to focus your mental attention onto that thought or mental image.

This ability to "imagine" things — which is sometimes referred to as "visualization" — will be of great importance as you continue to work with the Three Minute Meditation method.

The Breath Counting Meditation

In this meditation we'll turn our mental attention to an actual physical event — our own breathing process — instead of turning our attention to a mental image or thought of our favorite creature. The instructions are simple and clear, so don't think about it much, just give it a try.

Consider the act of breathing. At its most basic, each breath consists of two parts: the inhalation and the exhalation.

Begin by practicing this meditation while sitting comfortably in a quiet place, back straight, feet flat on floor, hands in lap.

Now simply pay attention to your breathing, and "count" four consecutive breaths.

Begin with an inhalation. Then, while you exhale, mentally label that out-breath with the number "One". Continue for three more breaths: Inhale... "One"..., Inhale... "Two"..., Inhale... "Three" ..., Inhale... "Four."

Strive not to lose the count, and also try not to alter or regularize your breathing in any way.

Do this Breath Counting meditation once *right now...* before reading any further.

About the Breath Counting Meditation

When enjoying a favorite hobby, like golf or knitting, your thoughts generally focus directly on just what you're doing. Swinging to connect with the ball, or counting stitches, become your "preferred" thoughts. Although your mind is likely to wander, as other thoughts enter, you keep returning to the action at hand. As you build Mental Muscle™ — and create a new "breath counting neural path" — it will become easier, and your mind will be less likely to go off to what David's teacher Jack Kornfield calls "la la land!"

Right now, consider the observing and counting of each breath to be your "preferred" thoughts. Other thoughts — such as memories, plans, fears, desires, lunch, or whatever else — are sure to flit into your mind. Just gently replace these unwanted thoughts with your "Inhale...One..., Inhale...Two..." and so on, as soon as you notice these thoughts creeping in. And creep in, they will! Of course it's difficult to stay focused! But strangely satisfying, as it becomes more natural.

> If you find yourself thinking about anything except the feel of your breath and the number of that breath, return to focus on the sensation of breathing, and on the number of the breath. If you are not absolutely sure what number breath you're on, immediately begin again with "Inhale...One..." No judging, no "I blew the count" thoughts, just back to "Inhale...One..."

Why Bother? Because We're Solving the Emotion Equation™!

Why are we emphasizing this seemingly trivial exercise? Who cares if it's "Breath Number Three" or "Breath Number Four," anyways? We don't — because it's not the *number* that's important. Numbering each breath simply forces you to pay extremely close attention to the breathing process. And it's the intense focus on the breathing process which *is* crucial.

> As we said earlier, a thought only becomes an emotion if it triggers a Fight or Flight Response. Re-focusing your attention onto the breath is one of the best ways to short-circuit a Fight or Flight Response.
>
> *That's* what's important about this simple exercise, since it's difficult to re-focus (especially in a stressful situation, when the Fight or Flight has already been triggered) without practicing in advance!

The beauty of the Breath Counting meditation is that, once learned, you can do it anywhere! Try it on the bus, or during a long, boring meeting. Like all "mind clearing" exercises (more on, and more of, these later), with a bit of practice the breathing meditation gives rise to a delightfully peaceful and calm feeling (the Relax and Release Response, if you recall, from Page 33). Now do it again, or read on, as you like.

> Start practicing your breath counting meditation anywhere — no one can even tell that you're doing it! Once it starts feeling natural (and you can get up to "four" without losing count), you're ready to apply this exercise to a real life situation!

Now Prepare to Give It a Try...

You'll *prepare* to use meditation to deal with a real life stress situation simply by bringing a thought into your mind, as you did in the Imaginary Animal exercise. Here's how to do it.

Choose a low stakes real-life situation that tends to trigger a mild Fight or Flight Response for you. Then prepare to use your Breath Counting Meditation to deal with it, by practicing — at first — on the level of the imagination.

For example: Imagine this (or a similar real life scenario that you know you'll experience soon): It's lunchtime, on a hectic day. You're waiting in line at the deli, or the pharmacy. Your lunch hour — or the time you've got left until you *have* to pick up the kids/meet your mother/make that appointment — is ticking away, and that clerk is soooo darn slow!

You feel your jaw muscles tighten, feel your shoulders get tense. Even though it's not really happening, you feel yourself travelin' down your normal "get grouchy on the slow line" neural path!

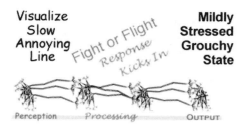

Visualize Slow Annoying Line — *Fight or Flight Response Kicks In* — Mildly Stressed Grouchy State

Perception   Processing   OUTPUT

Feel the grouchiness coming on? Good. Now add *this* to your imaginary scenario: Instead of mentally berating the overworked clerk, imagine that you notice what's starting to happen. "Aha," you say to yourself, "Grouchiness is kicking in, and my Fight or Flight Response is getting triggered."

Then you imagine yourself starting to count your breaths: "Inhale...One..., Inhale...Two..., Inhale...Three..." until it's your turn to pay. In fact, you actually *do* a moment or two of breath counting at the same time as you *imagine* yourself counting your breaths.

The line between imaginary exercise and real life Breath Counting Meditation is blurred as you feel the R n' R Response kicking in. Your shoulders release their tension and lower themselves. Instead of thinking about cursing the clerk, you just keep breath counting for a moment longer....

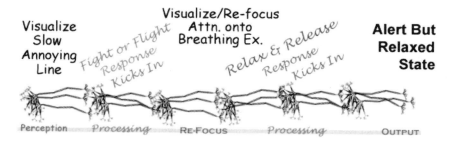

Now, if you're ready, it's time to walk the walk. Try using your Breath Counting Meditation during a real life low stakes stressful situation — just as an experiment — to see how it feels...

Chapter Four, In a Nutshell...

We're sorry to do this. But you really need to read the entire preceding section on Real Life practice. And do the two exercises. They are some of the most important parts of this book.

If you don't feel ready to use your Breath Counting Meditation during a Real Life situation, no problem! Just keep doing the "imaginary" exercise we just described, and it will help you get ready for the real thing (we'll talk lots more about this when we get to the "Visualization" chapter).

> If you are still working on being able to do the Breath Counting Meditation at all, that's okay too. Keep on reading, and do a practice breath count every few pages.

If your first Real Life breath count went well…that's great! If it worked for you in the situation you chose, it should work in others as well. So the next time that you start to experience a mild Fight or Flight Response trigger, don't get stressed. Don't get mad. Don't get even. Just do the Breath Counting Meditation, and see how it solves the Emotion Equation™. Remember: No Fight or Flight Response, no emotion!

> **IMPORTANT:** Why do we keep recommending that you work with a situation that triggers a "mild" Fight or Flight Response? Because — even if you have bought this book to deal with more serious problems, stressors, or issues — it will be easiest to begin using the techniques in low stress scenarios.

And whether you've been successful or not with the Breath Counting Meditation, or with its Real Life use, be kind to yourself. If you have a tendency to be self-critical, or to "push" yourself when in pursuit of a new skill or hobby, please keep reading or skimming your way to Chapter Six right now!

> As we say at in Step Six, when speaking of Compassion: using a mindfulness method as an excuse for self-criticism or anger rather than compassion is an irony that none of us needs...

Chapter Five:
The Meditator's Guide
to the Universe

In this and the following chapters, we're going to present some concepts that will help you to understand meditation more clearly and completely. We'll begin by describing a particular way of thinking about the world that almost all long-term meditators eventually seem to adopt. Initially, you may find it difficult to believe in this alternative worldview. But, as you meditate, you will find that it somehow begins to make intuitive sense.

> For some of us, this philosophical "Big Picture," may be intriguing. For others, not so. And it's fine to feel that way, because the main use of meditation is as a practical daily tool with almost instantaneous beneficial results. If you're not interested in theory, just skim the boxes until you reach the end of Step One, on page 65.

"I Stand Alone" — The Western Worldview

Most of us in this workaday Western world tend to hold onto one rather limited, but overwhelmingly popular, way of relating to ourselves and the world. We'll call this the "Western worldview" and begin by describing the "Western self-image".

When subscribing to the Western worldview, we see ourselves primarily as a body, a few cubic feet of skin-enwrapped flesh, with a specialized chunk at the top end called a brain. Complex chemical interactions in this brain chunk somehow give rise to instincts, emotions, thoughts, and self-awareness.

We believe that anything inside the skin is "me", anything outside is "not-me". This not-me part includes everybody else and everything else, from rocks to raccoons to real estate agents.

"We Are All One": The Meditator's Worldview

But there's more than one way to think of ourselves in relationship to the rest of the universe. For thousands of years, mystics and meditators (the two often go together, though they don't have to) of all persuasions have maintained an alternate opinion, which we call the "Meditator's worldview".

In the Meditator's worldview, the universe is, to paraphrase theoretical physicist Sir James Jeans, more like an "enormous mind" than an "enormous machine". And each one of us is more like an integrated thought in a great big mind than like an isolated little cog functioning almost independently in a great big machine (as in the Western view). Some people like to refer to this "big mind" as the universal consciousness. Others prefer to think of it as "God", the "Higher Power", or the "All-That-Is".

The analogies that follow may help to clarify this concept.

The Dream Analogy

"Row, row, row, your boat gently down the stream.

Merrily, merrily, merrily, merrily, life is but a dream."

We'd sung that song, like everybody else, since childhood, without ever really stopping to look for any particular meaning in it. Yet for thousands of years, philosophers of every culture have compared the unenlightened person to a character in a dream, whose understanding of reality is limited to the "reality" of the dream world that he or she inhabits.

Think about dreaming. In any dream, there are a variety of dream characters. But you'll probably believe yourself to be one particular character —that is, you'll know which character you are in the dream, even though that character might be somewhat different from who you are when awake.

You are also very "invested" or "engrossed" in your dream character. Whatever he or she does, whatever happens to "you" in the dream…feels very real…

As David puts it (and he has some wild dreams): "I've dreamed of being older, younger, of being a snake, even a Martian. But whoever I am in the dream, I know that it's me, in spite of the fact that my dream character may change from one part of the dream to another.

Yet although I almost never realize it during the dream, my "waking-life-mind" is creating both the "Dave-character-within-the-dream", and the rest of the characters in that dream."

Seen from the Meditator's worldview, we could say that each one of us is now like a dream character in a scenario dreamed by the "big mind". The big mind (or God, or universal consciousness) is dreaming both Nina and David, and everyone and everything else in this real-seeming dream that we live in. Since we see this universal dream from our own limited point of view (the Western view), the other people and things in it seem separate from us, although they're not. We are all simply characters in the same universal dream, being dreamed by the Big Mind (or the Mind of God, or the Mind of Universal Consciousness). And it's "just" a dream, no matter how real it feels.

Invisible Connections

A mushroom growing on the ground appears to be an individual plant. Yet the thumb-sized piece we call the mushroom is actually only a tiny, temporary part of a fungal network (known as a mycelium) that exists underground year-round, and which may be as large as a football field. Those thousands of mushrooms spread around a meadow, seemingly separate, are all organs or parts of a single organism.

In the Western worldview, a person is like our erroneous concept of the mushroom. Tiny, temporary and isolated. When we switch to the Meditator's worldview, we see the mushroom as an integral part of a mycelium field, and the individual person as an inseparable part of the universal consciousness.

The Cosmic Ocean

A wave in an ocean seems to have an individual identity of its own. It appears, and exists for a while. You can watch it, and listen to it, and surf on it. Then it disappears back into the ocean, of which it was composed. Try thinking of yourself as a wave in the ocean of consciousness.

While the Western worldview focuses on "me" (everything inside my skin, including my thoughts, emotions, and desires), the important element of the Meditator's worldview is that we are each much more than a tiny, isolated mind/body.

We are instead, as described in the three analogies above, each a tiny but important part of a collective consciousness which includes all that has ever existed. We've just momentarily lost sight of this fact when we were born into this culture, with its prevailing Western view.

Please take a moment now, return to the box on page 48, and do the Breath Counting meditation. Do it once or twice.

Your Own Worldview: A Pervasive Perspective

Taking either the Western or the Meditator's approach to life shapes our perceptions of some very basic issues. Attitudes towards birth, death, and everything in-between are affected by our choice of worldview.

Birth

In the Western worldview, birth is seen as a rather mechanical event combining egg and sperm like two chemicals that mix to form a compound substance with its own particular properties. Consciousness then results from a bio-chemical reaction in the newly-formed brain.

In the Meditator's worldview, some impulse or desire in the big consciousness to express itself in physical reality causes the interactions necessary to bring a man and woman together, then sperm and egg. Thus each individual is a "recycled piece" of the universal consciousness.

God

In the Western worldview, God tends to be seen as above and separate from the world. God is the creator of the universe, almost as a person might create and then run a business.

In the Meditator's worldview, God isn't separate from the world, but is the consciousness out of which everything is formed. So God is the entire universe, which includes me, you, Mother Teresa, and Al Capone.

From the Western point of view, when someone says "I am God", it probably means that they are crazy, and they expect everybody else to bow down to them. From the Meditator's point of view, when someone says "I am God", it may mean that they understand that everybody, and everything, is God also, because God is the "stuff" out of which everything, and everybody, is made.

Cause and Effect

In the Western world, individuals perform specific actions that have particular effects on the world. In the Meditator's worldview, everything you do is connected to, and dependent on, everything else.

Think about your neighbor's cat. Its movements in the neighborhood, in the Western view, seem random, and completely independent of anything else. Yet, in the Meditator's view, the cat is drawn to one yard because of a honeysuckle bush that attracts hummingbirds and avoids another yard due to the presence of a large dog.

The honeysuckle bush was planted by a family who left the Old Country after an earthquake in the 1880's. The other family bought a watchdog after a neighbor's house was broken into by thieves. In a very real way, the cat's movements today are connected to an earthquake in the past and the fear of potential crime in the future. This same "interconnected" viewpoint applies to any event: political, social, economic, or interpersonal.

Good and Evil

In the Western worldview, events and people that you like are called "good", those you dislike are called "evil". Good and evil are considered absolute terms. It is always possible to tell them apart, and to tell which is which.

In the Meditator's worldview, it's understood that good and evil are relative terms. Each is valid only when considered from a particular point of view. During the Civil War, a Northerner would consider General Grant good, and General Lee evil. A Southerner would think exactly the reverse.

Death

In the Western worldview, death of the body necessarily means death of consciousness, since consciousness is merely a by-product of the brain's bio-chemical activities. Even those Western viewers with traditional Judeo-Christian or other religious upbringings may find it difficult to reconcile their religious beliefs about life after death with their beliefs about physiological reality.

In the Meditator's worldview, death means some kind of re-absorption or recycling into the universal consciousness. Thus, it is easy and natural to believe in some form of life after physical death, even though the specifics may be presently unknowable. Virtually all of our spiritual leaders, from Moses to Martin Buber, and from Jesus to Thomas Merton, have deeply believed in the Meditator's outlook on life after death.

Living In The "Real" World

Of course, believing in the Meditator's worldview doesn't mean that you won't spend a lot of your day-to-day life in the Westerner's world. And, that being the case, it's convenient, even necessary to act as if cause and effect, life and death, good and evil, were real and meaningful.

A theoretical physicist knows that his kitchen table is composed largely of the empty space between electrons. However, he confidently uses it to support his lunch. An Australian Aborigine believes in "Dream Time" -- a mystical reality in which dreams and spirits rule the earth, determining the outcome of all events. Yet he also depends on his knowledge of animal behavior and local geography in order to live.

You can live, and act, in the world using the Westerner's view. At the same time, you can begin to open your mind to the possibility that the Meditator's worldview has a validity of its own. The following section may help you to accept the Meditator's view (on an intellectual level, at least) right now.

Why We Might As Well Believe

As you continue to meditate, the Meditator's worldview will begin to feel more right to you on a gut, or emotional level. But today, you probably feel doubtful about it, and wonder: Can the Meditator's worldview possibly be real?

Our answer to that is practical, rather than scientific or spiritual. And this same answer also works for what is perhaps humankind's oldest question: "Is there life after death?"

There seems to be a certain amount of evidence that some part of a person may persist after the body dies, although it's impossible to know for sure, until you die yourself. But we are sure, dead sure, that we just can't lose by maintaining a belief in continuing existence after the death of the body. "How can this be?" you may well ask. We'll tell you.

If we're right, and a continued existence of some sort does follow death, we'll be prepared. And throughout this present life, we'll have had the faith and support that comes from a belief in undying consciousness.

If we're wrong, and absolute nothingness follows death, we'll never realize our mistake. But we'll still have gained the same benefits from that belief during our life! It's a bet that we really can't lose!

On the other hand, let's say that we may choose to disbelieve in consciousness after death. However, if we're right, and nothingness follows death, we'll never have the satisfaction of knowing that we were right. And if we're wrong, not only will we be unprepared for whatever comes next, but we'll have cheated ourselves out of the benefits of belief in some type of life after death during this lifetime! What a lousy deal!

We feel exactly the same way about the Meditator's worldview. If we're wrong in our belief, we'll never know. And right or not, our trust in the Meditator's worldview can help us to live right now with increased acceptance and confidence!

Chapter Five, In a Nutshell...

Don't spend too much time now worrying about the philosophical underpinnings of "The Big Picture." Read the sections above, if you're so inclined. Especially the last one, about why "We Might As Well Believe" — it's the most important one, and might be of real philosophic value to you someday.

Otherwise just continue skimming your way to the next box, once you've finished reading this little "nutshell..."

Chapter Six:
MetaPhysical Fitness

It's often tempting to think in terms of specific, concrete "things" or "outcomes" rather than in terms of ongoing "processes". And it would be so convenient if "mindfulness" were an object of some sort, that we could obtain or achieve once and keep forever (whether we used it or not), like a rowboat or a law degree. But it's not.

> Mindfulness is an ongoing process, and it requires ongoing practice. It's rather like getting (and staying) in shape...

Getting in shape isn't too hard. A few weeks or months of weight lifting combined with the South Beach Diet and we look and feel great! Jogging and the Atkins Diet will work also, or Aerobic Parachuting and the Rutabaga Diet. But after just a few months of indolence and over-indulgence, we're again ready to enter the Goodyear Blimp Look-Alike Contest. Of course, even sporadic, feeble attempts at getting into shape are better than none, although the effects of such lackadaisical efforts may be almost imperceptible.

We really like the comparison of mindfulness with the idea of getting in shape. Like getting in shape, there are a wide variety of equally effective ways to go about meditating. Like getting in shape, anyone can meditate, although it sometimes *seems* easier or more natural for certain people than for others. (Usually someone other than ourselves.)

> Once a person has become physically fit (by using *any* diet and/or exercise method), everything they do both reflects their fitness and helps to increase it. They walk with bounce and balance; they climb stairs instead of taking elevators.
>
> Once a person begins to meditate (using *any* of a variety of mental exercises), everything that happens to them presents a great opportunity both to utilize and to improve their meditative skills. Fears and desires, annoyances and disappointments, all become grist for the meditative mill!

You Use It or You Lose It

Unfortunately, just as with getting in shape, if we stop meditating, we lose its benefits.

And, as with getting in shape, we have to begin meditating somewhere. Very old or infirm persons wouldn't start their exercise programs by trying to run the Boston Marathon, but might instead begin with daily walks around the block. A modest beginning, but certainly steps in the right direction!

Someone new to meditation, or someone lacking time and commitment to a meditative practice, surely wouldn't buy a one-way ticket to that monastery in the Himalayas. Even 20 minutes twice a day at home might be just too much to commit to. But a few of the Three Minute Meditations might be exactly what the (meta)physician ordered!

> As with exercise — for beginning meditators, it's better to start small, than not to start at all! And, once started, the benefits of meditation may become so appealing that mindfulness becomes part of the natural flow of life.

Martial Arts Of The Mind

The karate student practices in the "dojo", or karate studio. He or she practices a variety of punches and kicks, doing each one separately, carefully repeating each movement tens of thousands of times. A new neural path is created, then strengthened, for each physical motion.

After mastering each move in isolation, the student begins to practice more complicated combinations of blows, performing each sequence hundreds or thousands of times. Sparring with other students or instructors comes next. Finally, if one day martial skills must be used on the street, in a real combat situation, this practice has prepared the student to do so.

Consider, likewise, the beginning weight lifter. He or she practices the complex motion necessary to get the barbell overhead by starting off with a light weight, not the heaviest one in the gym. Once the hand/arm/body motion is memorized (or, we might say, the appropriate neural path has been created and strengthened), then and only then is it time to increase the weight.

Similarly, whitewater kayakers must learn a rather complicated technique known as the "Eskimo Roll", which enables them to turn their kayak right-side-up after it has turned bottom-up in a river rapid. They first learn this technique (that is, create a neural path for it) in a swimming pool. Once they feel comfortable "rolling" in the pool, they go out and purposely capsize their boat in a very small rapid, and then try to roll. Gradually, they progress to practicing in larger and more dangerous rapids, until they can confidently roll *anywhere* on the river.

> Students of any athletic discipline begin their practice under safe and controllable conditions. As their skills develop, they can apply what they've learned in more challenging circumstances. You will do the same with your meditative discipline...

You've already begun to practice the Breath Counting Meditation, a simple type of Three Minute Meditation is one of our "Clearing The Mind" Exercises. For now, you're doing it (we hope) either in completely calm surroundings, or on the level of imaginary practice (as described on page 50) or perhaps during *very* mildly annoying events. As you become more adept at meditating, you'll be able to use your meditations to short-circuit Fight or Flight Responses and defuse stress in increasingly difficult situations.

But for now, you'll simply practice in a safe setting. Or at times, instead of getting slightly anxious or a tad annoyed, you'll just turn your mental attention to Breath Counting as the slow deli clerk cuts into your lunch hour, or as the elevator refuses to stop at your floor, or when the omelet comes to your table, overcooked. This practice will improve both the quality of your life, and the quality of your meditation!

Chapter Six, In a Nutshell...

Each of the Three Minute Meditations is an exercise for the mind. Like the athletic exercises which prepare the body to excel at sports such as martial arts, weightlifting, kayaking — they build the Mental Muscle™ and the new neural paths that are needed to live mindfully.

These beginning techniques must be first practiced under controlled conditions (the kayaker practices in a pool, not a raging river) in order to later obtain benefits in "real life" situations. Thus you'll work with the slow deli clerk or the elevator that won't stop at your floor — and not with your most feared rival or most hated adversary — in your beginning meditation practice.

You'll gain confidence by practicing the Three Minute Meditations when you're alone, or under *mildly* challenging real-life situations, as we've recommended.

After practicing, you'll be able to apply your meditative skills to more serious mental and interpersonal predicaments.

Step One: What You Need to Know

Congratulations: You've already taken this step, Step One, by either skimming the boxes up to now or having read each word (your choice). You don't need be able to tell the axon end of a neuron from the dendrite end. You don't need to have memorized the various and sundry elements of the Meditator's Worldview. You only need to understand two things:

• First, you'll need at least a vague general understanding of the function of the brain and the mind (which is the non-physical but very real component of those three pounds of grey matter atop your neck). This general understanding will include the following facts:

> The 100 billion cells that make up your brain are called **Neurons.**

> Neurons link together to form the **Neural Paths** that underlie your words, your actions, and everything that you have learned.

> The more often you use any neural path, the stronger it becomes, and the easier it is to "travel" that path.

> Some neural paths are learned, others are "hard-wired" — that is, built into your brain since birth. The two most important hard-wired neural paths are the **Fight or Flight Response** (which causes the emotions known as Anger and Fear), and the equal but opposite **Relax and Release Response** (which *reverses* the effects of any Fight or Flight Response).

• Secondly, you'll need a sense that experienced meditators tend to have a different way of looking at the world than most people do.

These two main points will help you to understand why you're doing what you'll be doing as you use the rest of this book.

Even if you've just skimmed boxes to get to this one, you've taken Step One: Getting a very quick and basic Understanding of the Brain and the Mind, and of the Meditator's Worldview.

You've got plenty of theory. Are you ready for Step Two? Ready or not, it's time to do a Breath Counting meditation (page 48) right now, before reading on!

STEP TWO:
Clearing the Mind

Welcome to Step Two of *The Three Minute Meditator,* which is composed of Chapters Seven through Fourteen. Here we'll begin to introduce you to a variety of the Three Minute Meditation mind-clearing exercises themselves. This is the longest step, and in some ways the most important one, since it provides you with the basic "how to do it" — the "nuts and bolts" — of meditation.

In our Introduction, we spoke about ourselves and discussed how this book is organized. In Step One, we presented a general summary of how the brain works, and why learning to short-circuit the Fight or Flight Response by consciously triggering the Relax and Release Response is important. We also discussed the way in which many experienced meditators view the world.

As you read Step Two, you will learn some variations on the Breath Counting Meditation that you've already (we hope) begun to practice. A variety of new exercises will be added, so that you can experiment, and choose the ones that suit you and fit into your daily routine — at home or at work — the best. (Please note, by the way, that we use the words "meditation" and "exercise" pretty much as synonyms.)

Once again, especially important paragraphs will be boxed.

If you think it might be helpful, you can review the introductory material on the Breath Counting Meditation in Step One (page 48). Or else turn the pages, and try some exciting new meditations!

Important: If the Breath Counting Meditation seems hard, please just keep working at it, and keep reading, for three reasons:

- It gets easier with practice (like everything else). If you can only get as far as *"Inhale...One...Inhale...Two...Inhale...uh oh"* right now — well, after another few attempts, which only take a moment or two, you'll be able to get all the way up to *"Inhale...One...Inhale...Two...Inhale...three...uh oh."*

- Chapter Ten will help you deal with discouragement, doubt, self-criticism, and other common but unuseful thoughts that beginning meditators (and even experienced ones) often encounter. After reading it, you'll appreciate the value of reaching even one more breath in the breath count!

- Some of the new Three Minute Meditations that follow may be easier, and better suited to you, than the breath count. So please keep reading, even if the Breath Counting has seemed frustrating.

A Few General Thoughts...

As you'd expect after reading about the Meditator's Worldview, these steps tend to melt, blend, and overlap into each other. But we are certain that for most people, Step Two, *"Clearing The Mind,"* has the most critical information. In fact, you could easily spend an entire lifetime or three just on Step Two! We still spend about 80 or 90% of our meditation time with the mind-clearing exercises. This is how we build the Mental Muscle™ that enables us to use the mindfulness techniques in real-life stressful situations. That is, when we *really* need them!

Chock-Full of Thoughts

Minds are just chock-full of thoughts, many of which trigger Fight or Flight Responses and thus become emotions. You may sometimes be able to concentrate so intensely on a specific task that no distracting thoughts interfere. For a while. But soon enough a moment of restlessness, or doubt, or desire, or fear creeps in. And, thoughts being what they are, when your mind isn't strongly focused — when you're driving, or eating, or just relaxing by yourself — your mind may jump from thought to thought like the proverbial "drunken monkey" leaping aimlessly from branch to branch.

Most of the time, our mental attention is directed outwards, to other people, to the outside world. Our minds are full of thoughts that plan for the future or analyze the past. We constantly make judgments about everything that passes into our mental field of view: "I like this person... dislike that one... she's beautiful... he's a jerk."

"Grabby" Thoughts

Some thoughts may last a lifetime, as when we spend years being obsessed by the same strong desire, raging over the same old anger, or beating ourselves with the same seemingly "unmanageable" fears. It often feels as though a particular thought has grabbed hold of us — like a hijacking of the mind — and just won't let go.

If we're able to watch our minds, as we'll learn to do in Step Three, we find that grabby thoughts are almost always those thoughts that trigger Fight Responses or Flight Responses. More on this, later...

Just One Thing to Focus On

When we work with the mind-clearing meditations, we simply focus our attention onto *just one thing*, whether it's our breath, our steps as we walk, a candle flame, or whatever other object of attention that we choose.

While shining the spotlight of our attention on the chosen object of our meditation, we try not to be distracted by the thoughts that normally harass us. These thoughts will inevitably sneak in because they are so ingrained, and that's okay. But even a few seconds of mental clarity can feel really soothing. A variety of mind-clearing exercises will be presented in Step Two, so that you'll be able to choose the ones that work best for you.

> Each mind-clearing exercise helps to quiet the constant, ongoing stream of chatter in the mind, while building Mental Muscle™.
>
> Mind-clearing techniques are also our greatest tool for short-circuiting unnecessary Fight or Flight Responses (many of which are triggered by repetitive and unuseful "Grabby Thoughts").
>
> Eventually, as the mind begins to clear, we can move on to the Step Three, *Watching The Mind*.

Chapter Seven: How To Use These Exercises

Some general guidelines for using the Clearing the Mind exercises follow. These suggestions will help you choose which ones to use, and in what order. They'll also offer hints on issues — like diligence, body position, and doubt — that we know can be tricky for beginning meditators (as well as more experienced ones, like us!).

One Size Fits All?

Lots of things — from workout pants to diet methods — are often breezily presented with a "one size fits all" approach. Usually, though, one size doesn't really quite do it for us (especially since David is literally twice as big as Nina). Nor does this standardized approach work for meditation. Although many meditation methods (even some popular ones) have just one set of exercises or practices, we believe that each of us needs to learn how to best integrate meditation into our own unique daily life.

Meditation exercises are not "one size fits all." So you'll probably need to try a few before you find the ones that work best for you. Naturally, if you decide you like the Breath Counting Meditation best, that's fine — stick with it. But please remember...

Doing at least one — *any* one — of these exercises at least a few times a day is more important than reading about them. So feel free, if you like, to read only the boxes below, and scan the section titles, until you get to the new meditations.

Then you may (or may not) want to spend a couple of days or weeks doing a variety of The Simplest Clearing the Mind Meditations that follow, before you go on to the rest of the book. Or you may want to keep doing just one particular meditation that you like, while you continue to read on.

The "Crawl Before You Walk" Approach

Some meditation students like to spend a while working with all of The Simplest Clearing the Mind Meditations. These are easy because they are quite "cut and dried," almost mechanical. If you follow the simple instructions, you cannot go wrong. They are the "meat and potatoes" of meditation, and we enjoy doing some of them at least a few times each day. Practice these for as long as you like. If you did nothing but one or two of these exercises daily for the rest of your mindfulness practice, you would still derive great calmness and energy from your efforts. You don't have to do anything fancy to get results, as this tale indicates.

The story goes that an early Catholic bishop went to visit three old monks who lived on an island, because he'd heard that they believed in Jesus, and he wanted to teach them to pray in the proper manner. When he arrived, he discovered that their only prayer or meditation (referring to the Christian idea of The Trinity) was the simple "The Lord is Three, and we are three," repeated continuously.

The bishop spent days teaching the old men how to pray properly. Long, complex Latin prayers and invocations. Then he and his entourage sailed away, satisfied with a job well done.

But when his boat was only a few miles away from the island, the ship's lookout spied a mysterious blur overtaking them. It soon turned out to be the three monks, running over the surface of the water to catch the ship.

"Your Holiness," they panted as they came within shouting distance, "We've forgotten our new prayers!"

And the bishop was chastened, and bade them return to their former simple and effective practice...

A simple meditation that you *do* will provide much greater benefits than a "fancy" meditation that you *don't do!*

As the ancient Shaolin Kung Fu saying goes, "Do not fear the fighter who knows ten times ten thousand types of kicks. Fear the one who has practiced one kick ten times ten thousand times."

The "Shotgun" Approach

If you prefer, you can spend just a few minutes trying all of the following meditation exercises, in whatever order you choose, including the slightly More Complex Clearing the Mind Meditations. You may find that one or more seem to be a better "fit" with your own personal style of doing things. We'll discuss this issue of personal style and meditation choice right now, since it's an important issue for many beginning meditators.

Bats, Birds, Bees, and Barnacles (and Don't Forget the Parrots)

Speaking of personal style, David has worked directly with tens of thousands of people in his workshops, and we've realized (duh!) that people have different preferences in how they relate to the world. This also, of course, applies to how they relate to meditation, and especially to which exercises they prefer.

We introduced this concept, naturally enough, back in the Introduction, when we offered you both a visual image (our "Three Minute Meditator Pyramid") and our "Baseball Metaphor" as ways to understand the organization of this method. Now it's time to consider it in more detail.

Some (we call them the "Bats") are audio learners — they like exercises, such as the chanting meditations, which have sound components. They may like the verbal labeling meditations, and wish to whisper parts of a meditation that others would say silently to themselves.

Others are "Birds" (an eagle can spot a rabbit from a mile away!) and prefer a visual meditation, like the Draw-a-Breath™ or the Flame Watching exercises.

"Bees" are busy, and like the Walking Meditations (or even Jogging and Running Meditations).

"Barnacles" may not be very active physically, but they are very sensitive to sensations — how things feel and smell and taste — and may prefer the Tongue Block Breath, or the Very Simple Eating Meditation and Heartbeat exercises that come later on.

"Parrots" talk. (Yes, we know that parrots are birds, but we liked the alliteration of the four "b" sounds in our title.) They are very verbal. And some of us use speech — whether actual physical speech or talking to ourself — as a way of relating to the world. "Parrots" may enjoy the labeling type of meditations that we'll describe soon.

These personal preferences are why, though we think that The Simplest Clearing the Mind exercises are great to start with, we suggest that you consider using the "Shotgun" Approach as well, especially if none of the simplest exercises quite seem to suit you.

> Many of us have a preferred sense. Some of us would prefer to listen to a lovely piece of music rather than see a beautiful painting. Some of us like to jump right in and "do" when confronted with a new situation, while others prefer to "get the feel of things" first. Yet others like to talk a situation through, before they even consider starting to "feel" or "do."
>
> We refer to these different types of folk as "bats" (hearing), "birds" (seeing), "bees" (physically active), "barnacles" (physically sensitive), and "parrots" (verbal).
>
> If you have a strong preference for a particular sense — hearing, seeing, physically doing, feeling, or talking/reading — this may affect the type of meditation that will be easiest for you to do, and also easiest type for you to keep doing.

Progressive Meditation: What's Easy And What's Hard

You are really the only person who can say what's easy or hard for yourself. In general, we've tried to arrange the exercises in the order of difficulty that meditators and teachers we know tend to agree on. But although there was some agreement that the first five exercises were the simplest, there was considerable disagreement about the ranking of the rest. So you'll just have to try them all for yourself!

There is a certain progression to the exercises in Step Two. We begin by focusing the spotlight of our attention on first the *counting,* and then the *labeling* of natural processes, like breathing and walking. We then focus attention on *actual physical objects* — such as the sound of a syllable, a flame, a taste, or the movements involved in taking a simple step — without counting, labeling, or (we hope) thinking at all. In later Steps we will move away from natural processes and tangible objects to focus attention directly upon *emotions* or *ideas* such as "Compassion", "Non-Judging", "Impermanence", or the elusive "I Am".

Chapter Seven: In a Nutshell...

You may be a Bat or a Bird, a Bee, a Barnacle, or a Parrot. You may prefer to use either the "Crawl Before You Can Walk" or the "Shotgun Approach" strategies to choose which exercises to do.

But the bottom line is this: just read about a variety of meditation exercises right away, choose one or two or three that feel comfortable to you, and *start doing them!*

Memorizing *every* word or doing *every* exercise in this or any other book is worth less to you than spending a few minutes a day with only the simplest Breath Counting Meditation.

And even the simplest Breath Counting Meditation can be used to work with the Dead End Thought Strategy in Chapter Twelve — and that will cut out a chunk of daily stress, right away!

Chapter Eight: What To Do When It Hurts

Sometimes, as we look deeply into ourselves, old or hidden pain can arise. It may not happen to you, but if it does, please be sure to read this section carefully.

> If you are already under a doctor's or psychotherapist's care, you should definitely discuss this book with them before using it. By the way, psychotherapy and meditation make an especially effective combination, as we discuss in the Appendices! As you continue to meditate, previously unconscious material will come clearly into view, where it can be worked with.
>
> If you are in great mental pain now, perhaps you should carefully read the entire book before doing any of the exercises, and then start out with the "Compassion" meditations of Step Six. They are probably the most effective exercises in the book for dealing with suffering of any kind.

There are two distinct types of mental suffering. There's the suffering that occurs when we are not meditating, or before we've learned to meditate, when our thoughts, our fears and desires, cause us pain. This is the type of suffering that many of us experience on an *ongoing* basis. Since many non-meditators have little control over their thoughts, this kind of suffering is hard to deal with. It may possibly diminish if we can change various external circumstances in our lives. But it probably won't. Instead, it's more likely that the pain will either persist (or return after a brief interval) and eventually change the new circumstances for the worse!

The type of suffering that may arise during meditation is different, although it can, on the surface, feel the same. But it is suffering whose purpose is to *end* further suffering. So if painful feelings arise while meditating, try to remember that these are the *temporary* pains that will help us to *end* the *ongoing* pain, just as the pain of the extraction is intended to end the ache of the infected tooth.

When we see deeper into, and learn about ourselves, we sometimes see elements of our personalities that we'd prefer to deny. As long as we remember to use the Watching the Mind exercises (presented in Step Three) to *observe* our pain, rather than just getting lost in the contents of the painful thoughts, we can *utilize* this *temporary* pain to reduce *ongoing* pain.

We know, from personal experience, that this is a difficult concept to believe, especially when you (or we) are in a state of suffering. Using the Compassion exercise may be especially helpful to ease the pain. It's what we try to do, when in pain, if we can be skillful enough, or mindful enough, to remember to do so.

Chapter Eight: In a Nutshell...

If mental suffering seems to arise while doing these simple meditations, take a break from meditation for a day or a week, and use that time to read your way through the rest of this book. Eventually, you'll feel ready to try some of the Softening Around Pain and Compassion exercises. After doing so, you'll be ready to return to Step Two, with the softness and compassion that is so crucial to a mindfulness practice...

Chapter Nine: Guidelines for Doing the Exercises

There are really only three important general guidelines for doing the exercises.

The first is to be *diligent,* to commit yourself to remembering that you are meditating. This means that your attention is supposed to remain focused on the object of meditation, be it your breath, your steps, your feet, a sound, or a candle.

> Whenever any other thought intrudes, *as soon as you notice* that you are no longer focused on the meditation, bring your attention back to the meditation.

The second is to be *compassionate.* Spending time mentally yelling at yourself for not focusing on the meditation (because you momentarily thought of lunch, or work, or sex) is just more time spent not focusing on the meditation.

> No need to be critical when you lose your focus during a meditation — be kind (don't waste time berating yourself, that's just adding insult to injury!) and simply return your attention to the breath or other object of your meditation.

The third (which may help you with the second) is to realize that the thoughts which distract you from the meditation are actually *helping* you. They give you the opportunity to notice that you're no longer focused on the meditation, so that you can return your attention to it.

> It's good when your mind wanders off sometimes during a meditation! Think about the process of paper training a puppy. It starts when Spot looks as though she has to pee. You place her on the newspaper. She wanders off. You gently, patiently bring her back. She wanders off again. You bring her back.

> *It is the act of being returned* to the newspaper that paper trains the pup. If the foolish little thing never left the paper, you wouldn't have the opportunity to train it. So you don't kick it when it wanders off, nor do you give up in disgust. It's just the nature of a puppy to wander, and you appreciate each opportunity to correct its behavior during the training session.
>
> *Likewise, it is the act of noticing that the mind has wandered, and gently, patiently, returning the attention to the meditation, which helps us learn to focus the mind.*
>
> Your success in meditation is not judged by how many thoughts you can count in a row, or how long you can stay focused without distraction. To paraphrase David's teacher Stephen Levine, your success is indicated — when you notice that your mind has fallen from the meditation to thoughts of lunch or sex or money — by your ability to use compassion to pick yourself up, dust yourself off, and return without self-criticism to the meditation: *"Inhale...One...Inhale...Two...Inhale..Three..."*

Twin Examples

In David's inspiring early experience:

"When I began to meditate, I was "plagued" both by distracting thoughts and self-criticism. I'd try to focus on my breathing, but a typical meditation session might have gone something like this: "breathe in, breathe out...wow, I'm meditating...uh-oh, I'm not supposed to be thinking about meditating, I'm supposed to be focusing on my breathing...in, out...hungry...uh-oh...drat, I can't do this, I'm no good...in, out, in, out, in, out...hey, I've got it now!...feelings of pride...uh-oh, better go back to breathing...in, out, in out...wonder what's for lunch, hmmm, hope it's spicy, I remember when we ate that...uh-oh, lost it, I'm an idiot, I'll never be able to do this, oh well...in, out, in, out...wonder if it's time to stop yet...etcetera". Sometimes I'd get lost in an exciting daydream or a session of planning for some future event, and my period of distraction would then last for minutes at a time, far longer than I was ever able to stay focused on my breath!

"Now that I'm more experienced, I still have plenty of sessions like that! But many times, I can just *quickly notice* that a thought has crept in, and *go right back to my preferred business at hand*, which is meditating.

So a current session might look more like this: "breathe in, breathe out, in, out, in, out...ahh, a lunch thought...in, out, in, out...Doing Well!...ahh, that's a pride thought...in, out, in, out...". Of course, sometimes I still spend more time being distracted, than being focused! But I notice the distractions more quickly, and return to the meditation!"

As Nina describes her first stellar attempts at meditating:

"At first, I felt frustrated because I kept wondering whether or not I was 'doing it right.' I'd start meditating and immediately (being a perfectionist) begin evaluating and criticizing my own performance: Breathe in, breathe out...Is this how it's supposed to feel? In, out...I'm feeling really restless...In, out...I kind of want to crawl out of my skin...in, out, in, out...I wonder if most people have this much trouble getting started? I'll bet no one else has as much trouble doing this as I am. Maybe it won't work for me ...maybe I should just give up right now... In, out... in, out..."

"Once I decided simply to return to the meditation every time I began to grade my efforts, I was finally able to stop worrying about how I was doing and just focus on meditating. When I started to apply compassion to those interfering thoughts, I saw how much unnecessary pain I was creating by being so self-critical.

"My meditations still get restless and judgmental at times, but now I'm better able to watch my thoughts and to see how my drive to 'do it perfectly' gets in the way of simply doing it!"

> If you like, read about our own feeble attempts to meditate, back when we started. It's still hard sometimes, but like most things, meditation gets easier with practice (as you build those neural paths).

On Diligence and Commitment

It is important to be diligent in your attention to the meditation. That means that *as soon as you notice* that your attention has strayed from the meditation, you are committed to bringing it gently, but firmly, back. Just like you return the puppy to the paper. That means not spending even an extra second on that interesting thought or exciting daydream. (So forget David's mind's favorite bogus trick of losing his focus for him by saying "But wait — *this* is a really *important* thought that has popped into my mind — I'd better stick with it, and come back to the meditation in a minute!")

Wasting Time with Self-Criticism

Don't waste even a second on self-critical thoughts like, "Darn it! There I go, thinking again". Simply *let go* of whatever thought it was that just passed through and come back to the meditation. Just for these three minutes, the meditation is your *preferred* thought — any others can wait.

> Being diligent in returning your attention to a meditation when thoughts have intruded is a bit like training yourself to wear a seat belt. As soon as you notice that it isn't buckled, you put it on, *every time*, even if you're only three blocks away from your destination. Soon it becomes a habit (and a healthy one, at that).
>
> And remember: During a meditation, a second spent in self-criticism ("I'm soooo not good at focusing!") is another second spent not meditating.

On Body And Hand Position

Luckily for you, we don't require a full lotus position for meditation (can't do one, ourselves, without enriching our chiropractors)! It's probably best to meditate (except for the walking-based meditations) while sitting up straight. Not ramrod rigid, but not slouching either, with your feet flat on the floor. Then again, you'll sometimes want to meditate while lying down, or while on the bus, or when standing in line. You may even want to meditate while in the bathroom (Nina enjoys meditating while taking a shower). So don't worry much about body position. Sit up straight when it's convenient, and see if it makes any difference to your concentration.

However, for many people find that it's useful to maintain a particular and *consistent* hand position while doing most of their meditating (yoga folks call this a "*mudra*"). David favors having some part of the thumb tip of each hand very lightly touching the curled tips of his fore and middle fingers. It feels natural to him, and doesn't attract attention when he does it in public, since it's not a particularly unusual hand position.

Nina likes to rest her hands on her legs just above her knees, palms down. Whatever hand position you choose, after a bit of experimentation, is fine — it's using the same hand position consistently which is often helpful, for the following reason.

> Don't worry about the lotus position, unless you are already a yoga practitioner. But once you become familiar with the process of meditating, simply re-creating the hand position that you consistently use will help you to enter into a meditative state of mind.
>
> Learning to maintain a standardized hand position can help to act as a "memory cue" or "trigger" for mindfulness — that is, it starts you off on the neural path that leads you to this serene and highly aware state.

Having established a hand position "trigger" can be especially useful in stressful situations, like a job interview, where you cannot take "time out" to go and meditate (unless you fake a bathroom break — a useful tactic at times). But simply touching thumb to forefinger while taking a deep and mindful breath can help to remind you of the peaceful place that you find in meditation, and give you energy to continue the interview with confidence.

Competitive Meditation

It's easy to get competitive, or goal-oriented, with meditation (or with anything else, in this high-pressure culture of ours). The late Tibetan guru Trungpa Rimpoche used to call this "Spiritual Materialism"!

> Try to think of meditation as dance, rather than a race. In a race, the goal is to reach the end faster than anyone else, or faster than you've ever done it before. In a dance, the goal is to enjoy what you're doing while you're doing it. So try not to worry about whether your meditations are "improving", or about whether you're "doing it right". Just do it!

Even in a race situation, excessive concern about how you are doing (looking back over your shoulder too often) will actually break your stride and decrease your performance.

What To Do With Feelings Of Doubt And Resistance

Minds being what they are, at some point yours is going to say to you: "This just won't work" or "Why bother?" These thoughts and feelings are the results of old neural paths — such as the popular "When I can't get good at something quickly, I get frustrated, then mad (or discouraged) and quit." If you can learn to use the mind-watching exercises described in Step Three, you'll be able to use these very thoughts of doubt or resistance themselves as objects of focus for your attention. Once mind-watching becomes a practiced and ingrained response, it's amazing how everything becomes "grist for the mill," as Stephen Levine is fond of saying.

Facing Frustration: Two Common But Un-useful Paths: Anger and Angst

Animals tend to be Fight or Flight "specialists" in their focus on a single type of response. A gazelle will always prefer to run than fight, and a grizzly bear is likely to do the opposite.

Likewise, many of us tend to have one or the other of two common neural paths when faced with learning a new skill (especially a difficult one). Like a deeply worn rut of a path running across an empty lot, these neural paths can be so well-established, that they are automatically set into motion, hard not to follow, and hard even to notice.

For some of us, frustration (with the learning process) triggers the Fight part of the Fight or Flight Response, and anger results, as pictured on the following page.

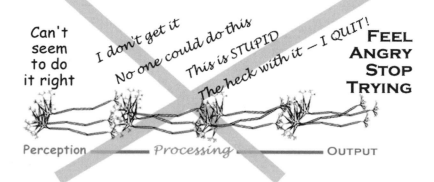

Frustration ➜ Fight Response ➜ Anger ➜ Quit

For others, frustration triggers the Flight part of the Fight or Flight Response, leading to feelings of depression, being "no good," helplessness, with a side of anxiety — in a (German) word, *angst!*

Frustration ➜ Flight Response ➜ Angst ➜ Quit

Of course, some of us are lucky enough to tend towards both anger and angst — a double whammy indeed!

Chapter Nine: In a Nutshell

The diagrams you just viewed tell the story. Some of us tend toward anger. Some towards *angst*. And, some of us are lucky enough to tend towards both! But regardless whether we "prefer" anger or *angst* as a response to frustration, the solution is that same:

Keep working on the Breath Counting Meditation, while you continue to read the rest of the book.

Just as smelly old manure can be turned into valuable fertilizer, you can use even thoughts of doubt and resistance to hone your meditational skills, merely by watching them. These thoughts will then become your teachers, instead of your tormentors.

But we need to take care that old and well-established, but un-useful, neural paths — like the path of frustration to anger, or the path of frustration to *angst*, as described above — don't prevent us from learning important new skills, like meditation.

If deeply engrained paths like these trouble you, please just continue reading, and you'll learn strategies to help you overcome unskillful neural paths and replace them with more helpful ones, because:

• **Triggering an unskillful neural path created in your past...**

• **Brings it into your present...**

• **Which affects both your present, and your future!**

Allowing an old Frustration to Anger neural path to force you to quit using this method will not just make you feel mad right now. It will also delay or prevent you from learning the most useful skill there is, and affect your future as well...

Chapter Ten:
The Simplest Clearing
The Mind Meditations

Most of the following mind-clearing exercises operate on what we call the "distraction and subtraction" principle. This means that:

• We give the mind a very simple but consuming set of instructions to follow, which just happen to…

• Replace the ongoing mental "chatter" that often fills many of our minds, and

• Trigger the Relax and Release Response, which relaxes us and…

• Short-circuits any Fight or Flight Responses that might arise in reaction to some fleeting thought and which would…

• Result in the emotions (like fear or anger) that are likely to disrupt both your meditations and your life. Without these emotions…

• The "normal" mental monologue of memories and plans for the future, of angers, fears and desires — can be stilled for a moment. The mind is too busy with the meditation exercise, too distracted by it, to keep up its usual chatter and story-telling.

Our minds, of course, are very good at bringing things into the view of our mental attention: chatter and story-telling, thoughts and emotions. What's two times two? The mind instantly shows you the answer. Imagine your favorite animal? No problem! (Right?)

Unfortunately, although schools and parents and the media are very good indeed at helping us put things into our minds, we are rarely encouraged to do the opposite. So most of us have never practiced taking attention away from thoughts. Many of us (ourselves included, until we began mindfulness practices) are unfamiliar with the serenity and spaciousness of a calm mind, having never experienced one.

When asked how he could carve an elephant from an immense block of stone, the master sculptor replied: "I simply cut away everything that doesn't look like an elephant." Carving away the excess thoughts from your mind — subtracting the mental monologue — will leave you with a clear and peaceful feeling, and eventually allow you to understand what really goes on in there!

After temporarily subtracting these above unwanted thoughts — especially the fears, angers, and desires — from the contents of the mind, you will gradually be able to directly observe the thought processes of the mind, with the mind-watching exercises of Step Three: *Watching the Mind*.

Eventually, you'll be able to use your mindfulness skills to intervene in un-useful thought processes, even during a difficult situation or a crisis. But for now, merely removing "excess" thoughts from the mind for a moment as you sit quietly, will be your goal.

Please begin by doing the original Breath Counting Meditation (page 48). Then read the entire text of the following exercises as you try each of them once or twice, while deciding which to keep doing.

Your Breath Counting Meditation

This first Three Minute Meditation involves our most basic need. We can live for days without water, weeks without food and perhaps years without sex or a job. But one scant minute without breathing is a long time, for most of us. Yet how often do we really focus our attention exclusively on this most crucial of functions? Fortunately, for a person in decent health, breathing doesn't take much thought —and many of us haven't usually given it much — until beginning to read this book.

Begin by practicing this meditation while sitting comfortably in a quiet place, with your hands in the thumb to forefinger position described on page 79. We'll repeat the instructions for this meditation here, just in case you need them.

Consider the act of breathing. At its most basic, each breath consists of two parts: the inhalation and the exhalation.

Begin by practicing this meditation while sitting comfortably in a quiet place, back straight, feet flat on floor, hands in lap.

Now simply pay attention to your breathing, and "count" four consecutive breaths.

Begin with an inhalation. Then, while you exhale, mentally label that out-breath with the number "One". Continue for three more breaths: Inhale... "One"..., Inhale... "Two"..., Inhale... "Three" ..., Inhale... "Four."

Strive not to lose the count, and also try not to alter or regularize your breathing in any way. If your mind wanders, or you lose the count, just return to: Inhale..."One"...

The beauty of this meditation is that, once learned, you can do it *anywhere*! Try it while waiting on line, or at the laundromat (no one can tell that you're doing anything unusual)! As the old saying goes: *"Don't just sit there — Meditate!"*

The "Step Counting" Meditation

The purpose of this exercise is simply — very simply — to force you to focus your mental attention onto your walking process for a moment or two. This, of course, will build Mental Muscle™, no matter how simple it seems.

Choose a situation in which you have to walk a short distance (not more than the length of a long room, at most). Perhaps you're sitting at your desk, and need to walk to the printer, or to the bathroom, at the other side of the room.

• Just count the number of steps it takes you to get there, by counting "one" as your foot hits the floor for the first step, "two" as your other foot hits the floor for the second step, and so on.

• As in the previous exercise, try not to lose the count, and also try not to alter or regularize your walking in any way.

If your mind wanders, or you lose the count, just try it again, as you walk back from the printer or the bathroom.

No need for even s second of self-criticism, no need for anger or discouragement, just a "do-over": Step..."One"...Step..."Two"...

The "Walking Breath" Meditation

Walk a bit more slowly than usual, focusing your attention on the ins and outs of your breath. Begin each inhale and each exhale with a mental label of "In" or "Out". Maintain a thumb to fingers hand position, unless that feels unnatural now. The "Walking Breath," in our opinion, this is one of the most rewarding of the meditations (especially for busy folk, and "bee" types), so we'll box it, for emphasis.

> • Without trying to control the breath too much, see if you can begin each in-breath and each out-breath exactly as one of your feet hits the ground. Do that for a moment.
>
> • Now notice how many steps you take during each inhalation, and how many steps you take during each exhalation.
>
> • Then count each step as you walk and breathe, so that in your mind you are saying "In, Two, Three, Four...Out, Two, Three, Four...In, Two, Three, Four...Out, Two, Three, Four..." or perhaps "In, Two, Three...Out, Two, Three..."
>
> • Continue to substitute "In" or "Out" in place of each count of "one", to help you stay focused on the breathing as well as the walking.

Your own personal breathing rhythm may be different from the above. Exhales may take longer than your inhales as in: "In, Two, Three...Out, Two, Three, Four..." Or inhales may take longer than your exhales as in: "In, Two, Three, Four, Five...Out, Two, Three..."

The step count is likely to vary from one breath to the next — just pay close attention, so that you can accurately count your steps during every inhale and every exhale. Just breathe, and walk, and count. As in all meditations, if your mind wanders, gently bring it back as soon as you notice that it's gone. Once having practiced this with walking, Bees may like to up the ante by applying the "Walking Breath" to hiking, jogging, or running.

> This is a perfect exercise to use as a "mini-meditation" — as we will describe a little later. Just choose a task (like walking from desk to printer) that involves walking for a few seconds, and apply this meditation each and every time you do that task. Or do it while you jog!

The "Breathing By The Clock" Exercise

This meditation is very "mechanical," and provides for an extremely powerful concentration that kicks in almost instantly. We find that some people like it, and some don't. But it can be done anywhere or anytime — standing, sitting, or lying flat on your back — that you can see a clock or a watch, and it offers the opportunity to practice building Mental Muscle™ in a minute or less.

You simply look at your watch or clock while you breathe. Inhale for a certain number of seconds, and exhale for a certain number of seconds. How many? That's up to you, and you'll have to experiment a bit to come up with a comfortable time for each in and out. When teaching this in a group, David usually starts people (with normal lung capacity) off by breathing in for three seconds, then out for three seconds (his favorite speed is fifteen in, fifteen out, but he's a harmonica player). Here's a breakdown of how it works:

> • Look at a clock or a watch, as you exhale.
>
> • Start emptying your lungs, so that you're ready to begin inhaling right when your timepiece is ready to click off a second.
>
> • Inhale to get your lungs reasonably but not uncomfortably full while your watch or clock ticks off three seconds, then...
>
> • Switch to the exhale as the watch hand or digital number hits the fourth second, and...
>
> • Continue to exhale as the watch ticks off three seconds, so that you end up reasonably but not uncomfortably empty, then...
>
> • Repeat for a while.

If three seconds feels like too long, try two seconds per inhale and two seconds per exhale. If three seconds doesn't feel like enough time, try five.

The ideal amount of time is that which makes it a bit of a challenge, but not an uncomfortable one. This forces you to keep your attention on the breath, since you don't want to run low on air towards the end of an out, or be too full at the end of an in!

The Breath Labeling Meditation

The "parrots" amongst us — the verbal types — may like this way of focusing mental attention on the breathing process. For some, the use of words is a very powerful way to focus.

When labeling the breath, we'll want to start in the simplest way possible: just labeling each inhale and each exhale with the words "in" and "out," as described in the box below, so that labeling each word takes exactly the same amount of time as your inhale or your exhale.

• Sit comfortably in a quiet place, back straight, feet flat on floor, hands in lap.

• Begin with an inhalation. While you inhale, mentally say the word "in" to yourself — extending the word "innnnn" for as long as you inhale.

• Then, while you exhale, mentally label that out-breath with the word "out" — extending the word "ouuuuttttt" for as long as you continue to exhale.

"Innnn...ooouuut....inn...ouutt...innnnnnn...ooooouuuttt..."

• Try not to alter or regularize your breathing in any way. If your mind wanders, just return to... "innnnn...ouuutttt..." for a few breaths more. No self-criticism, no angst, no anger.

Chapter Ten: In a Nutshell...

We hope that you've tried the above exercises, and found at least one that seems as though it might suit your personal style, and lifestyle. If not...

If any of the previous meditations "felt right," please feel free to spend a few days using it. If not, please read on to check out new exercises in Chapter Eleven, which are about the same level of difficulty as the ones you're just tried, just different.

If you've already found a meditation that feels right, you may want to jump to *Chapter Twelve: "Dead End Thoughts" and Using the Meditations in Daily Life* for some real life practice. But don't forget to return to Chapter Eleven for lots more meditation exercises to experiment with!

Chapter Eleven:
More Breath Meditations

We think that the following exercises may be the tiniest bit trickier than the ones we've already described. But you may not, so don't take our word for it — just try 'em for yourself!

Hold It: More on the Breath Labeling Meditation

After you've done the Breath Labeling Meditation a few times — just mentally saying the innnns and the oouuutts — explore a third part of the breathing process, the "hold."

Most of us never pay much attention to this part of the breathing process — unless we are consciously holding the breath while underwater, or to avoid a bad smell. However, when we pay very close attention to our breathing, we find that sometimes an exhale does not instantly follow an inhale, or vice versa. Instead, there is a fleeting moment in which breathing has stopped moving: the "hold."

Sometimes, as swimmers and divers know, the hold is very conscious, and controlled by closing off the back of the throat to keep from inhaling or exhaling through the nose (demonstrate this for yourself by "holding your breath" with your mouth open).

Other times the hold occurs when the diaphragm, the large plate-shaped muscle that flexes up to force air out, and flexes down to bring it in, stops moving for a moment. In this case (which most people would describe as "just not breathing for a moment," rather than "holding the breath) it doesn't matter if your nose and mouth are open or closed.

> Once again, consider the act of breathing and its two main parts: the inhalation and the exhalation. This time, consider also that you sometimes have a tiny "hold" between an in and an out breath, or an out and an in. Consciously or unconsciously, for a fraction of a second or for a longer time, there is neither inhale nor exhale.

- Sit comfortably in a quiet place, back straight, feet flat on floor, hands in lap.

- Begin with an inhalation. While you inhale, mentally say the word "in" to yourself — extending the word "innnnnn" for as long as you inhale.

- Then, while you exhale, mentally label that out-breath with the word "out" — extending the word "ouuuutttt" for as long as you continue to exhale.

- If there is a moment between inhale and exhale, or between exhale and inhale, when the breath is not moving at all, label this mentally with the word "hold." (Or "hooooold" if the breath stops moving for a slightly longer time.)

"Innnn...ooouuut....inn...out...innnnnnn...hooold...ooouutt..."

- Just for practice, label a few breaths that you've consciously put "holds" into — although usually you'll want to try not to alter or regularize your breathing in any way — just label what's happening, trying not to either add or to avoid "holds."

- As you did before, if your mind wanders, just return to labeling "innnnn...ouuutttt..." (or if appropriate perhaps to an "innn...hoolldd...ouutt...") for a few breaths more.

Hiccups, Burps, and Sneezes

If, during a Breath Labeling Meditation, you should happen (and it does happen to even the most dedicated of us) to interrupt your breathing with a hiccup, a burp, a sneeze, a swallow, or any other natural function — just label it.

"inn(hic)nnn...oooouuttt(swallow)...innnnnnn...ooouuttt..."

The Draw-a-Breath™ Meditation

This one is "for the birds" — that is, for the visually-oriented. It's a very powerful focus exercise that can be practiced anywhere you have a pen or pencil and a piece of paper (David invented it to present in his corporate workshops — it's great if you want or need to meditate during long meetings). It may also help you notice any "holds" that occur when you breathe.

In the Draw-a-Breath™ all you do is create a visual representation of your own breathing. Here's how (we won't put this whole exercise into a box, as it has too many charts):

It's easiest to do with lined paper at first, but if you need to, draw two neat parallel lines, about ¾ of an inch, or an inch apart. Label the top one as "Full," and the bottom line as "Empty," as shown.

FULL

EMPTY

The top line represents the state of your lungs almost completely full, as they are at the end of a long inhaled breath. The bottom line represents the state of your lungs being pretty empty, as they are at the end of a long exhale.

As with all (English) writing, you work from left to right. Put the point of your pen on the "empty" line, at the left edge. Breathe normally. After you've exhaled, begin drawing an upwards diagonal line until you're pretty full. Try to time your drawing so that by the time you're full, your pen point reaches the top line.

As you begin to exhale, start drawing a downwards diagonal line. The following chart shows how you'd draw four breaths: three slower and deeper breaths, then one shallower and "sharper" (a faster inhale crisply followed by a faster exhale) breath.

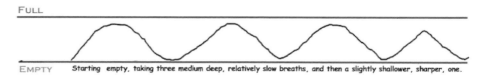

FULL

EMPTY   *Starting empty, taking three medium deep, relatively slow breaths, and then a slightly shallower, sharper, one.*

A more rounded contour represents a gentler breath. A more pyramid-shaped breath represents a sharper breath. Slower breaths take up more left to right space. Faster breaths take less left to right space. This next diagram represents five breaths and the very beginning of a sixth. The first breath slow and even, the next three fast and sharp, then a very slow one that ends with a really deep exhale (below the line), and ending just after the sixth breath begins.

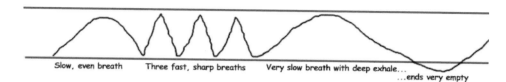

Slow, even breath   Three fast, sharp breaths   Very slow breath with deep exhale...

...ends very empty

You can do this for as long as you like, of course, just by jumping down to the next set of double lines when you run out of room.

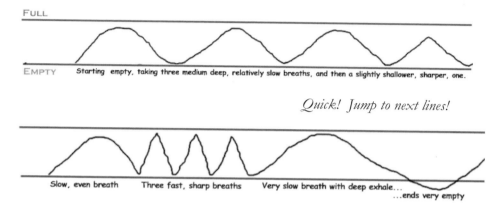

FULL

EMPTY   Starting empty, taking three medium deep, relatively slow breaths, and then a slightly shallower, sharper, one.

Quick! Jump to next lines!

Slow, even breath   Three fast, sharp breaths   Very slow breath with deep exhale...

...ends very empty

Once you really get the hang of this, you can add the tiny "holds" — the spaces between the inhales and exhales that most of us never even notice unless we are consciously "holding our breath." Sometimes our in breaths are sharp, with a crisp change from in to out, or from out to in. Sometimes the change is slow and gently, almost imperceptible.

And often, there is a tiny pause when no air is moving, between an in and an out. The state of "holding" is simple to represent: a horizontal line. This line is long if the hold is long, and short if the hold is short. The "hold" line is near the top if you are "holding" with your lungs full, and near the bottom if you are holding with your lungs empty.

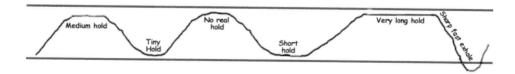

Medium hold   No real hold   Very long hold

Tiny Hold   Short hold   Sharp fast exhale

Get good enough at this, and you can throw in a little symbol of some kind for a burp or a hiccup, if you like!

> This is the ideal breath meditation for a boring or a stressful meeting, so it's worth a bit of practice (even if it seems confusing at first). You look as though you are carefully taking notes, but you are actually building Mental Muscle™!
>
> And don't worry about missing the content of the meeting. With a bit of practice, you'll have no trouble shifting your focus back and forth from the speaker's words, to your draw-a-breath chart!

The Tongue Block Breath

This easy but effective meditation came out of both the harmonica and the yogic traditions, and may especially appeal to the "barnacles" (those who are sensitive to bodily sensations) amongst us.

When playing harmonica, "tongue blocking" is a method of playing low and high notes simultaneously, by blocking out the middle notes with the tip of the tongue. During David's "Zen and the Art of Blues Harmonica" workshops, he noticed that many students found tongue blocking to be an excellent attention focuser. In the popular Kriya yoga style, an important technique involves placing the tongue tip so that it partially blocks the incoming air, which helps emphasize attention on the breath.

> • With lips partly open, touch the tip of your tongue to the roof of your mouth, less than an inch behind your upper front teeth.
>
> • As you inhale through your mouth, notice the coolness of each breath on the sensitive underside of your tongue.
>
> • As you exhale, notice that your cheeks puff out just a bit more than they normally would, due to your tongue blocking part of your partly closed mouth opening.
>
> • Count each breath up to four (or longer, like eight or ten if you like), with some appropriate mental label.
>
> "In Cool, Out One." "In Cool, Out Two."
>
> • Or if you prefer, forget about counting and simply notice the sensation of the air as it passes by this strange tongue position.
>
> "Parrots" may want to label this process verbally: "In Cool, Out Puff." "In Cool, Out Puff."

You can add this new tongue position to any of the breathing meditations: the basic ones, the chore-based one that's coming soon, or the Walking Breath. And it's inconspicuous enough to do in any place or anytime (which, of course, is where you *should* be doing it!).

The Mouth and Nose Breath Exercise

Here's another very simple breath meditation that may help some — especially the barnacles — to stay focused on the breath.

> • Breathe in through the mouth, then out through the nose. Or breathe in through the nose, and out through the mouth.
>
> • Parrot-folk may want to use a label: "In mouth, Out nose." If you like the breath counting, you can combine this exercise with counting: "in mouth...out nose One...in mouth...out nose Two..."
>
> As you are probably starting to notice, there are lots of specific techniques that can be used to help you focus your mental attention.
>
> That's because it's not really *what* you are focusing your attention on that's important — it's how *diligently* you maintain that focus, and how quickly but kindly you *return* your focus to the chosen meditation when you've lost it, without self-criticism, doubt, anger, or other common but un-useful reactions!

Yoga Time: Alternate Nostril Breathing

Not all yoga involves exotic poses that require balance, strength, and years of practice. If you can breathe through your nose (some of us can't, in hayfever season), and pinch your nose shut when you pass an especially ripe garbage can, you can learn the ancient yogic art of Alternate Nostril Breathing.

> • Start by making sure that you can breathe through your nose (if you can't, go on to the next exercise). Empty your lungs to a comfortable degree.
>
> • Put your thumb on one side of your nose, and your forefinger on the other, as though you were just about to pinch it shut.
>
> • Press either nostril shut with your forefinger (from the side, not front, so that it doesn't look like you're doing [con't next page]

anything too gross). Breathe in through the nostril that's open. Hold the breath for a bit if you feel like it.

• Now remove your forefinger from the first nostril and use your thumb to press the other nostril shut. Exhale through what is now the new open nostril.

• Repeat a few times. In through one nostril, out through the other.

The thumb — forefinger motion is easiest if you just hold your thumb and finger an inch apart, and move your whole hand from side to side, just enough to close one nostril, and then the other.

For variety, you can do the in-out (or the in-hold-out) using one nostril only, then switch and do an in-out (or in-hold-out) using the other nostril, then repeat.

Note to Yoga Practitioners Only: You're probably used to doing this exercise with a specific hand position (probably closing the nostrils with the ring finger and thumb, with other fingers held out straight), and possibly with a specific ratio of in to hold to out (these range from 1:1:1 to 1:4:2, with lots of variations). Feel free to keep doing it this way, but non-yogis shouldn't worry about these specifics.

And if you already do yoga, but don't apply a meditative mindset to the physical poses, you're missing half the fun (or the benefits, rather). Why not think about applying the same mental focus that we are recommending that you use with alternate nostril breathing to every yoga pose, if you are not already doing so? We'll talk about this some more in Step Seven: *Living in the Now*.

When It's Hard: The "Combo" Breath

Some people have a hard time staying focused for very long on a single breathing meditation. If this is true for you — or true at certain times, such as during stressful situations — try what we call a "Combo" breathing meditation.

When you just can't seem to stay focused, try a Combo Breath. In the Combo Breathing Meditation, you do four breaths (or you could decide to use five, or three) using one type of breathing meditation, then switch to four breaths of a different one.

For example, you might do four breaths worth of Breath Counting, then four breaths of Breath Labeling, then four breaths of Mouth and Nose Breathing, then four breaths of Alternate Nostril Breathing. Or more simply, go back and forth between four breaths of Breath Counting and four breaths of Breath Labeling.

Don't spend so much time thinking about what you're going to do next that you "miss" a breath, and use your favorites!

Chapter Eleven: In a Nutshell...

There's not too much to add here. Try — or at least read — each of the exercises. Some of them may feel more "right" to you than others. If possible, do all of them, a few times at least.

Building up a "repertoire" of different meditations will be very helpful when you begin to integrate them into different situations in your daily live. Please do remember the old adage "Different Strokes for Different Folks," and try them all to see which fit YOU best!

Chapter Twelve:
"Dead Ends" and Using
Meditation In Real Life

Dead End Thoughts

As David's first harmonica hero, Mr. Bob Dylan, put it in a song: "You ain't a-goin' no where." And that's what Dead End Thoughts do to us — take us...nowhere.

 When you're driving on your way to an appointment — perhaps to somewhere you haven't been before, but you know it's still a ways off — and you come up to a side street marked with a big yellow "Dead End" sign, what do you do? It's a no-brainer! No need to waste a thought on it. Just don't turn down that street. It's clearly marked as a dead end. It doesn't go anywhere that you want to go. Right?

Yet many of us allow ourselves, on a daily basis, to turn into a dozen dead end streets of the mind, only to get mired in the muddy cul-de-sac where they end, or lost in a morass of alleyways that go nowhere.

What are Dead End Thoughts? They are repeated thoughts which lead to neural paths that we identify, after careful reflection, as not being useful in any way.

For example, thinking of your least favorite politician while you're having dinner (and allowing the Fight or Flight Response that this triggers to upset your digestion) is probably not very useful to you. Just like turning into a dead end isn't useful, when you're trying to drive to the other side of town.

Soon we'll teach you to identify your own Dead End Thoughts. And then give you a specific strategy will help you to avoid allowing them to take you where you don't want or need to go.

Dead Ends or Dandelions

Once you know where a dead end street is, and you know that it is a dead end, it's usually pretty easy to avoid turning into it (except when you're tired, or not paying attention, or don't really care).

Unfortunately, it's not always easy to avoid Dead End Thoughts, even after we've identified them. This is especially true if you don't have much Mental Muscle™ at your disposal, yet.

So we sometimes refer to this type of thought (in addition to calling it a Dead End Thought) as a Dandelion Thought. Think about your garden, filled with tomato and pepper plants, and perhaps the odd gladiola or herb bush. When you spot a dandelion growing in there, do you have to think about it? "Hmmm…do I want a dandelion in between those tomato plants? Let me see…" Of course not! As soon as you notice it, you…

Pluck It and Chuck It

That's right, you pluck it out and you chuck it away, and you don't give it another thought! Naturally another dandelion will sprout up. But there's no need to get mad at the dandelion, or to pay it much attention. Even when it grows back. Once again, you just pluck it and chuck it. Every time the dandelions return to your garden, you just pluck 'em and chuck 'em, then go about your business.

Sometime we like to think of Dead End Thoughts as though they were like dandelions growing in our garden. Every time we see one, we just *Pluck It and Chuck It*.

No need to think much about it (as long as you already know how to identify a dandelion). No need to be angry (dandelions are pretty, make decent wine, and are fine out in the meadow): you just don't want them in your garden)…

Identifying Dead End Thoughts

In order to work with our Dead End Thoughts, we must first identify them. And every one of us, of course, has a different set of Dead End Thoughts. But regardless of type, identifying even one or two of them and working on them daily can have a very nice effect on your daily stress level!

A quick warning: David liked to lift weights when he was young, and he encouraged some fellow students to try the sport. As he (and we) has said before, "Never start with a 300 pound weight. You learn to do a particular lift with a very light weight. Once you've gotten it down — trampled down a solid neural path for the body motions needed — that's when you start adding weight."

> As we discuss the different categories of Dead End Thoughts, you'll see that some are "heavier" than others. Start off working with one or two lightweight ones, and in later Steps we'll help you with the heavies.

Here are some of the criteria we use for identifying Dead End Thoughts:

• They occur relatively often.

• They are unwanted (that is, they cause us pain in some way, most commonly through anger, fear, self-criticism, or unuseful desire).

• They have no useful purpose *at the present time*. This can change — an "I really hate my boss's son, whom I work with every single day" thought can be a Dead End while you've absolutely got to stay at the company in question, and a useful motivational thought once you decide to look elsewhere for work. Similarly, "I'm overweight" is a Dead End Thought, until the moment that you decide to go on an exercise and diet regimen.

• Generalized or specific self-hating or excessively self-critical thoughts are almost always Dead End Thoughts (unless you've done something *really* bad, and are able to use shame or self-criticism as a motivator to do better in the future, or to make amends).

Following are a few other categories of Dead End Thoughts. Once you've read about these, you can identify others on your own.

Out-of-Place Dead End Thoughts

Some Dead End Thoughts would be fine, if they happened at the right time. Thinking about food is a Dead End Thought if you're trying to finish a job on a tight deadline, or sitting in a class that you're interested in. But at the deli, considering lunch choices? Of course it's appropriate and useful.

Even useful thoughts (such as non-repetitive planning) or pleasant thoughts (like an entertaining memory) can arrive in your mind during a time or situation in which they are not useful. In this case, consider them to be Dead End Thoughts, for as long as you think they should be.

Leaving the Job, On the Job

One of the most common types of Dead End Thought involves bringing the job home with you — or bringing to any non-workplace location. Not just in your briefcase or backpack, but in your mind, in your neural paths. When you are not either working or doing useful planning for work, work thoughts are probably Dead End Thoughts.

Nina clearly saw a pattern of Dead End Thoughts — and saw the need to pluck and chuck — while walking in the woods on a beautiful day:

"I began to watch my mind, and realized that I was feeling angry about something that had happened two years before.

As I walked through the woods, surrounded by nature, instead of enjoying the sounds, smells, sensations of being outdoors, my mind fell into a painful and well-worn path. I could feel myself getting angry again – and going through a very familiar chain of anger, resentment, frustration, and anger … to the point where I felt as stressed as if the drama were still happening.

"I realized that I had completely lost track of the present moment and was recreating pain from my past. With that realization, I began to watch my mind. The pain of reliving a difficult time was transformed into a moment of insight when I understood that *I had a choice*. I could continue to re-play the anger in my mind, or I could pluck and chuck that Dead End Thought, and simply choose to let it go. Just some thoughts… passing through. No need to allow my mind to be hijacked by them, to let my moments in the woods be ruined. Amazingly, this simple mental action had a profound effect on my sense of well-being."

Deadline Dead Ends

Those of us who have to work under tight time constraints are often tormented, at 4:30 pm, by those "I'm in big trouble if this isn't done by 5 pm!" thoughts. It makes good sense to keep an eye on the clock when you're on deadline, but the angst of the aforementioned thought won't help you finish — it will only take time and energy away from your ability to focus on the task at hand.

Dead Ends, 24/7

We consider some thoughts (such as excessive self-criticism, unreasonable fears, unnecessary angers, and unskillful desires) to be Dead End Thoughts no matter when they occur.

Another 24/7 Dead End category is that of unfulfillable desires. Too tall? Too short? Don't want to get old? Wish you'd gotten married twenty years ago? There are skillful ways to work with thoughts like these, but allowing them to run rampant in your mind is not one of them!

Unfortunately, these type of thoughts tend to be grabby ones, and thus fall in the "don't start weight lifting with a 300 pound weight" category. So for now, when choosing a Dead End (or, if you prefer, a Dandelion) Thought to work with, please *do not* choose a very heavy one!

A Few Words on Grief

Many years ago, at a workshop, a participant asked David, "Is grief a Dead End Thought?" An excellent question which may deserve a book of its own, our short answer is that grief and sadness can be Dead End Thoughts, if they are "excessive."

Missing a friend or relative — some of the time — decades after their death may be very appropriate, if it does not prevent you from living your own life. Wearing black and moping for months after the demise of your goldfish, or of a casual love affair, may be excessive, and the thoughts which result in your behavior may indeed be Dead End Thoughts. But only you can tell, and Compassion, which we will talk about in a later step, is the key...

If You're Not Sure

If you're not sure whether a thought is a Dead End or not, don't be in a rush to label it. Simply being painful or unpleasant does not make a thought a Dead End Thought. We are not suggesting that you repress fear or anger or desire — in fact, we want you to look carefully at any thought and evaluate it before giving it the Dead End Strategy. So take your time, and evaluate every potential Dead End Thought for any possible utility value. To review:

There are many categories of Dead End Thoughts, but each one shares three characteristics:

• It occurs relatively frequently.

• It is unwelcome, and causes you pain in some way.

• It has no useful purpose, at least during the time period in which you declare it to be a Dead End Thought (for example, thinking about lunch may be a Dead End Thought while you are working, but not while you're lunching).

The Dead End Thought Strategy

The good news is that it's simple to treat a Dead End Thought like a dandelion in your tomato patch, and just Pluck It and Chuck It. The bad news is that it takes a certain amount of Mental Muscle™ to do it. Here's what to do:

• Make sure that you've practiced at least one of the meditations in the preceding chapters.

• Look at this Dead End sign, then close your eyes. Can you see it, in your imagination? If not, can you say "Aha, a Dead End Sign!" to yourself?

• Choose a Dead End Thought using the criteria described above — and not a heavy one. Go light.

• Commit yourself to turning your attention away from the Dead End Thought, and onto your breathing meditation, every time you perceive that thought.

• Now consciously bring the Dead End Thought into your mind.

• After a second or two, imagine the dead end sign popping up, or imagine hearing the words "Aha, a Dead End Sign!"

• Turn your attention forcefully onto your breath, which will short-circuit any Fight or Flight Response, or take your attention off any desire thought, and trigger the Relax and Release Response. Like a dandelion, Pluck It and Chuck It!

> If you practice the above process often enough, you'll create a brand new neural path like the one pictured below. But the key is *practice* — enough to grow a strong, robust, automatic neural path so that we can Pluck and Chuck our chosen Dead End Thought instantaneously, without effort.

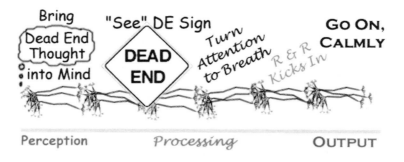

Bring Dead End Thought into Mind | "See" DE Sign | Turn Attention to Breath | R & R Kicks In | GO ON, CALMLY

Perception   *Processing*   OUTPUT

> And once you've established this new neural path to deal with a Dead End Thought — and practiced it enough so that it becomes automatic — you can activate it almost instantaneously whenever the same Dead End Thought enters your mind without your permission!

Event-Triggered Dead End Thoughts

Sometimes a Dead End Thought is triggered by an actual event. This adds one step to the process, but the Dead End Thought Strategy remains the same as described above. The only difference is that you'll add the triggering event while you do your practice. So, in the following case, you'd purposely walk by the mirror, and if your "Bad Hair Year" Dead End Thought was triggered, turn your attention straight onto your favorite breathing meditation.

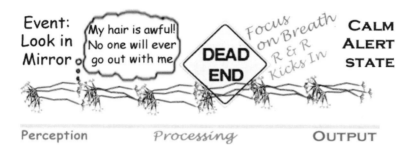

The Dead End to End All Dead Ends

The Dead End Thought Strategy can be difficult to do successfully, especially if you have not yet built up enough Mental Muscle™ to turn your attention onto a breathing meditation at will. It's possible that you'll find, when trying to do it, that you get "hijacked" onto the path of anger ("This is stupid. I quit!") or the path of angst ("I can't do this. Sigh. I might as well stop trying…").

Should this happen to you, please just go back to whichever of the breathing meditations seemed easiest for you, and practice it for a while under calm and quiet conditions, until you feel ready to try the Dead End exercises again. And please remember that any thoughts which discourage you from using meditation are the biggest Dead End Thoughts of all…

> If you found the Dead End Thought exercise difficult to do, you are probably using too heavy a Dead End Thought. Try it with an even more minor annoyance, or a very mild desire indeed.

> If necessary, please return to *Chapter Ten: The Simplest Clearing the Mind Meditations* and work with your favorite one under calm and quiet conditions, until you feel ready to return to this chapter.
>
> The more you practice this with *any* Dead End Thought, the easier it will be to use the strategy with other Dead End Thoughts!

Integrating Meditation into Your Daily Life

In addition to choosing a few Dead End Thoughts to work with, it's time to start, as the title of this section says, integrating meditation into our daily lives.

> Please make sure that you've practiced and are starting to feel comfortable with at least on meditation that is easy to do when you are sitting down, and one that's easy to do while walking.
>
> Once you've done that, start looking for opportunities — situations in which:
>
> • You are likely to experience stress, and
>
> • Which contain an opportunity to use at least one of your "favorite" meditations for at least a moment or two.

David always uses the Walking Breath meditation at the national publishing and music conventions he attends, which can be hectic and stressful for him:

"Instead of scurrying and worrying from one appointment to the next, I walk and breathe, walk and breathe — so that each step soothes and centers my mind. Then, when I arrive at my next meeting, I'm more relaxed, and ready to deal with whatever may arise."

When he gets to that meeting, he may also, notebook in lap, use the Draw-a-Breath™ Meditation:

"If I feel stressed out during an appointment — or even when I have a difficult phone call to make in my office — I may spend a minute splitting my attention between the words of the person speaking and drawing my breath. I have no trouble getting the gist of what they're saying, it calms me, and it may help keep me from saying something un-useful 'just to be saying something,' which I often tended to do when I felt insecure during a meeting."

Nina added an "aerobic" dimension to the Walking Breath:

"My office is on the fourth floor, so I need to go up and down several flights of stairs at least half a dozen times each day. Instead of taking the elevator, I've made using the stairs into a mini-meditation. As I walk up or down, I count the number of steps that I take during each inhale and during each exhale.

"Instead of worrying whether I'm on time or not (too late to do anything about that, once I'm on the stairs), it's a wonderful way to center myself as I head to the next meeting. I don't have to carve out time from my day for this mini-meditation. I also get to accomplish something that enhances my life physically, emotionally, and spiritually without adding a minute to my schedule. What a deal!"

Situational Meditation

As you can gather from the above examples, what you are doing, or where you are, may affect the meditation you choose to use at any given moment. Clearly, for most of us, it would be inappropriate to do a Walking Breath meditation during a sit-down with the boss. But given the wide variety of meditational options available, it's not difficult to integrate meditation into the fabric of daily life.

The Draw-A-Breath™ exercise is perfect for group meetings and lectures, and both the Breath Counting and the Tongue Block Breath exercises are virtually imperceptible to the outside observer, so they can be done anywhere. Alternate Nostril Breathing, on the other hand (or the other thumb and forefinger), is a bit more, umm, odd-looking to the uninformed, so it may be best done privately.

> Different meditations fit different situations. Once you know a variety of them, you can pick and choose to get the best fit.

Mini-Meditations

It's often easy to insert a very short meditation — a mini-meditation, if you will — into tiny timeslots in your daily life, at home or work. For example, every time you go from your desk to the printer, you might do a Walking Breath Meditation. Every time the phone rings, you might do a single breath count before you answer it.

> The opportunities for this kind of ongoing practice are virtually unlimited, if you choose to take advantage of them.
>
> Since the effects of meditation are *cumulative*, even when performed in very short increments, you can build lots of Mental Muscle™ by doing lots of mini-meditations throughout the day!
>
> David, for example, rarely answers the phone until the third ring. This gives him ample time to do a few seconds of a breath-labelling meditation (one of his favorites)...

Chapter Twelve: In a Nutshell...

You've now read about or tried close to a dozen different meditation exercises. We hope that you've found one or two or three that "just feel right," and that you start using them, both to deal with Dead End Thoughts and to integrate into the fabric of each day!

> Learning to meditate without using it in daily life is like spending the time to learn to drive, then never sitting behind the wheel.
>
> And it doesn't take much time, once you've learned how to do the basics. You can even fit "mini-meditations" into time slots of just a few free seconds — as you walk from table to fridge, or while you wait for a page to download from the 'net.
>
> Also, eliminating only one or two Dead End Thoughts from your daily mental routine can cut out a surprisingly large percentage of your daily stress quota.
>
> So work with at least one Dead End Thought, and try some real life walking and breathing meditations yourself, whether in between tasks on the job, during a quiet walk in the country. Or, in a stressful situation, while taking a quick break "to go to the restroom."
>
> Feel free to continue with the simpler meditations while you read more of the book. Or, try some of the more complex meditations in the next chapters. It's up to you!

Chapter Thirteen: Interpersonal Applications

For those of us who are not hermits — meditating merrily by our lonesomes in a remote cave somewhere — other people may be an important source of stress. So it's crucial to start applying our meditation techniques to interpersonal stress situations.

As we've said, it's unskillful to start learning to weightlift with a 300 pound weight, or begin to learn to kayak in a raging river. Likewise, it would be overwhelming and unproductive to try to start using our new mindfulness tools when faced with our most loathed colleague or the person we fear the worst.

So, in the next section we'll explain how to start in a safe way. Please try to be patient, because mastering the process described may take months or even years. However, the first stages are easy and satisfying, and from the very beginning, you'll reduce stress while learning a lot about yourself and your mind!

> If you are interested in using your meditation techniques to reduce stress, fear, or anger when interacting with other people, please read the entire section above, and those that follow. This will take time and practice to master, but it's simple enough so that you can start the process right now, using what you've already learned.

Completely Shifting Attention Versus Splitting Attention

Up to now, our real life use of meditation techniques have involved *completely shifting* the focus of our attention from a mildly stressful situation (such as when a slow deli clerk starts to trigger a Fight or Flight Response) to a *full focus* on the breath.

From This... **This...**

To:

[speech bubble:] This @#$% clerk is so slow...grrrr!

[crossed-out speech bubble:] This @#$% clerk is so slow...grrrr!

[speech bubble:] Innn... Out... Innnnn... Ooouuuttt... Innnnn...

The strategy of working with Dead End Thoughts by turning our full attention onto one of the meditations is also a great example of this.

However, in the following exercises, we'll be *splitting* our attention — that is, keeping part of our attention on the annoying situation, while turning *part* of our attention inwards onto the breath.

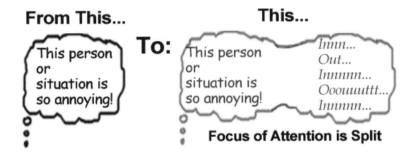

From This... **This...**

To:

[speech bubble:] This person or situation is so annoying!

[speech bubble:] This person or situation is so annoying! Innn... Out... Innnnn... Ooouuuttt... Innnnn...

Focus of Attention is Split

In the following interpersonal exercises, we will practice splitting the focus of our attention between an annoying person or situation and a breathing meditation. Read on if you would like to learn how to deal skillfully with the most challenging people in your life.

IMPORTANT: This is a key concept to understand and work on as we'll find additional uses for attention splitting in later Steps of the book...

How to Get Started

Begin by doing any of the meditation exercises we've described above *while* listening to the radio or tv. Don't tune to a station or a show you hate. If possible, find one that you feel neutral about, and spend just a few moments splitting your attention between the meditation and the words you hear. If you are using a tv, don't look at the screen, just yet.

Notice that if more of your attention is on the meditation, less will be on the words you hear. If you start paying more attention to the words, you may lose your focus on the breath. Play with the balancing of your attention, just as you might play with bass and treble balance settings of a sound system. If the bass is turned up too far, you lose the treble (high) sounds. Too much treble and the sound gets shrill, and loses the boom of the bass.

After a while you'll get a sense of how to balance the two different *foci* (a fancy word for more than one focus, it sounds better than focuses). This may take a few tries, at a minute or three each. Your goal is to staying focused mostly on the meditation, while keeping enough mental attention on the words of the radio or tv so that you have a general sense of what they are saying, although you may miss a word — or even a sentence — or two, every so often.

You may want to try experiment with this exercise in a real-life group situation — a lecture (or other setting with one person talking and a group of at least a dozen or so listening) is a great place to do it. Of course, it has to be one in which you *don't* need to be listening very carefully to the content of what the speaker is saying! And if you want to appear polite, look at the bridge of the speaker's nose every so often (while you continue to count, or draw, or tongue block your breath). This makes it look as though you are paying attention!

Escalating the Exercise

After you've done the previous practice, and can balance your attention as you choose (which may take a few days, or even a week or so of three minutes a day practice) — turn to a radio or tv station that you mildly dislike. Choose a sports channel if you don't like sports, or a business news channel if that is not an interest of yours.

Work on maintaining the balance between foci again. Most likely, it will be a bit more difficult. Why? Because the now slightly more annoying words may now tend to start triggering either thoughts or even a mild Fight or Flight Response. So be prepared for this (review the section on fear or anger "symptoms," page 32, if you need to) and be ready to re-focus your attention back onto the breath if a response is triggered, and your mental focus gets "hijacked." No self-criticism, just a rapid, but calm, return to the breath.

To up the ante, use the tv and begin watching the screen as you meditate — it's harder to stay focused, with both sound and picture.

Eventually, with lots of practice, you may be able to watch your least favorite actor or athlete or politician on the screen, while short-circuiting the Fight or Flight Responses that will repeatedly occur. Every time you notice a response starting to kick in, you simply refocus more of your attention onto the breath.

Working with Difficult People... ...in Real Life

After you've spent some time working with the neutral radio or tv show, and then with the slightly or the very annoying show, you'll find that the exact same technique can be used with an annoying person! In fact, that boring relative at the party, or the abrasive co-worker, can provide a challenging and even interesting meditation object, just by splitting your attention between the person and your breath, as you did with the radio or tv.

> Splitting attention in this way may well change your reaction to the difficult person and your skill in handling the situation as you continue to build Mental Muscle™.

Difficult Relationships and Dead End Thoughts

Often, we will find that it is a recurring Dead End Thought (as in the following example) which makes a relationship or interaction difficult. By using our Pluck It and Chuck It strategy every time the thought arises during an interpersonal interaction, we short-circuit the Fight or the Flight Response which causes us distress.

This tends to be easier to do in a short-term situation. In this example, while cornered at a party a really boring person, we use the opportunity to practice the Dead End Thought Strategy every time the "He's so boring!" thought comes up. It's a win-win event: we are polite to the bore, and we build Mental Muscle™.

By practicing in mildly annoying situations with people that we don't have to interact with over the long run, we gain — eventually — the degree of Dead End Thought practice and Mental Muscle™ which will allow us to use the same technique on the relative who chews with his mouth open, or the co-worker who can't stop gossiping. And, in time, with people even more difficult than these.

Chapter Thirteen: In a Nutshell...

Unless you're a hermit, dealing with other human beings may be the most difficult thing you do on a daily basis. So practicing the attention-shifting and attention-splitting exercises in this chapter may take a while to provide positive results, but it's important enough to be worth working on. Don't be embarrassed to work with the radio or tv — David often uses his least favorite radio personalities as a focus for his efforts (and some of them occasionally still make him blow his stack!).

> By practicing the progressively more difficult exercises described above, you can develop the ability to deal with difficult people without triggering a full-fledged Fight or Flight Response.
>
> Naturally, the more difficult the person or situation, the more Mental Muscle™ you'll need to turn your focus back to the breath! We'll offer additional advice and exercises on the subject in later parts of the book.

Chapter Fourteen:
More Complex Mind
Clearing Meditations

In these following exercises, you'll be focusing your attention on a physical sensation, rather than merely labeling a physical action with a number or a word as we've already done. Since this is a slightly less cut-and-dried thing to focus on, your attention is apt to wander more. So you must be diligent in noticing that the "puppy" of your attention is wandering off, and gently bring it back to the sound, or the foot, or the flame.

These meditations are somewhat harder to do during that boring meeting or at the convention, since they require a bit more action than the simpler mind-clearing exercises. But with ingenuity, you'll find moments of privacy to practice the chanting or the slow walk, and candle-lit restaurants are natural places to do a flame meditation (while your new date, or the spouse with whom you are annoyed, is in the restroom).

> Although we've grouped these under the title of "More Complex," as we've noted, difficulty may lie in the mind of the meditator. That said, the Chore Based and Higher Count breathing exercises at the end of this chapter are definitely harder to stay focused on, at least for us.
>
> But try all of them, or any that appeal to you. After all, not being able to do them perfectly allows us the opportunity to practice returning to the breath — or other focus of meditation — without self-criticism. And that's a skill as important as the meditational focus itself.
>
> Oh — and from now on, we won't be putting the meditations in boxes. You'll have to read the whole thing if you want to try the exercise!

About The Simple Chanting, Or "Mantra" Meditation

This simple chanting or "mantra" (a repeated sound used as focus point) exercise is probably the world's most widely used meditation.

It's somewhat similar in nature to Maharishi Mahesh Yogi's Transcendental Meditation™, or "TM" system which the Beatles helped bring to the Western world in the late 1960's (except that it won't cost you $385, or require you to bring a white flower to the TM Trainer). As we've mentioned, TM was each of our first organized meditational experiences, and even though we no longer practice it, we'll always feel a debt of gratitude to both the Beatles and the Maharishi, for popularizing and publicizing this age-old technique in the West (and for all those great tunes).

The Simple Chanting Meditation

• Sit in a comfortable, upright position, in a quiet place. Place thumbs and fingers together, if you like.

• Now focus your attention on a pleasant-sounding one or two syllable word.

Yogis seem to prefer OM or AUM. Many non-yogis like to use the word ONE. AMEN may be especially appropriate for those of a Christian persuasion. The TM folk also like two syllable mantras (many of theirs sound quite like AMEN). Choose any one of these to use right now.

• Begin by slowly whispering the word (let's say you've chosen OM) to yourself.

• Stop whispering "OM", and just think "OM". Perhaps you'll picture the word OM, written out in your mind. Perhaps you'll imagine hearing it in your mind, or imagine saying it.

• Keep your attention focused on that OM, in whatever form it may seem to appear.

Of course, your mind will wander. You'll find yourself thinking about tomorrow, or about how well-focused you are on the OM. Maybe you'll have a doubtful thought ("I can't do this") or a pleasant daydream.

When Attention Strays

When your attention strays from the OM (or other mantra), bring it gently but firmly back. Let go of the daydream, or the doubtful thought, or the desire thought for now. You can think about those things as much as you like, later. For now, you're just thinking OMMMM...

That's all there is to it. The more you do it, the longer you'll be able to stay with the OM. A few seconds at first, then 10, or 15, or half a minute. For many meditators (the Bats among us), mantras seem to be an especially powerful focus for the attention. That's why they're so popular!

Christian, Jewish, and Buddhist Chants

If you enjoy practicing the Simple Chanting Meditation, you might eventually like to try repeating a more complex and difficult chant. Any very short Christian prayer that you've memorized will work, like the "Prayer of The Heart": "Lord Jesus Christ, have mercy on me." If you come from the Hebrew tradition, try the most important prayer of the Jewish faith, the "Shma": "Hear oh Israel, the Lord our God, the Lord is One." (Pronounced: Shma' Yis-roy-el' Ah-doh-noy' Eh-lo-hay'-nu, Ah-doh-noy' Eh-chord').

The Buddha's last instructions to his disciples were to repeatedly chant the phrase "Nam Myoho Renge Kyo" (Pronounced: Nahm Me-yo'-ho Reng'-yay Ke-yo'). A greatly over-simplified translation of this might be, "I devote myself to the law of the Universal Consciousness". This form of meditation is now known as "Nichiren" Buddhism, and has proponents and groups worldwide.

Consult your local priest or rabbi to obtain additional Jewish or Christian chants, which will add greater depth to the practice of your chosen religion. Or create a meaningful chant of your own.

The Slow Walking Meditation

You'll probably want to begin practicing this one in a private place, since it looks a bit funny. Pick a spot where you can walk for at least 8 or 10 feet in a straight line.

• Now walk *very* slowly, so slowly that you have enough time to mentally label *every part* of every step.

• Say "lifting" as you pick your "first" foot up.

• Say "moving" as your foot travels through the air.

• Say "placing" as you put that foot down again.

• Say "shifting" as you shift your weight onto that foot.

• Say "lifting" as you begin to pick up the other foot. And so on.

"Lifting, moving, placing, shifting...lifting, moving, placing, shifting..."

At first, take a minimum of eight to ten seconds to complete each four part (lifting, moving, placing, shifting) step. This is truly life in the slow lane! Whenever your attention wanders, bring it back to your walking process.

As you get used to focusing on your feet, you can try sometimes walking faster, labeling only the lifting and placing portions of each step. If you prefer, you can say "up" and "down" instead of "lift" and "place". Or try slowing it way down, and take 30 to 40 seconds (some people in meditation workshops call this "the Zombie Walk") for every complete step. If balance is a problem, speed up a bit, or do it next to a wall or rail that you can put a hand on, for support.

Other thoughts intruding? Get right back to that focus on the active foot!

A Very Simple Eating Meditation

This one is simple, although not always easy.

• For just a minute or three, count the number of times you chew each mouthful of food. That's all there is to it.

If thoughts intervene — if your mind starts telling you a story — finish chewing the mouthful you're working on, swallow, and start counting the chews of the next mouthful.

Should this food-based exercise seem difficult, or bring up painful thoughts, put it aside until you've working with the compassion exercises. Then you may want to come back to this one, or go to the additional meditations around food and eating in the Appendix section of the book...

The Flame Meditation

• In a darkened room, from ten or fifteen inches away, stare intently at a candle's flame for one or two minutes.

• Whenever your attention wanders, return your gaze to the heart of that tiny fire. Try not to think about the candle, or this exercise, or why fire looks as it does, or your boss, your cat, or politics. Just keep returning your attention to stare at the flame.

• Abruptly blow the candle out, and close your eyes.

• Within a few seconds, you'll begin to see the image of the flame again, apparently projected onto the inside of your eyelids. Watch that image for as long as you can.

It may change color, or shape, or seem to slide around. It may disappear, and then come back in a slightly different shape, color, or form. But you'll recognize it, if you concentrate. With practice, you'll be able to perceive the image for at least as long as you watched the actual flame.

The combination of focusing on both the real flame and then the afterimage can be very exciting and challenging. Birds, artists, and other people who are visually oriented may achieve an exceptionally strong concentration with this exercise.

For Friends, Couples, and People with Pets: The "Shared" Breath

For a very intimate experience with a close friend, relative, or lover, try this exercise. David learned it from Stephen Levine, who learned it from Richard Boerstler, of The Clear Light Society. We don't know who Richard learned it from, but it's a wonderful thing to do!

• Decide which of you will be the active partner.

• The inactive partner simply sits or lies comfortably, eyes closed, and breathes normally.

• The active partner sits nearby, close enough to see the rising and falling of the inactive partner's chest with each of their breaths, close enough to hear each in and out breath.

• The active partner tries to match as exactly as possible the breathing rhythm of the other.

This means beginning the in breath exactly when the inactive partner does, and inhaling exactly as long, beginning the out breath exactly when the inactive partner does, and exhaling exactly as long. Is there a hold between in and out, or out and in? The active partner will have to match that, as well.

It's not easy to do, and requires intense concentration! On each exhale, the active partner may want to release the breath with a gentle sigh... "ahhh".

The inactive partner should try not to "help" the active partner by making breaths unusually regular or loud, neither should they try to hinder the other by holding their breath or breathing especially softly.

This exercise promotes a strong feeling of connection, compassion, and love between the partners. It's almost as though one breath is being shared between two people — sometimes it actually feels as though the two bodies are somehow merged. Couples will find this a lovely trust-builder, and especially powerful if eye contact is maintained. You can even do the Shared Breath with a pet (you'll probably need to take the active role).

Many nurses, therapists, and some physicians use this meditation with their patients. It can be done with the inactive partner sleeping or comatose, and may be very calming and soothing for someone who is ill, as well as for the healer. David uses it in all his hospice work and hospice workshops (and it may be part of the reason that his large harmonica/meditation sessions, sometimes featuring thousands of participants, are such a powerful experience!).

The Heartbeat Meditation

Every second your heart beats at least once. If it stops beating for very long, you're history. So counting or labeling each beat is an amazingly powerful attention focuser, even if you only do it for one minute or less. Since this exercise involves a mental focus on physical sensation without physical action (unlike, say, the walking exercises which involve focus on action), it may appeal to the barnacles amongst us.

Warning: If you are a hypochondriac, or have any heart problems, don't do this exercise until you feel very comfortable with the mind watching and Softening Around Pain exercises that follow in Step Five.

Put your hand over your heart, or locate the pulse in your wrist with a few fingers. Count each beat or pulse to four, or ten, like you've done with the breath. If you lose count, start again.

Or, label each beat or pulse by mentally saying "beat" every time you feel one. This is similar to what you did with the four part (lifting, moving, placing, shifting) Slow Walking Meditation.

For many, the exciting (and scary) part of this meditation is that the heart skips a beat every minute or two. It is never absolutely certain whether the next beat will happen, or not. So you have to pay very close attention.

Doctors say that unless you average more than four or five per minute, skipped beats are not necessarily indicative of heart problems. But it's still a bit unnerving, when it occurs. If a fear thought comes up after a skipped beat, just notice it, notice that you've stopped counting or labeling, then go back to focus on the heartbeat. You can always worry later, after you're done meditating. Or, perhaps, with sufficient meditation, you won't even want to worry quite as much!

Variations on the Breath Counting Meditation

Since the reason to do this exercise is to build Mental Muscle™ (rather than to follow some very specific and unchangeable protocol), you can vary the way in which you do the Breath Counting meditation.

Higher Counts (Macho Meditation?)

Experiment, for example, if you like, with extending each count up to eight or ten. Is that easier or harder to do than a count of four? Want to be meditationally macho (or macha)? Every once in a while, see how many consecutive exhales you can count without losing yourself, and your count, in a thought.

As David describes an exceptionally high count during his early days of meditating, reached one foolishly competitive afternoon during a ten-day retreat:

"Pride was my downfall: 'Inhale...439, Inhale...440, Inhale...441, Inhale...442, Wow, I'm really doing great! I bet I've gotten further than anyone else here, me! David! — Uh oh, what number breath *was* that last one? — #%X@!!!... Oh #%X@!!! How could I be so stupid! Oh well.....Inhale...One, Inhale...Two, Inhale...' "

He now occasionally gets up to a thousand, and tries to avoid the "Oh #%X@!!!" part if he loses count around 997 — just goes back to Inhale… "One"…!

> If not otherwise indicated, at first practice each of these meditations for three minutes, or longer if you prefer. Once you've learned the exercise, do it for as long or short as you like, from three seconds to three hours!

The Chore-Based Breath Count

Try this meditation after you've practiced at least a few sessions of Breath Counting meditation. You'll be doing this one in conjunction with a specific task or chore that you do on at least a daily basis (preferably something very short, and more or less mindless). Taking a short break from work to get a drink of water (average count, four breaths), removing a page from the computer printer (average count, six or seven breaths) or making popcorn in the microwave (average count, forty breaths) work well.

Simply count the number of breaths it takes to do the task (numbering each exhale, and without, of course, trying to control the speed or regularity of your respiration). Naturally, thoughts try to intrude, but for the duration of this particular task, your "job" is to get an accurate count of your breaths.

Some people seem to find this meditation slightly easier, or more compelling, than the more basic Breath Counting Meditation. It has the added advantage of helping you to integrate your meditation practice right into your daily life. This same exercise can be done while counting steps rather than breaths — try that if you like.

Start out with short, simple tasks, and if you lose count, you know what to do: Go directly to breath number one, without spending time on self-judgement or other thoughts!

In fact, if you like this exercise you may eventually want to try doing it with more complex tasks, that you are likely to lose your count during. This will give you the opportunity to practice re-starting the exercise without even a moment of self-criticism, which of course is far more important than keeping an accurate count!

When we are both in good meditating shape, we sometimes try (and often fail) to keep an accurate breath count while doing a seemingly easy errand that involves interpersonal contact (like walking into a store, buying a loaf of bread, and leaving).

IMPORTANT: Being able to lose our count and quickly return to "Inhale...One" without self-blame or negativity is actually more important than keeping the count correct in the first place.

Chapter Fourteen: In a Nutshell

The meditation exercises in this chapter, in addition to the ones you've already learned about, provide you with a good set of tools.

Step Two: What You Need to Know

Just to review: the short-term reason that you're doing these meditation exercises is quiet the mind, to find and enjoy the relaxed but alert place that concentrated mental focus on the breath — or on other objects — will bring you to.

The longer-term, or more general reason, is to build the Mental Muscle™ that will allow you to use meditation during a stressful situation — whether those stressors are in the mind or in the outside "real" world — to short-circuit the Fight or Flight Response.

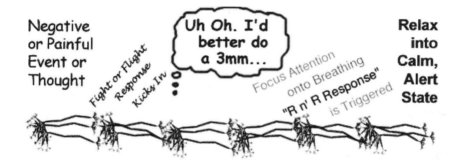

If you stopped reading right now, and simply spent the rest of your life practicing whichever of the above Three Minute Meditations seem to fit your personal style and your life, you'd get great benefits from the practice. Why? Because...

...The neural path *outcome* depicted above — a calm but alert state — is the ideal place from which to decide what to do next, instead of reacting from a state of fear or anger!

But to take it one level deeper, please go on to Step Three: *Watching the Mind* — and begin working with it while you continue to fit the exercises of Step Two — Clearing the Mind — into the fabric of your daily life.

STEP THREE:
Watching the Mind

Welcome to Step Three of *The Three Minute Meditator*. In this step, you'll learn to observe and explore your own mind, by looking at various types of thoughts and neural paths generated by the brain. (As you recall, we consider the brain to be the "physical" part of the mind.)

We'll study "Watching the Mind" in a number of different ways. Some will involve learning new ways of relating to the mind, like our "at the movies" analogy. Others will involve learning more about specific types of neural paths and thoughts, then investigating them in a series of Watching the Mind Exercises and meditations.

> "Watching the Mind" offers us a new way to relate to our thoughts. Instead of becoming involved in the specific **content** of each thought, we begin to see the **process** by which thoughts arise and pass away.

Once you learn to watch those ongoing "movies" in your mind (just as you'd watch a show on your new widescreen HDTV), you'll also learn to be able to "get up and leave" or "change channels," or hit the pause button on the DVD — whenever you choose to do so!

> Since this may be a very new concept for many readers, it may be useful to read Chapter Fifteen in its entirety (don't worry, it's short), rather than only skimming the boxes.

In Chapter Sixteen, you'll review the basics, then learn about a new type of neural path, in which an event triggers a thought.

We'll go on to discuss self talk, thought chains, and desire-based neural paths. Then, in Chapter Seventeen, you'll learn how it's possible to "map out" the highways, byways, and dead end streets of what we call the "Neural Neighborhood."

And after we provide you with a variety of Watching the Mind Exercises towards the end of Step Three, you'll use them to do some neural path "mapping" of your own.

Please read the above paragraphs if you'd like a very short outline of what you'll find in Chapters Sixteen, Seventeen, and Eighteen. Lots of interesting material, but not all of it easy.

Please don't worry if some of this may seem confusing at first. If, while working with these chapters, you ever feel frustrated, discouraged, or in doubt — simply go back and do some mind-clearing exercises from Step Two. This will help you build the Mental Muscle™ that you'll need to do the mind watching exercises in Step Three!

IMPORTANT: Learning to watch the mind is very useful — it is a lifelong study (or many lifetimes, if you like that kind of thing) — but don't spend too much time here now. Instead, just get the general idea of mind-watching, try some of the mind-watching exercises, then go on.

Learning to watch the mind without going on to Softening Around Pain and the other steps would be like learning all about the personalities, relationships, strengths, and weaknesses of your team — then never going on to practice batting or throwing!

Chapter Fifteen: How to Watch a Movie

When we first discussed Watching the Mind, we said that after doing some mind-clearing, it would be possible to observe our thoughts as though they were "scenes on a movie screen." We would like to take the movie analogy a bit further now. Please imagine settling down in your theatre seat, or beginning (alone or with a group of friends) to watch a DVD in front of your 108" HDTV screen with 4000 watt surround sound capabilities. And consider these two distinctly different ways of watching a movie...

If we choose, we can focus our attention very narrowly on that humongous screen, and absorb ourselves in the **content** of the film that is playing. When we watch in this way, if sad events occur on the screen, we will feel sad. If happy events occur, we'll feel happy. If the filmmakers are skillful propagandists, it will be simple for them to manipulate our beliefs and feelings. For instance, the German movie "Das Boot" (The Boat), about a German submarine crew struggling for life, was upsetting to many audiences in this country because it virtually forced them to root for the Nazi submariners.

Alternatively, we can focus our conscious attention more widely, on the entire **process** of "watching the show". Then we will be aware not only of the action on the screen, but also of the fact that it is "just a movie." So, as we watch the play of light and color on the screen, we will also be conscious of many other aspects of the situation. Some of these are obvious, and based on the film itself. Does the plot make sense? Is it original, or derived from older films? What genre is it: mystery, sci fi, romance?

The process of watching the show involves being very aware of some aspects that involve *our* relationship to the action on the screen. Have we seen this film before, or is this the first time? What feelings does each scene or character evoke for us? Do we like or dislike having those feelings? Do we feel manipulated by some agenda on the part of the director or the producer of the movie?

Other process aspects of which we are aware are interpersonal. Are we watching alone? With a friend? With a group? Is the theatre crowded or empty? Are the other viewers absorbed, or bored? Well-behaved, or noisy? Can we hear them eating popcorn? Does that sound bother us?

> Think about watching a movie. You can allow yourself to be caught up in the content of the show, perhaps to such an extent that you forget that "it's just a film."
>
> Or you can sit there in your seat, paying attention to the entire process of "watching a movie," keeping track of the onscreen action just enough to analyze each scene and special effect, second-guess the director, observe the reactions of other viewers.
>
> Or you can go from one mode to the other, enjoying the movie, even being enraptured by it, while still understanding on some level that it's just light projected through a lens or digital process onto a screen...

Relating To Your Mind Rather Than Reacting To Your Thoughts

We can relate to our own minds in these same ways — content or process — as we can relate to watching a movie. The type of thinking that most of us do, most of the time, is "content" thinking.

We become absorbed and engrossed in the **content** of each passing thought. Is that a fearful thought arising? We focus our attention on the fearful thought, our "Flight Response" is triggered, and we experience the emotion of fear. Is that an angry thought arising? We pay attention to it until it triggers the "Fight Response" and we get mad. If two conflicting thoughts happen to arise at the same time, like a dessert-desire thought and a fat-anxiety thought, we feel upset and/or confused.

Most of us are so involved in the content of each thought that comes into our mind — whether it just occurs once, or whether it's a repetitive thought — that perhaps it seems we are actually nothing but the sum, the total, of our thoughts.

But when we learn to look at the **process** of our thinking, to watch our thoughts, to watch the process of our neural paths — we realize that they are not "us," any more than a rock, or a book, or anything else that we can see outside of ourselves is us. And we can begin, as Stephen Levine says, to "relate *to* our mind, instead of *from* it."

Since this is such an important concept, we're going to repeat it. "Relating to our mind, instead of from it" is a technique that will free us from hurtful old mental habits — by allowing us a choice of action — not an automatic knee-jerk response.

Relating *to* your mind means mentally "stepping back" to watch exactly what your mind is doing, without getting hung up in the content of any particular thought. It means being able to notice a fearful thought and say "Ahh, there's a fearful thought" without automatically reacting by becoming fearful. It means being able to notice a sexual thought and say "Uh-huh, there's a sexual thought" without automatically reacting by becoming consumed with desire and/or guilt.

> When we learn how to relate to our mind, we can *choose* how to react to any thought, instead of having our old habitual or automatic reaction to that thought. As we've said, once you learn to short-circuit the Fight or Flight Response that a thought may trigger...you become the master of your mind, not the other way around.

Do I WANT to Watch My Mind?

We'd be remiss if we didn't admit that looking at what's really going on inside your head may be somewhat of a daunting task. So it behooves us to ask: Is your mind a bit on the wild side? And never mind what your answer is — we'll respond: *Ours are!* Most people, we believe, will (in a candid moment) admit to feeling at times overwhelmed by repetitive thoughts, emotions, or desires that demand excessive mental time, space, and emotional energy.

Imagine thinking that you were the only person in the world who needed to go to the bathroom a few times every day. You'd be acutely aware that you must continually perform this dirty, "unnatural" act, but you might never see anyone else do it.

Einstein hit the can? Your favorite movie star or news commentator? Queen Elizabeth? Go to the bathroom? Impossible!

It's just as painful, if slightly less ridiculous, not to realize that everybody has the same kind of "drunken monkey" mind that you do (swinging heedlessly from branch to branch, a simian accident waiting to happen). Few people are open enough to talk to you about the fears, phobias, and fantasies in their minds. So your own mind is the only one whose swirling multitude of strange thoughts you can easily know. Understanding that we're all in roughly the same mental boat helps us take our own bizarre ruminations just a bit less personally.

As Nina notes:

It's easy to look at other people and believe that their lives have fewer challenges, problems, quirks and eccentricities than one's own. That's because we are comparing their "outsides" with our "insides." It's like comparing the picture perfect exterior of a neighbor's house — white picket fence and all — against the sometimes chaotic disarray that we see inside our own Home Sweet Home.

But opening the front door — or perhaps the bedroom closet door in that idealized house next door — may well reveal the skeletons, or at least some very dirty laundry, in a heap on the floor.

Similarly, the recesses of another person's mind are invisible to us. Mr. or Ms. I.M. Perfict may appear to be calm, cool, and collected to your gaze, yet be mercilessly harassed by their own repetitive, painful, drunken monkey mind thoughts. Please be assured that everyone has a mind which is capable of making them miserable. Fortunately, the techniques based on meditation and mindfulness that you are learning will help you be able to work more skillfully with your innermost thoughts and feelings. By doing so, you'll also worry less about what other people think!

Chapter Fifteen: In a Nutshell

Most of us never even consider the possibility of observing the mind and its thoughts as though they were something "outside" of ourselves. Instead, every thought and feeling that we notice seems to be part of "us."

With just a bit of practice — and a bit of the Mental Muscle™ that you'll get from doing the exercises in Step Two — it's not too hard to start seeing at least some of your thoughts as though they are objects outside of you, as though they were scenes in a movie that you were watching...

It's really important — especially if you feel at all nervous about investigating uncharted territory inside your head — to realize that just about everybody has a wild and crazy mind, filled with the same type of untamed, tangled thoughts that run through your own mind. We just never get to see the strange stuff in most *other* people's heads — only the strange stuff in our own!

In the following chapter, we will provide another way to turn the great power of our mental attention onto the mind itself, so please keep on reading.

Chapter Sixteen: A Quick Visit to the...Mind?

If you were planning a move to a new city (or wanted to learn more about the one you live in), you might buy a guidebook and find lots of great information. Historic buildings and terrific restaurants, museums and monuments, the best roads and routes to travel by car or public transportation, as well as places that the tourist or resident would be wise to avoid, and the reasons why — it should all be in there, carefully marked on accurate maps.

Every guidebook reader knows what the terms "museum," or "restaurant," or "questionable neighborhood after dark" mean. But you may not be quite as familiar with the various kinds of thoughts and other elements that make up the paths in your "Neural Neighborhood" (more on this, later) — though they're the mental equivalents of the geographical elements in the guidebook.

Learning to look at your mind as though it were a fascinating place that you were visiting is a great way to relate to your mind (rather than just reacting to its thoughts as we all usually do). Let's begin with a bit of review from Chapter One. If you're sure you remember all this neural path stuff, just skim it.

Then we'll add some new elements to our knowledge of neural paths, including:

• Self Talk and Thought Chains
• Overgeneralization and Awfulization, and
• Desire Paths

These are all things that we're apt to encounter when we visit the landscape of the mind! Understanding what these things are — and where and when you'll find them — will help you to successfully map and navigate *your* Neural Neighborhood, using the exercises in the latter part of Step Three.

Knowing the whereabouts of both the useful paths and the dead ends in your mind will improve your life exponentially! It's even more valuable than knowing where the best restaurant, least crowded highway, or most dangerous bar is, in your physical neighborhood, or in a city that you plan to visit!

Neural Paths 101: A Brief Review

• Brain cells — called neurons — link together to form "neural paths." These chains of brain cells underlie all of our actions, our emotions, and our words.

• Many neural paths follow a three part pattern (we'll give you some examples below): A *perception* leads to a *process* which leads to an *outcome*.

Perception ➜ Triggers Process ➜ Outcome (Action or Emotion)

• Some neural paths are what we call instinctual, or built-in, or automatic, or hard-wired. The frog perceives a tall, birdy-looking object, an automatic neural path process is triggered as the neurons connect up, and PLOP! The end or output of that neural path is the frog jumping into the pond to avoid the stork's razor-sharp beak!

• Humans have instinctual or hard-wired paths, too. As with the frog, these are usually triggered by the perception of an event. Perceive a taxi leaping the curb and coming straight at you? An automatic neural path instantly connects, the well-known "Fight or Flight Response" kicks in, and the end result, the output, is that you leap to safety.

See Taxi ➜ Triggers Fight or Flight Response ➜ Leap to Safety

• In human beings, the Fight or Flight Response can be triggered by a thought. When we "think of something scary," the flight part of the Fight or Flight Response kicks in. Our heart races while our digestion stops cold and our muscles tighten. The output? Well, since there's nothing useful that can really be done to physically fight or flee from a thought, so we just "feel scared." This is what's happening, in neural path terms:

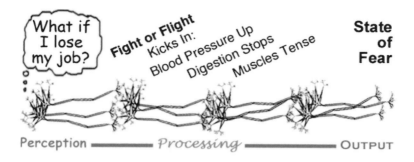

• Humans have another type of neural paths: learned neural paths. Every time we learn something new, a new neural path is born — in fact, you might say that learning is the process of creating new neural paths in the brain.

• When a learned neural path is repeated often enough, whether it is the neural path that underlies tying a shoelace, memorizing a times table, or the neural path that links hearing a critical comment from a loved one to an emotion of anger — it becomes automatic. No thinking necessary.

• When one of these "automatic learned paths" is put into action by perceiving, say, a criticism from a spouse or friend — the rest of the process (including, in this case, the "fight" part of the Fight or Flight Response) happens so quickly and automatically that the output of anger is almost instantaneous...and hard to avoid.

Hear Criticism ➔ Triggers Fight Response ➔ Anger

• Just as a path which you've tramped down through a weed-filled empty lot is much easier to follow than no path at all — a well-established neural path is easy to follow. So easy to follow, in some cases, that it's hard *not* to follow it, even when it doesn't take you where you want to go!

> Before reading on, make sure you understand these concepts:
>
> • That fear, anger, all learning, all desire, and just about every other human process is caused, at its most basic level, by a neural path.
>
> • That both the perception of actual events and the perception of "mere" thoughts trigger neural paths which then activate the "Fight or Flight Response," resulting in the emotions of anger or Fear.

Events or Thoughts, and Neural Paths

As we just mentioned, some neural paths are triggered by an actual event — that is, we perceive (see, hear, feel, taste, smell) something in the "real" world. Some of these event-triggered neural paths are instinctual — built-in, automatic. See that taxi veering towards you, or the saber tooth tiger leaping and no thought, no lengthy processing is needed — your Fight or Flight Response kicks in to let you fight or flee your way out of the situation (we hope).

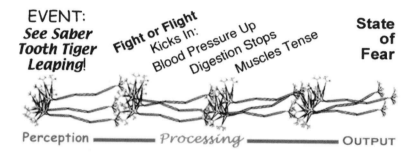

As we also mentioned (and diagrammed), other neural paths are triggered when we perceive nothing more real than a thought in the mind. If we have "practiced" this type of thought-triggered neural path, it can result in a Fight or Flight Response so quickly that it, too, has become automatic, almost hard-wired into your brain.

A thought of your least favorite person comes into your mind, and before you know it (literally), your blood pressure rises, your digestion stops cold, and your fists and jaw and shoulders tighten as the Fight Response kicks in.

> Some neural paths are triggered by events. Others are triggered by nothing more "real" than a thought that enters your mind.
>
> Either way — event-triggered or thought-triggered — they can produce a Fight or Flight Response so quickly that the process seems almost automatic, like leaping to safety when something big comes at you fast.

Events + Thought Neural Paths

Before we can start to navigate our neural neighborhood, there is one more type of neural path we need to learn about.

400 years ago Hamlet put it rather well when he said (Act II, Scene ii) "…there is nothing either good or bad, but thinking makes it so." We'd put it similarly, if less strongly:

> Sometimes it's not the event that matters, it's what you *think* about that event.
>
> Because an event can trigger a thought — or trigger a chain of linked thoughts — that go on to trigger a fight or flight response, which then results in an emotion of anger or fear (or both). We'll discuss this in the following pages.

As David often illustrates this point by telling his audiences: "Your Martian buddy, riding shotgun, is delighted by those flashing red and blue lights following your car as you speed down the highway going thirty miles an hour over the speed limit. *You're not.*"

Self Talk and Thought Chains

What's the difference between you and the Martian (aside from number of eyes and so on)? He simply perceives the event of the colorful, beautiful, flashing lights. That's it, for him.

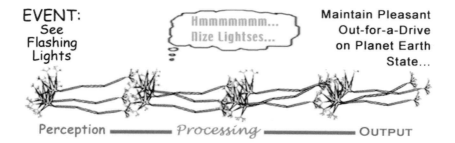

You perceive the event, and then proceed to "talk to yourself" about it (psychologists, not surprisingly, call this "self talk") — by adding a thought to the event: "Oh no! Another speeding ticket!" And perhaps that thought is followed by another: "That's the third one this year!" And yet more, in a now long chain of thoughts: "I'll lose my license." "I'll lose my job." "I won't be able to pay my mortgage." And so on. By now, as a result of this thought chain, your Fight or Flight Response has kicked in, and the result is either anger, or fear, or both.

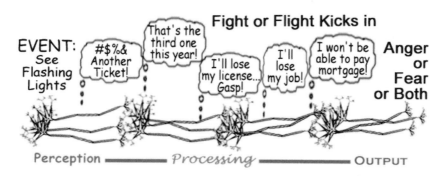

Consider a slightly more realistic example: Your friend doesn't meet you at 1 pm, when he said he would. By 1:15 pm (or 1:30, if you're a more patient soul than either of us) a chain of self-talk thoughts has ensued, such as this thought chain leading to a Fight Response: "He should have been there when he said he would be…He's never on time…He's always late!..He has no right to treat me like that…I can't stand it! #$%!!!"

Or like this set of linked thoughts leading to a Flight (fear) Response: "I wonder why he hasn't come or called? Maybe he doesn't care enough to bother. I guess he doesn't really care about me at all. No one cares about me…"

Or perhaps: "I wonder why he hasn't called? Maybe something is wrong. Maybe there's been an accident. A terrible accident. Oh my God…"

And so a Fight or a Flight Response is triggered — you've either made yourself angry because he didn't show up or call, or made yourself fearful that he doesn't really care about you (nor does anyone else), or have begun to fear that there's been a disaster. Maybe all three.

However, when you hear, on the news, that your friend was stuck for an hour on a train whose engine had broken down (and with no cell phone reception), your emotions change drastically. Had the news of the train breakdown somehow reached you before he was supposed to arrive, your response would have been totally different. Thus, your thoughts and self-talk about the event played a crucial role in your emotional reaction to this situation.

"Aaargh" and "Eeek" Versus Self-Talk Responses

Sometimes an instantaneous Fight or Flight Response is hard-wired right into a neural path, such as when we step into the pothole on the dark road and find ourselves falling. In other anger or fear-producing situations, we may have traveled a neural path so often that a response, whether fight or flight, has become automatic. Picture someone that you've really disliked or feared for years, and — Presto! Practice makes perfect, and an anger or a fear response follows the thought of that hated or feared person in no time at all.

We like to call this type of immediate response, whether hard-wired or well-practiced, an "AAARGH! Response" (for instantaneous anger) or an "EEEK! Response" (for instantaneous fear). Because Aaargh! and Eeek! are what we're likely to say when this these types of neural paths are triggered.

It's true that some of our self-talk thought chains have been used so often, are so well practiced, that they've become automatic, as in the following diagram. These, like all Aaargh! and Eeek! Responses, require a goodly amount of Mental Muscle™ if we want to be able to short-circuit them.

(Elapsed Time Approximately Three Seconds!)

Fight or Flight Kicks Right In!

EVENT: Spouse is Late — S/He was late yesterday. — S/He was late last week, too. — S/He's ALWAYS LATE!!! — AAARGH!!! — Anger

Perception ——— *Processing* ——— OUTPUT

On the other hand, when some self-talk thought chains trigger a Fight or a Flight Response, there can be a span of a few seconds — or a few minutes — in which we basically *"talk ourselves into"* a Fight or a Flight Response. This can provide even those of us who have limited amounts of Mental Muscle with a brief window of opportunity that can be used to short-circuit the response. But in order to do this, we must not just notice that we are engaged in self-talk, we must become aware of our Point of No Return ("PONR").

Here's an analogy. Imagine a six-foot section of telephone pole, balanced upright on one end. If we notice it falling as soon as it starts to lean, we can bring it back to the vertical with one hand. If we don't notice until it's halfway to the floor, only a champion weightlifter could prevent it from hitting the ground. Likewise, only a small amount of Mental Muscle™ may be needed to short-circuit a Fight or Flight Response if it's noticed early on.

Notice Your PONR: The Point of No Return

If we can notice that an event, a thought, or a self-talk thought chain has *started* to trigger a Fight or a Flight Response, we can sometimes have time to short-circuit the response *before* it really kicks in, by re-focusing our mental attention onto the breath. As we've said, it's easier to short-circuit a Fight or Flight Response when it has just started — because once it is in full swing, it has a momentum of its own.

Or consider the common cold. A cold often starts with a few subtle symptoms: a scratchiness in the throat, a slightly stuffed-up nose. If we know the early symptoms of a cold, we can apply some vitamin C, extra rest, and a dose of Grandma's chicken soup to try to catch it early and avoid the three days in bed that a raging cold could require for recovery. Or three weeks if it turns into pneumonia.

What we call the PONR ("POH-ner," rhymes with loner) is the Point of No Return — that is, the point at which the Fight or the Flight Response has reached its full strength and become almost irreversable.

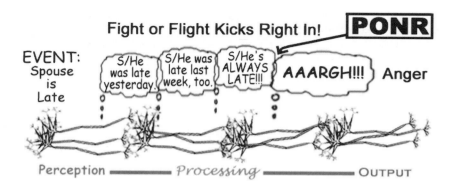

Immediate Aaargh! and Eeek! Responses just don't give us enough time to act before our Fight or our Flight Response reaches the PONR. But some self-talk situations do — if we learn to look at what we are saying to ourselves, we can sometimes avoid unnecessary anger or fear.

Playing with the PONR

There are two simple things that you can do to practice noticing your PONR. The first is to review the "symptoms" of anger and fear, as described way back on page 32. The second is to go back to the "Escalating the Exercise" on page 111. The balancing between the breath and the negative trigger of the disliked radio or television program will help you to notice your PONR — it's when you lose focus on the breath, and get mad!

We often "talk to ourself" about events that happen (self talk). This self talk can be described as a series of linked thoughts, which we call "thought chains." Unfortunately, these thought chains can trigger a Fight or a Flight Response.

Thought chains may take slightly longer to trigger a Fight or Flight Response than, for example, stumbling into an unseen pothole (the "Eeek!" Fear Response) or seeing a picture of your least favorite politician winning an election or a debate (the "Aaargh!" Anger Response).

This increased time span occurs because you need to "think your way through" the thoughts in the chain. Of course, with lots of practice, a thought chain neural path can become automatic, with the thoughts occurring so quickly that the Fight or Flight Response is triggered in no time at all! Please take a moment and read the above examples.

Learning to notice your "PONR" — Point of No Return, or the point at which a full-scale Fight or Flight Response kicks in — can be very useful, so please read the section above, and go back to practice with the "Escalating the Exercise" meditation on page 111.

Our self-talk and linked thoughts often follow habitual patterns. Often, these tend to be negative and result in a Fight or a Flight Response, and its attendant emotion of anger or angst. Two of the most common of these self-talk patterns are described below.

Self-Talk Habits to Avoid: Over-Generalization and Awfulizing

The kind of self talk or thought chain that triggers a Fight or Flight Response often involves one of two unuseful and closely related mental habits. "Over-generalizing" is when we consider a *particular* event, and make ourselves believe that it represents a situation that is true in *general*.

Please re-read the example at the end of the last section, about the friend (or perhaps spouse) who doesn't show up on time. In the first example of thought chaining, your self-talk takes this specific instance (that he has not arrived on time or called today) and turns it into a general issue ("he's never on time"). If your self-talk uses words like "always" or "constantly" or "never" — you may be generalizing. Of course, generalization can be realistic (maybe it's true that he "never does show up on time."). But if you often find these words in your self talk, it may behoove you to see what's actually true, and what's over-generalization.

"Awfulizing" is just what it sounds like, as exemplified in the two self-talk examples just above — both the speeding ticket thought chain and the he-didn't-show-up thought chains. In the speeding ticket example, and in the second and third versions of the he-didn't-call example, thoughts link up from bad to worse. The self talk gets more and more dire: from "another ticket" to "I'll lose my job," and from "I wonder why he didn't show up on time?" to "No one cares about me." Or from "I wonder why he didn't show up on time?" to "He must have had a terrible accident."

Often, it is not simply a real world event that triggers a Fight or Flight reaction — it is our thought or thoughts about that event. Our mind tells us stories about what has happened.

The stories that your mind makes up to tell you may well be worse than the incident itself! Especially if your self talk or your thought chains tend toward "over-generalization" or "awfulizing," both of which pretty much are what they sound like. Either is likely to trigger a Fight or Flight Response, landing you in a state of anger or fear.

Name Your Poison: Anger or Angst

Perhaps you remember the Emotion Equation™ from page 30. In this psychological "formula," an event or thought (or a thought chain) triggers the Fight or Flight Response, and the result is an emotion. But which emotion will it be — since the fight part of the response will result in anger, and the flight part of the response in fear? Understanding this dichotomy (two way split) will help you map out your Neural Neighborhood, so let's consider it further.

As we said in Chapter One (page 32) and again at the end of Chapter Nine, many people tend to be disposed more towards either the

Fight part or the Flight part of the Fight or Flight Response (grizzly bears fight, and gazelles flee). Since the Fight or Flight Response is such an important influence on our emotional life, knowing which part (Fight or Flight) your self-talk or thought chains tends to trigger — or knowing that you are equally likely to trigger either one, or both simultaneously — can be very useful.

> For now, just be aware that for some of us who are grizzly bear-like, self-talk tends to trigger the fight part of our Fight or Flight Response.
>
> For others, who are gazelle-like, self-talk tends to trigger the flight part of the response.
>
> And there are some lucky ones amongst us (including David) who are equal opportunity fighters and flee-ers! We'll offer you an exercise to work with this, a little later.

Sub-Conscious Self Talk: The Chatterbox Mind

Often, we are not even completely aware of all of our thoughts. Rather than an organized chain of thoughts proceeding with some kind of logic from a triggering event, they lurk below the level of consciousness. Thus many of us suffer from an internal monologue that runs intermittently — a critical, judgmental, internal voice that seems to love to offer gratuitous, and usually negative, comments. These comments slink through our mind half-noticed, and, like small leaks in the bottom of a large boat, often have a long-term or cumulative effect, which is not a pleasant one.

David used to use the first line or two of the Beatles song "I'm A Loser" to berate himself with:

"Anytime I did anything that didn't work out perfectly, I'd subconsciously croon 'I'm a looo-oo-ooser...' to myself, thus reinforcing negative feelings.

He also found himself a victim, at one time, of a strange and subconscious neural path based on McDonalds™! Whenever he would pass the Golden Arches, he'd find himself feeling discouraged and depressed. Eventually he realized that a girlfriend had recently left him for a guy named Ron, and every time he encountered one of the world's most ubiquitous fast food emporiums, the following neural path would run *just beneath* his awareness:

Pass and Perceive a McDonalds™ → Ronald McDonald → She left me for Ron → Flight Response → *Angst*

Nina's internal critic could be equally harsh:

"Ongoing self-talk used to make it hard for me to relax in a group. Judgmental comments often ran just beneath the threshold of my awareness. If I didn't speak, my internal commentary would snipe: 'I'm being too quiet, they'll think I'm boring.' If I did say something, my self-talk might say: 'I sure sounded stupid!' I couldn't win. I'd spend more of my time wondering feeling anxious due to the self-commentary than being present in the moment and enjoying the social occasion."

Not all self-talk is on a conscious level, and easy to notice. Once we began to clear and to watch our minds through meditation, we were able to see some of our mostly subconscious neural paths (at least sometimes), and began to let go of these self-hating habits (described above in awful detail).

Before we gained a bit of mental clarity from meditating, we just couldn't see these negative neural paths. And if you can't notice, and catch yourself in the act, you can't change a self-sabotaging behavior.

Take it from us: you'll feel happier and more positive when you begin to navigate your neural neighborhood with a bit more awareness and a better sense of direction!

Deeper than the Sub-Conscious

Beneath even sub-conscious Self Talk lie hard-wired paths that have evolved over millions, if not hundreds of millions, of years. Yet some of these may affect our daily behavior. And the same kind of self-awareness that we are explaining here can help us to bring even these deeply hidden paths into view, where we can gain some degree of control over them, if desired.

Some of these ancient and hidden paths involve our most basic needs, such as interpersonal (and sexual) relationships, and nutritive (eating) issues. In our opinion, they often affect the relationships between males and females, and usually *not* for the better.

Men and Women, Solving Versus Sympathizing

Here is a common interpersonal and inter-gender issue, which we believe goes back into neural paths formed during pre-human evolution. Although not true of every male/female relationship, we've seen it in our own personal experience and in the relationships of our friends, students, and colleagues. Here's how it works.

The woman describes a problem, major or minor, to the man. What does she want to get by doing this? A sympathetic response, empathy, acknowledgement of the problem.

The man hears her describe the problem, then does one of two things. He may try to offer a solution to the problem, then feels frustrated when that is unwanted (because remember: the woman doesn't want a solution, she wants a sympathetic response of some sort). The frustration triggers a neural path (probably involving self-talk such as "She doesn't *want* me to help! Grrrr!") leading either to the Path of Angst or the Path of Anger.

Or perhaps he can't offer a solution, in which case he feels frustrated (and perhaps inadequate or fearful), again triggering a neural path leading either to the Path of Angst or the Path of Anger.

Either way, the woman feels unheard and has not received the empathetic response that she wanted, triggering — you guessed it — a neural path (probably involving self-talk such as "He just won't listen!") leading either to the Path of Angst or the Path of Anger.

Eating When You're Hungry, or Not?

On a different activity but with similarly evolution-based neural paths, humans and their ancestors were gatherers and hunter/gatherers. If you or your clan found a fruitful berry patch, or killed a mammoth, you didn't just eat enough to feel reasonably full, and put the rest in the refrigerator.

Our evolutionary history around food and eating issues may well affect the way we eat today. Although you don't need to study human and pre-human evolution, the knowledge that how we evolved affects us today — coupled with the *Watching the Mind Exercises*, can give us insight into our behavior, and increase our ability to change it, as well.

Acknowledging the effects of our evolutionary history on our behavior can help us to change that behavior now, for the better. By *Watching the Mind*, we identify self-talk, thought chains, and other elements of the neural paths that may date back millions of years!

Desire and the Seven Deadly Sins

While anger and fear are certainly frequent human emotions, the hands-down favorite neural path for many of us is desire. As David pointed out in *Neural Path Therapy*, if we consider Pope Gregory's list of The Seven Deadly Sins, compiled way back in the sixth century, five of the seven worst things that a person could do (in Gregory's opinion, at least) were avarice, gluttony, lust, envy, and pride — all related to issues of desire, appetite, or craving.

These "desire" thoughts and the neural paths that they trigger are commonly experienced — who hasn't wanted another cookie, or a million bucks, or to have a romantic liason with someone inappropriate. However, these thoughts are rarely explored (other than by giving in to temptation, which is *not* the type of exploration that we're talking about here).

Recent studies at the University of Amsterdam (Laan, Both, and Spiering, 2007) indicate that our behavior around sex follows the same Perception-Processing-Output formula that underlies fear or anger. The perception of certain sights or smells (or — we believe — thoughts, though they were not part of the Amsterdam studies) trigger the body's "sexual response process" almost instantaneously. The mental response we call "sexual desire" comes afterward.

As with fear or anger reactions, we can study these desire-based neural paths in our own minds, noticing the "symptoms" (the events and thoughts that trigger the paths, whether the sight of a chocolate cake on the counter, or the thought of an old lover) and being aware of the Point of No Return — at which we feel almost "forced" to react to those symptoms, and reach for the cake or the telephone…

> In the "Watching the Mind Exercise" section, we'll offer you some exercises and meditations to explore the thoughts and neural paths involving desire.

Chapter Sixteen: In a Nutshell

This chapter began with a quick review of how neural paths shape our behavior. Fear, anger, all learning, all desire, and just about every other human process are the result of these brain cells that form chains or paths in our grey matter. So if you're not completely clear on this important subject, you may want to at least review the boxes in the first part of this chapter.

We then go on to consider how events often produce a series of thoughts ("self talk") which affect our reaction to those events. We discuss two of the most common types of self talk: "Awfulization" and "Over-Generalization."

> Awfulization and Over-Generalization, with the addition of desire thoughts, comprise for many of us the bulk of what we've called "Dead End Thoughts" in Step Two. They just don't go anywhere useful!
>
> Understanding and observing our self-talk — whether conscious, sub-conscious, or even pre-conscious (formed by evolution) — will help us to short-circuit the Fight or the Flight Responses that it can trigger. Especially if we practice noticing our "PONR." That is, our "Point of No Return," the point at which it becomes difficult to re-focus attention onto the breath…

Chapter Seventeen: Your Neural Neighborhood

In this very short chapter, let's continue our metaphor of the mind as a geographical location that we can learn to navigate with a bit of careful observation. You've probably already got some experience along these lines — if you've lived in the same neighborhood for a while, you know quite a bit about it (even without that guidebook). You know the good places to eat, the pleasant places to hang out. And also know the places to avoid — the dead ends and detours, and the places that might not be so safe to wander in after dark.

You've bought, found, or created some kind of map, whether written out on paper or in your head, that helps you go where you want to go, and avoid the places that you don't want to go. Having the same kind of "map" for the neural paths of your brain is both possible and useful. After all, it's important to know where to hang out, and where not to, when you stroll through your mindscape, as well as your landscape...

> Thoughts and the neural paths that they trigger are the basic building blocks of human activity, and are also the mental equivalents of the buildings and streets and byways of your neighborhood. Knowing these mental roads and ruts, the good places in the mind to hang out (or the bad ones to avoid), and the dead ends are just as — or even more — important than knowing their physical counterparts in your town or city.

How to Map Your Neural Neighborhood

Mapping your neural neighborhood is a highly individualistic thing to do, and it can be accomplished in many ways. The way that will be most effective for you has a lot to do with who you are, just as who you are (Bird, Bee, etc.) has a lot to do with which of the following meditations and exercises you may find most effective.

Diagram It Yourself...

Some of us — the Birds — will find the visual feedback of diagramming our own neural paths to be useful. A few of the following exercises will help you to do this, either by providing a simple "fill in the blank" diagram of a common neural path, or teaching you to create Draw-a-Breath charts that enable you to see the actual thoughts that distract and distress you...

...Versus a General Sense of "What's in There"

Others of us — including, perhaps, the Barnacles, who like to get "the feel" of things — will want to use meditations such as Counting Thoughts and Counting Particular Thoughts to get the lay of the mental land.

Listing "Your Top Ten"— And Those Grabby Thoughts

Analytical and verbal types — the parrots amongst us — are likely to find the "Top Ten" list and the "Grabby Thought" work to their taste. But perhaps the most important — yet easiest — of this step will be simply to choose just a few Grabby Thoughts to work with in Parts Four and Five. By using Visualization techniques and Softening Around the Pain of even a few repetitive (but unuseful) thoughts, you can almost instantly improve the quality of your daily life by a noticeable amount!

As with just about everything else, Watching the Mind is a matter of "different strokes for different folks," as described above. But no matter who you are — bird, bat, or barnacle — choosing a few Grabby Thoughts to work with in Parts Four (Visualization) and Five (Softening Around Pain) will reduce your stress and increase your mindfulness, right away!

Chapter Seventeen: In a Nutshell

One of David's corporate workshops is called *How To See It Coming, Before It Hits the Fan*™. In this presentation, he teaches groups two important skills. As usual, he uses the harmonica to teach his participants to focus attention on their breathing, then teaches them to use this new ability to short-circuit Fight or Flight Responses. But he also trains each participant to map his or her own Neural Neighborhood, so that he or she can prepare and practice — in advance — to use their new abilities in specific situations that they know will arise.

Forewarned, as the old saying goes, is forearmed. And it's that advance warning, that knowledge of one's Neural Neighborhood, that allows us to "See it coming, before it hits the fan." In other words, it is the "seeing" *before* the "hitting" that allows us to take skillful steps *before* fan time makes it too late to avoid a mess!

The following Watching the Mind exercises and meditations will be useful to you in the long run, since they'll help you to identify the specific neural paths that you most need to work on.

Chapter Eighteen:
The Watching The Mind
Exercises

In these exercises, *thoughts in the mind* will provide the focal point for our attention. In other words, we'll be using thoughts as our meditation objects, just as we've already used our breath, or the process of walking, or a mouthful of food that we are chewing.

As we did with our breaths and our steps in the breathing and walking exercises, we'll begin by counting objects, and then by labeling them. Only this time, instead of observing and counting or labeling external objects such as breaths or footsteps, we will watch our own thoughts. Later (when we get to Living in the Now, Step Seven), we'll be able to focus on the direct sensations that our thoughts produce.

Watching the Mind involves noticing our thoughts — and learning to treat them as objects in the mind. For now, we *will not* try to change these thoughts, or their effect on us. We'll just learn first to notice them, to count them, and to label them. Of course, treating thoughts in this way may change the way they affect us — that's okay if it happens, or okay if it does not.

Completing the exercises of Step Three will soon allow us, by using the techniques of Steps Four and Five, to reduce any painful effects that these thoughts — whether fear, or anger, or desire — may have on us.

So don't spend too much time with Step Three. Its purpose is mostly to help us understand our own minds better by identifying common thoughts and neural paths. And to start noticing *when* they occur. Doing some of the following exercises even one time may be sufficient for this purpose, especially if you create a quick record of the results.

• A Hint: For many of the mind-watching meditations, it may be useful to keep a pen and piece of paper handy, where you can reach it to jot down a word or two, or keep a quick count, without much effort.

The Thought Counting Meditation

This exercise will help you start withdrawing your attention from the *content* of your thoughts, as discussed on pages 127 and 128.

• Sit comfortably, with some type of timer or alarm clock handy. If none is available, make sure you can see a clock. Set the timer for one minute, or time yourself by the clock.

• Now close your eyes, and begin to count your thoughts. As soon as a thought appears in your mind, count it, but don't "get into" the content of that thought. If you do, you may only end up with a count of one thought for your entire minute!

Think about a bird watching competition. Competitive bird watchers go out, armed with binoculars, to try to identify as many species of bird as they can in one day. They don't study each bird for hours, or even minutes. As soon as they see one — that's it — on to look for the next. And right now you're a *thought* watcher, so you'll do the same with your own thoughts, for these sixty seconds!

You've already gained some skill at returning the focus of your attention to a meditation (from practicing the mind-clearing meditations). So you'll probably be able to let go of each thought after counting it, unless it's one of those particularly stubborn thoughts, which we'll deal with below. And then return the focus of your attention towards looking for another thought to count. If no thoughts seem to come up, either say to yourself "no thoughts" (which is a perfectly valid thought itself, and should be counted), or else just relax and enjoy a moment of spontaneous mind clearing!

So keep a count of your thoughts. This will include thoughts such as "Gee, I haven't had many thoughts yet!" or "Uh-oh, was that thought number seven or number eight?" Some thoughts will flash by like speedy and exotic birds, perhaps as quick mental pictures or even as single words. Others will lumber into sight like penguins, and take their time leaving as well. Some people will have only a few noticeable thoughts in a minute, others will have dozens and dozens.

• For those who tend to have lots of thoughts, counting them with pencil in hand, using the "four lines and a slash" method may be helpful, as pictured here for a count of 23 thoughts...

Working with "Grabby" Thoughts

It's easy to lose your count if a Grabby Thought grabs *you*. If this happens, there are a few ways to deal with it.

If a thought arises, and its content is so "grabby" for you that you just "can't" let go of it, try to remember what thought it is or even describe it in a few written words. That information will be useful, even though it seems to be preventing you from doing this exercise right now.

If it seems possible, you may be able to try to treat the thought as a Dead End or Dandelion Thought: by turning your attention back onto your breath for a few breaths. Try to count the innnns and outttts, then continue counting all thoughts.

Fear thoughts, anger thoughts, and desire thoughts tend to be the hardest to let go of, for most people. These thoughts trigger the physiological reactions — like the Fight or the Flight Response, or a Desire Response — that we've discussed. But remember:

> It's not the fear or the anger or the desire thought itself that's the problem — it is the inability to control your mind and body's reaction to that thought that creates a problem.

By the way: many, if not most, of our Grabby Thoughts are also Dead End Thoughts — the ones that do not serve any useful purpose. But it is possible for a Grabby Thought to serve a useful end (in which case it is not a Dead End Thought). And some Dead End Thoughts are not all that grabby (they are just mildly annoying). Please review the section on *Grabby Thoughts* on page 68, if you need clarification on this subject. And we'll do lots of work on loosening their hold on us in Step Five.

This isn't an easy exercise, but there's no way to do it wrong. It's sole purpose is to learn to look, for this moment, at your thoughts as objects, like birds, or rocks, or passing automobiles. Nothing to take personally — just thoughts...

Preparing for The Thought Labeling Meditation: Your "Top Ten"

In the last meditation, we paid *no* attention to the content of the thoughts that we were counting. Now, we are going to pay just barely enough attention to thought content so that we will be able to *label* each thought.

> Please begin by making a brief mental or written list of the *types* or categories of thoughts that are commonly featured in the movie of your mind. These are also likely to include the "grabbiest" thoughts you have. This list may prove very helpful, indeed.

You might call them "Your Top Ten," since they play over and over in the mind like the hit songs of your favorite radio station. David finds that he has just seven main categories, which we'll list below, in general order of popularity. Perhaps your Top Ten list will be as high-minded and spiritual as his:

"*Planning* thoughts are those in which I try to decide exactly what to do, specifically ("I'll write to John, then have lunch") or generally ("perhaps I should go to law school").

Desire thoughts include wishes for anything, from sex to a new Mac to world peace.

Fear thoughts include any type of worry: hypochondria, money, work, you name it.

Happy or appreciative thoughts are often noting pleasurable sensations such as the sun on my face, or the smell of onions cooking, or remembering or anticipating pleasant events.

Judging thoughts are those in which I approve or, more likely, criticize anything or anyone.

Righteous thoughts are a popular sub-category of my judging thoughts, in which I make the judgement that I am right, and someone else is wrong.

Angry thoughts could be those directed at myself (in which case I consider them as falling into the specialized sub-category of self-hating thoughts), or at anybody else."

The Thought Labeling Meditation

• Study your Top Ten Thought List for a moment.

• Sit comfortably, and observe each thought as it swims into awareness. Observe it only long enough to decide which one of your categories it fits into, mentally label it ("Ah, a desire thought.") then go on to look for the next.

If absolutely no thoughts seem to be forthcoming right now, simply relax and enjoy a few seconds of effortless mind-clearing.

If a thought doesn't seem to fit into any of your categories, just make up a more or less appropriate new category, ("ahh, that's one of those 'What-If-I-Had-Been-Born-An-Eskimo' type of thoughts") and go back to looking for the next thought.

As in the last exercise, if a "grabby" thought arises, if some physiological response occurs — flight, fight, or desire — just notice what thought, and what type of thought, it is. And just keep labeling it: "Fear…Yep, still Fear…Uh-huh, Fear again…" Sometimes, as indicated by a recent UCLA research project on meditators (Lieberman et al, 2007), simply labeling a painful stimulus is enough to reduce, or at least change, its effect on us…

• After the meditation, see if you can tell which thoughts occurred most often. Which thoughts were easy to let go of? Which ones were hard to let go of?

Thought Labeling with Breath Exercise

You may find it easier to do the previous meditation if you combine it with a breath labeling or counting exercise. In this variation, sit comfortably, and do your favorite breathing meditation…until you notice a thought creeping in. Then, instead of trying to turn your attention instantly back to the breath — as we hope you usually do — label the thought. *Then* turn your attention back to the breath. Until the next thought arises. Label that thought. And so on.

If thoughts *never* intrude while you are breath counting or breath labeling: congratulations! You're in better shape than we are, so just go back to the exercise before this one, and label some thoughts *without* benefit of breath!

The Thought Labeling Meditation with Draw-A-Breath™ Exercise

This one is just what it sounds like. Consider your list of "Top Ten favorites" from page 153. Decide on an appropriate acronym for each type of thought. David uses "P" for Planning Thoughts, "F" for Fear Thoughts, and so on (rocket science, it ain't). As you do your Draw-A-Breath™, add the appropriate acronym whenever a thought intrudes, then return to drawing your breath.

A typical session of a half a minute or so of David's practice might look like this: He draws about two-and-a-half breaths (first line), then is distracted by a sudden Fear thought (F). Maybe he misses a breath or three while grabbed by the fear, but he turns his attention back to his breath at the beginning of a slightly shallow in breath (at the end of the first line).

A Planning thought (P) distracts him after he draws another breath (beginning of line two), then he notices that he has lost his focus and returns to breath drawing somewhere near the beginning of a rather gradual in breath (middle of second line)...

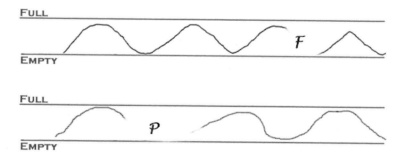

In the example that follows (originally presented in *Neural Path Therapy*), David was teaching this exercise to a woman who had recently begun exploring her thoughts. What does this chart represent?

After two breaths (represented by the first two "hills"), a planning thought (P) almost disrupts the breath drawing, but not quite. After a few more breaths, a vague food thought (she uses F for Food Thoughts) appears for a second, but doesn't interfere with the task.

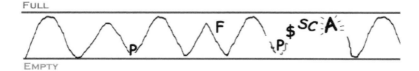

FULL

EMPTY

Then (two thirds of the way to the right) a more intense planning thought (P) arises, leads to a worry about money ($), and — uh-oh — the client gets "grabbed" by the money worry. The breath is forgotten (ragged line). When she eventually notices that she's stopped drawing her breath, there's a microsecond of perception — "I lost my breath focus" (not marked, it happens too fast). This is instantaneously followed by a few moments of self-criticism (SC) "I've got the attention span of a fruit fly. I'm no good at anything." leading to an angst-filled episode (A) in which the strong emotion provides her with a convenient additional distraction from the chosen task, and the drawing of the breath is entirely forgotten.

Eventually, she realizes that any further investment in self-criticism is just keeping her from the breath drawing. She exhales (with a wry sigh, perhaps?), and halfway through that out breath starts drawing again. Later, reviewing the chart, she can see a Grabby Thought Neural Path:

Planning thought ➔ money worry ➔ which triggers a Fight or Flight Response, which then leads to ➔ a self-criticism followed by ➔ an angst emotion.

So when you get "lost in a thought" or "grabbed by a thought" for a while, just mark the thought with a letter and return to Drawing-a-Breath™ as soon as you notice that you've been distracted. When you get good at this, you'll be able to notice that you "got lost" or grabbed and return to the exercise in the middle of a breath, and be able to draw the rest of that same breath!

> Doing the above exercise, and then looking for Grabby Thoughts or Thought Chains (and taking a few notes on what you notice) will help you to map your Neural Neighborhood!

The Particular Thought or Grabby Thought Counting Meditation

You can choose any thought, or category of thought, to notice in this exercise. Eventually, you will get the most benefits by choosing one of your "grabby" thoughts, as they are the thoughts that you most need to practice working with.

However, it will be more skillful to start off with a non-grabby or very mildly grabby thought, until you become familiar with this meditation.

A Hint: When you are ready to work with really grabby thoughts, reviewing the "symptoms" of the Fight Response or the Flight Response (page 32) may be useful if you have chosen anger or fear as the grabby thought you'd like to work with.

• In this exercise, you are going to try to remember to count the number of times in the course of an hour or a day that your own self-selected particular thought arises. That's all there is to it.

• You may want to keep count on a piece of paper, so that you don't forget your score.

Try not to get angry with yourself for having these uncontrollable repetitive thoughts. If you do get angry or self-hating, the Compassion exercises later on will help you to treat even your own mind with a touch of mercy. But for now, your task is simply to try to notice how often these particular thoughts occur. In the following Steps, we will work to reduce their effect on you.

David:

"I usually do this exercise with my judging/righteous thoughts, since they are, for me, the grabbiest. I love to be *right*, to judge others, and it's hard for me to let someone else be wrong without their admitting it, to just let go of me being right and them being wrong. On a seriously righteous day, I can count dozens of judging thoughts! Doing so helps me to be aware of the hold that this particular thought has on me, and to diminish it."

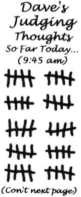

Dave's Judging Thoughts So Far Today... (9:45 am)

(Con't next page)

157

"Rube Goldberg" Thought Chains

In a Rube Goldberg cartoon, strange events are chained together to cause a final event. To create a Goldberg alarm clock, for example, the sun comes up, and its rays through a magnifying glass burn the rope that holds up the cheese, the cheese falls down so that the mice come out, the cat goes after the mice, the dog goes after the cat from under the bed where he was sleeping, which pulls out a slat so that the farmer falls on the floor and is woken up in time for milking!

Our minds often use self-talk to create similar absurdities, chaining together thoughts in strange ways. For example, when Nina is running a few minutes late for a meeting (which is not unusual), the following thought chain may arise:

"My thought chain begins with a relatively realistic perception ('I am going to be late.'). Then the thought escalates, via self-talk, into fear ('I'm always late and everyone gets angry.'). Now it becomes a full-fledged fantasy: I imagine myself entering the room, and all eyes turn reproachfully to the latecomer, while an angry buzz of commentary fills the room.

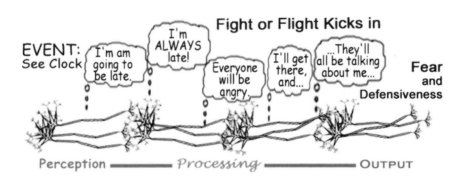

"If I don't notice that one of these perception-to-fantasy-to-emotion thought chain/neural paths has taken place, I can make myself feel fearful and defensive towards my colleagues for their behavior in *my* fantasy, before I even arrive at the meeting! Since I became aware of these thought chains, my ability to cut them short has increased, and their ability to affect me has diminished. Now I can even see the humor in the thought chain fantasies that I used to create! (Of course, I could simply learn to be on time!)"

The Thought Chain Labeling Exercise

After you've spent some time with the Thought Counting and Thought Labeling meditations, try a Thought Chain Labeling exercise in which you specifically look for two or more thoughts which often occur together.

You may find, for example, that the guilt thoughts you had perceived as happening spontaneously are actually a result of prior angry thoughts, which themselves are a result of helplessness thoughts. You may find it convenient to write this out like Nina did, above.

Or you can photocopy the "blank form" below and use it to create a thought chain diagram of your own — just fill in the Event or Triggering Thought that starts the chain, a few words about each subsequent thought, and the Emotion that you end up with. However you choose to do it, becoming aware of your thoughts in this manner can really help you to understand why you feel the way you do.

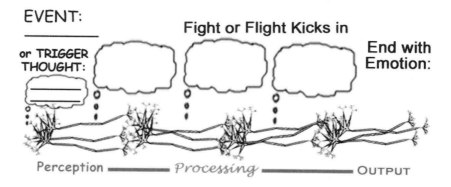

About Desire-Based Neural Paths

The term "Desire" covers a lot of ground. At one end of the spectrum, some desires — such as the desire to take a breath when you've been swimming underwater and just popped up for air — are natural, and even essential. Others, like a desire to have a waterfront mansion in Malibu, or a desire to romance your boss's spouse, may be unskillful.

In the first instance, because mansions in Malibu are expensive and you may not really need one. In the second, because it's most likely a really dumb idea, if not unethical. Other desires, for lost youth or lost love, may be unattainable no matter what we do.

> As with other types of thoughts, we will work on counting, listing, and labeling our desire-based thoughts and neural paths, as well as looking at what triggers them.

The Breath Desire Exercise

• Do a very short Breath Labeling Exercise ("innnnn...ouuuttt...inn...ouuttt..."), for just a few breaths.

• End on an exhale.

• But don't inhale automatically.

• Instead, just hold your breath — maintaining the "lungs empty" state — for a second or three or ten (depending on your aerobic condition).

• And notice how your body really, really, wants more air. Once you've noticed this, inhale. Please.

If you have any kind of breathing difficulty, be especially gentle with this exercise, or discuss it with your health care provider before you try it.

Don't be harsh on yourself, holding your breath until you gasp and convulse like a goldfish on the carpet. Instead, just relax and notice this completely natural desire, hard-wired into our neural paths, which we usually fulfill without a second's thought. Then take a deep, satisfying, well-appreciated inhale.

Without this hard-wired desire, we could not stay alive. Yet sometimes, as with many desires — learned or hard-wired — we must repress it. David, who occasionally goes diving for abalone (a large underwater mollusk which can only be taken legally without the use of SCUBA™ apparatus), has learned that attempting to breathe underwater is an great way to let the abalone catch you.

The Chew and Swallow Desire Exercise

Here's another easy one — and a great way to practice building Mental Muscle™ around desire issues anywhere and anytime, with no one the wiser (except you).

• During a meal, once you are no longer very hungry, chew a mouthful much longer than you usually do.

• Notice the desire to swallow and take another mouthful.

• Repeat the first few steps a few times, then return to eating normally.

The number of chews will be different depending on whether you are eating a steak, a piece of bread, or a spoonful of yoghurt.

This "desire to swallow" is a learned desire, a habit which has formed a neural chain, unconscious though it usually is. Some of us chew more, some "wolf" our food. Noticing habitual and learned desire-based neural paths — and what triggers them — will help us to deal with them more skillfully.

Other Desire Exercises

If unfulfillable or unskillful desires are an issue for you, it may be useful to do some more exercises on the subject. For example, turn back a few pages to review The Particular Thought Counting Meditation, and then try counting desire thoughts over the course of an hour or a day, or during the commute to work.

Chocolate
Thoughts
So Far Today...

You can also make a practice of labeling any desire thought that arises, simply by saying to yourself, "Ahh, that's a desire thought." And a "Top Ten" type list of your desires might be a useful thing to have, if this is an area that you'd like to work on…

Considering Desire Thoughts as Dead Ends

Perhaps you've already chosen a "lightweight" desire — not your most powerful, obsessive, compulsion — to use as a Dead End Thought. If not, now might be a good time to look at whether there is an appropriate desire to use in this way. As David puts it, in his workshops, and in the book *Neural Path Therapy* (which is focused entirely on issues such as these):

"Many desires are hard-wired into us, for what were originally very good reasons. Without food or water we'd die, without sexual attraction we'd die out, as a race, at least. This was all very well amongst our distant ancestors — until thought entered the picture, in the minds of *Homo sapiens*. Whereas previously, hunger or sexual desire neural paths were triggered only by either hard-wired responses based on actual need, or on the actual perception of a food or sex object in the real world, these desires could now, in human brains, be triggered by nothing more than a fantasy, a ghost, a thought.

"The next time you become aware of any mild desire — "Hmmm, I could use a sandwich." or "I think I'd like to read the paper for a while." — play with it. Instead of immediately seeking to satisfy the desire, whether need or greed, turn your attention to one of the breathing exercises. Just notice whether doing this affects your reaction to the desire. As you breath, try also to focus in on the physical sensation of the desire, rather than on any thoughts about it. Notice if the desire stimulates self-talk ("But I've been working for hours, I deserve a break.") — if so, the breath focus should take your attention away from the "story" that your mind is telling you about the desire.

"In this exercise, you're not necessarily trying to avoid the satisfaction of the desire. You're just investigating the nature of desire itself, as an object in the mind, rather than as some internal marching command that you must instantly obey."

Identifying Desire Triggers

As we mentioned earlier when speaking about desire, it seems as though neural paths involving desire follow the same perception to processing to output pattern as most other neural paths. We believe that at the very beginning of most situations in which desire raises its beguiling head, a thought or event has been perceived, which then triggers a physiological or mental reaction, resulting in the "feeling" of hunger, sexual need, greed, or any other desire.

- You might wish to choose one particular type of desire and see if a trigger event or trigger thought seems to precede it.

- As soon as you perceive your chosen type of desire arising, try to think back to the time just before it arose.

- A desire trigger might be a smell, a sound, a place, a taste, or a sight. Or it might be as subtle as a thought of a smell, sound, place, and so on.

You can use either a light or a heavyweight desire, since you are not trying to affect the progression of this desire — only to investigate whether any particular stimulus, real or on the level of thought, triggers it.

There are almost as many ways of working with desire — including giving in to it — as there are types of things that we desire. The exercises just presented above offer different ways of observing and relating to desire.

Try them with "lightweight" desires: the urge to have a sandwich or a snack when you don't really *need* one, or the urge to "just check the news online for a moment" when there are more useful things to do.

Desire "Triggers" often precede some of our more consuming desires, so identifying them will be useful, even though we won't work with these burning wants, yet. Instead, we'll offer suggestions for skillful handling of more intense desires and perceived needs in Step Five.

The Dead End Thought-Watching Exercises

We hope that you've identified — and been working with — a few "lightweight" Dead End Thoughts, as we suggested in Step Two (pages 100 – 103). If not, please go back and do so.

If you've been practicing the "Pluck It and Chuck It" strategy, here are some other entertaining things that you can do with Dead End Thoughts.

• Count your Dead End Thoughts. You can do this whether they are "pluckable and chuckable" or not — so it can be a useful strategy that will later help you to soften around the pain of Dead End Thoughts that seem, at present, too grabby to Pluck and Chuck.

• Label your Dead End Thoughts. Simply apply a one or two word descriptive label, any time one arises. Doesn't matter if it's a grabby one, or one that you can Pluck and Chuck. Just give each one a name, every time you notice it.

• Look for Dead End Thought triggering events, or triggering thought chains. Is there some specific thing that happens right before a particular Dead End Thought arises? Perhaps you notice a billboard advertising something that you can't afford, or you've just looked in the mirror, or a relative has just called. Be a detective, looking for clues to your own mind!

> If you have found it useful to work with the "Pluck It and Chuck It! Strategy" for Dead End Thoughts, you may find it fruitful to try the above Dead End Thought Exercises. If you haven't, please go back to Step Two and try again!

Chapter Eighteen: In a Nutshell

There's not too much to say about Chapter Eighteen, which contains the actual *Watching the Mind Exercises*. Some of them are easy, some are hard, and all are useful for understanding that sometimes insubordinate and often inscrutable entity which exists at the top of our spinal column: the human brain (and the mind which it supports).

> Please read about and try each of the exercises at least once, because doing so will help you to notice those particular thoughts and neural paths which produce the emotions, words, or actions that you most want or need to work with.

Step Three:
What You Need to Know

What's the point of Step Three? First, we've learned that our thoughts can be seen as just another type of object, which we can observe just as we watch a movie. This allows us to bring our thoughts and neural paths into the light of day by noticing that they exist, by listing them, counting them, labeling them. This is *Watching the Mind*. As we begin to map our Neural Neighborhoods, we learn to identify such specific and exotic creations of the mind as:

- Self-Talk and Thought Chains

- The PONR — Point of No Return

- Awfulization and Over-Generalization

- The Choice of Anger or Angst

- Grabby Thoughts

- Desire Triggers

Then — forewarned and forearmed with the knowledge of *which* thoughts and neural paths are likely to occur in *what* particular situations — in Steps Four and Five we use the Mental Muscle™ that we've built up from Step Two's *Clearing the Mind Exercises* to control our reactions to the thoughts we've learned to watch.

Please don't spend a lot of time — yet — with the Watching the Mind exercises. Read about them, and try each one a few times, or more often if you like. Make a few lists, of "Top Ten" and Grabby Thoughts, of Desires and Desire Triggers.

Then go on to Steps Four and Five, and learn how to use the Visualization and Softening Around Pain techniques to skillfully navigate the neural neighborhood that you've begun to map. *But remember that all of these steps work together.*

So don't forget to keep on doing your favorite Clearing the Mind exercises from Step Two *while* you work with Step Three — because that's what will give you the Mental Muscle™ you'll need to apply in Steps Four and Five!

STEP FOUR:
Visualization, Plus...

Welcome to Step Four of *The Three Minute Meditator*. In this very short but very important step, we will describe a crucial tool that can shorten your path to mindfulness. We'll also describe a technique that we call Progressive Neural Desensitization (PND), which uses visualization to help us deal with painful thoughts and events. This step will end with a Relaxation exercise. Practicing some "PND" and Relaxation will also help us to prepare for Step Five, *Softening Around Pain*.

Chapter Nineteen: Visualization

You already know how to "visualize." Back at the beginning of Chapter Four, you did the Favorite Animal "Meditation" (we put the word "meditation" in quotes, because the exercise seems so simple and natural that some might not call it a meditation — although we think they'd be wrong). Something magical occurred: a few simple written words on our part somehow resulted in a mental image on your part.

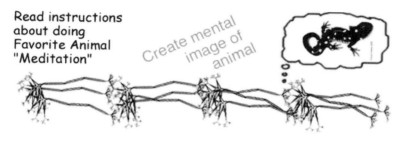

Read instructions about doing Favorite Animal "Meditation"

Create mental image of animal

What is Visualization? Why is it Important?

Visualization is the art of creating mental images. Anyone can picture an elephant, a rabbit, or a Volkswagen in their mind's eye. Most of us can produce a clear enough mental image of our own neighborhood to describe the houses or buildings next to our own. It is reported that inventor Nicola Tesla could visualize a new engine in his mind, allow it to "run" for a few hours, and then "see" which parts showed wear or metal fatigue! He was one serious visualizer!

The fact that our brains and bodies react so strongly to pictures in the mind's eye makes the ability to visualize very important. A tremendous amount of evidence indicates that after we've spent some time clearly visualizing ourselves performing an activity, it actually becomes easier for us to do. Olympic champions and master musicians use visualization to rehearse — on the level of the mind — what they plan to do in the stadium or the concert hall.

This technique works in almost any sphere of human endeavor, and the key element seems to be the degree of "real-ness" of the visualization. So it clearly pays to spend some time practicing and strengthening this most useful skill.

Since mental images in the form of thoughts can have a tremendously powerful effect on our bodies and minds — often triggering the neural paths that result in our emotions, words, and actions — practicing this skill will better allow us to use it to our advantage.

Improved visualization skills will help us with all of the Three Minute Meditations, but most importantly with the crucial *Master Skill Visualization Exercise,* which is the last visualization exercise in the book. Don't miss it!

In a way, the term visualization is a bit of a misnomer, since this technique's effectiveness is increased when senses other than the visual can be incorporated into every exercise. In the following exercise, try to re-create, in your mind, a vivid sense of sight, feel, smell and taste.

The Lemon Meditation

Picture a lemon in your mind's eye, as clearly as possible. As yellow as the sun, its thick skin minutely wrinkled, and just a touch oily to the hand. Dig your fingernail into the peel, and see a tiny spray of citric oil arch out into the air. Pull some peel off, to expose the white fibers covering the juicy, wet, pulpy insides.

You smell the tartness as you bite deep into the lemon, and taste the sourness. The saliva leaps into your mouth.

If you were able to visualize the lemon with any clarity, you probably salivated even before you imagined biting into it. And that's the point of this "Body/Mind" exercise.

Most people would consider salivation to be a bodily process outside of their conscious control. And yet we salivate when we think of lemons. Just the thought of the taste of citrus somehow stimulates a gland in the mouth to produce a secretion.

Practice your visualization with this lemon exercise. Can you "train" your salivary glands to spring into action at the first thought of lemon? At the word "lemon"?

More Visualization Practice

We'll continue to use visualization skills in many of the exercises, so practice a few more. Try to use as many senses as you can, when doing them.

Think about a short trip or commute that you have taken many times. Can you imagine the roads and highways, or the buses or subways that you must use? Can you smell the flowers near the bus stop (or the stinky exhaust of passing trucks?) Can you hear the sound that the train makes, roaring into the station? Or feel its vibrations as you ride it?

Can you picture the inside of your house or apartment? Can you visualize the different rooms, doorways, or windows, as though you were yourself moving from place to place? Are there smells as you pass the kitchen, or can you feel the sun on your face through the living room window?

How about some *wild* visualizations, just for fun? Can you picture Frankenstein's monster? Now put him into a tuxedo! Change the tux to a yellow tutu! Make him do the Charleston, then replace him with an image of... Brad Pitt! When will we ever stop having fun?!!!

The Meditation Visualization Exercise

Since, as we've said and many experiments and real life experiences conclusively demonstrate that mentally rehearsing an action — with as much "real-ness" as possible — will help us to perform that action in real life.

> So please spend just twenty or thirty seconds (or more) a few times each day, picturing yourself *actually using* a Three Minute Meditation technique in a real life situation.

For instance, you might picture yourself doing one of the walking meditations as you return to the office from lunch. Try to experience the scene that you've mentally created as clearly as possible. Feel your feet as they hit the floor, and feel your thumbs gently touching your forefingers. See the surrounding area, and hear or smell any appropriate sounds or odors.

After you've done this a few times, try to visualize using meditation to deal with a *slightly* more stressful scenario. Perhaps you can *picture* using a walking meditation on the way to the boss's office for a meeting, or on the way to a dinner date with a friend who can be just a bit trying!

Do you have a particular Dead End Thought that you've been working on? In Chapter Twelve's *Dead End Thought Strategy*, we've already suggested (without using the word "visualization") that you prepare to use the strategy "in real life" after practicing on the level of thought, by consciously bringing your chosen Dead End into the mind. You may find this easier to do now, after practicing some visualization on purpose just now!

> Is there a particular situation in which you'd like to use meditation techniques (but perhaps one that seems just a bit too heavy to attempt at the moment)? If so, try working with it, not in real life — yet — but instead by visualizing it, and working with it on the level of thought.

Once you feel comfortable with the above exercises, the adventurous amongst you may wish to jump to the back of the book, and try...*The Master Skill Visualization Exercise!*

Visualization And Health

For thousands of years, the fakirs of India have demonstrated their abilities to control various bodily functions to an astounding degree. Using techniques of a meditative type, a top-shelf fakir can suspend respiratory and circulatory functions for prolonged periods of time, and even a run-of-the-mill one can lie on a bed of nails or walk on burning coals. So it appears that the mind has a far greater degree of control over the body than is generally believed in the West.

A number of body/mind sciences, such as "Psycho-Neuro-Immunology" (PNI) deal with just this subject. If people can mentally control a glandular secretion like saliva (just as you did in the Lemon exercise), why *shouldn't* we be able to stimulate or retard other glandular functions, or rebuild a damaged immune system? The preliminary evidence indicates that we can — at least to some extent — and visualization is the technique most often used. While we'd never say that visualization is any kind of cure-all, if this subject interests you, we recommend reading Joan Borysenko's *Minding The Body, Mending The Mind*, and Bernie Siegal's *Love, Medicine, and Miracles*.

Not a Miracle, But Magic Nontheless

Of course, the body/mind connection does not *only* manifest itself in exotic or miraculous ways. Every time you raise a finger, or take a step, a thought in your mind is somehow motivating a physical response in your body.

The ordinary things that we do every day never seem quite as wonderful as someone else's feats. But, is the fakir's ability to *not* breathe on demand any more impressive than its opposite? Just because everybody can do it, makes it no less magical. It just tells us, once more, that we are *all* magical, and capable of great things, with sufficient Mental Muscle™...

The First of Two Secrets about The Secret

Of course we've noticed the popularity of Rhonda Byrne's "The Secret," in which she describes the "Law of Attraction" with its three step program of "Ask, Believe, and Receive." (And to be honest, we're envious of that popularity — but that's a Dead End Thought for us, of course!)

We'd *like* to believe that simply maintaining a positive attitude, dealing skillfully with negative thoughts, and asking the universe to provide whatever we desire will bring said desires to our door. But we've found, sadly, that in addition to maintaining a positive attitude, visualizing what we want to happen, and dealing skillfully with negative thoughts, we also generally have to do some work, on levels both mental and in real life, to attain what we want.

Visualization is a powerful technique. But it works most effectively *within* our own minds and bodies. In our experience, its effect on the material world or universe is much harder to document. We know with certainty that the act of honing body and mind will help us to accomplish what we desire. But, as we see it, "act" is the operant word, although "belief" may surely *help* us to act...

We applaud and appreciate the role of *The Secret* in helping so many people hear about the importance of thoughts, and their power over us. We agree — and gladly admit — that our thoughts (and neural paths) and our expectations can have a profound effect on our experiences. What we said in the box at the end of Chapter Nine...

- Triggering an unskillful neural path created in your past...

- **Brings it into your present...**

- Which affects both your present, and your future!

...is surely in alignment with many statements in *The Secret*. However, we must respectfully state that we believe that a clear plan or method, and lots of Mental Muscle™ (built up by practice, just like a biceps muscle or the abs), are the ingredients that must be present before the central tenets of a program such as *The Secret* can be put into practice at all, whether effectively or not.

Regardless of whether the "Law of Attraction" will bring that BMW convertible to our driveway or eternal youth to our bods — our perusal of *The Secret* did not seem to provide us with a clear plan for enhancing positive feelings nor a good way to minimize negative ones. Asking the universe for help in doing this can't hurt. But we believe that Understanding the Mind, Clearing the Mind, and Watching the Mind are apt to be more immediately effective, from our own experience. Understanding that *The Three Minute Meditator* provides a set of skills that are complementary to *The Secret* will enhance efforts to increase positive energy while minimizing the negative.

And that's our first of two secrets about The *Secret*. The second? You'll find it near the back of the book, on page 237.

Chapter Nineteen: In a Nutshell...

Visualization seems so simple that it may be tempting for some to skip this chapter. But since it's an incredibly powerful tool for meditators — a word or two to the wise — please don't! Why is it so useful? Let us count the ways:

> • Visualization allows us to rehearse skills on the level of mind.
>
> • This allows us to use meditation to tackle issues, in a relatively safe way, which we might not yet be prepared to deal with in real life.
>
> • Diligent mental rehearsal using visualization will eventually help us to use our meditative skills with these difficult issues, later on, in real life.
>
> If you are interested in or a fan of Ms. Rhonda Bryne's *The Secret*, you may want to read the preceding paragraphs...

Chapter Twenty: Progressive Neural Desensitization and Relaxation

Progressive Neural Desensitization, or PND for short, may sound like a mouthful. But it's really only a variation on the Dead End Thought Strategy, the Splitting Attention Interpersonal Exercises, and the visualization exercises that you've already done. Here's another very short chapter, in which we describe how it works.

Progressive *Neural* Desensitization

Often, when working with fears that affect behavior (and a fear that affects behavior, such as a fear of flying which prevents one from completing important business travel, is called a "phobia"), psychologists teach their clients to use what is called "progressive desensitization." For example, if the client has a fear of snakes, the therapist will help him into a relaxed state, then show him a very mildly negative stimulus — say, a cartoon of an earthworm.

When the client can maintain the relaxed state while looking at the cartoon of an earthworm, the therapist substitutes a picture of an actual earthworm. Progressively more powerful negative stimuli are used as, with practice, the client gets better at maintaining a relaxed state while observing the stimulus object: a cartoon of a cute little snake, a picture of a small snake, a stuffed animal snake toy, a video of a large snake.

The PND Process

In Progressive *Neural* Desensitization (PND), all the work is done in the brain — no pictures, no stuffed snakes. Here's the general process that you'll use to desensitize yourself to painful thoughts, regardless of the specific content of any particular thought.

Once you have desensitized the thought, it will be easier to soften around it, in Step Five.

• Begin with a moment of your favorite breath focus exercise.

• Bring the thought of a mildly painful event or memory, a fear for the future, or an unpleasant type of self-talk that you experience, into your mind.

• Try to balance your attention between the breath focus and the thought.

From This...   **This...**

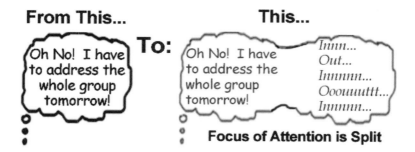

Focus of Attention is Split

• It's like being on a see-saw: you'll focus too much on the thought, and forget the breath, or focus too much on the breath, and forget the thought. Just try to stay balanced between the two mental objects.

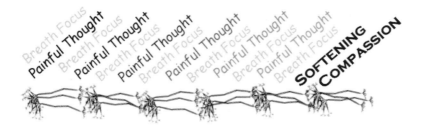

• With practice, you'll find that the thought has less power to affect you, to trigger a fight or fight response.

• Complete the exercise with a moment of conscious softening: shoulders, stomach, jaw, hands (you may wish to practice the Relaxation Exercise that follows, before you do this).

Then, if you can, end with a moment of compassion for the pain that you, and every other human being, is subject to. We will talk more about Compassion in Step Six, but if you are in pain of any sort, please feel free to go there right now...

On Relaxation

Being able to relax the muscles of the body at will is a useful ability, and one that visualization skills can help with — especially if you are someone who carries a lot of tension in the body.

You may find it easiest, in the beginning, to practice this exercise while lying in bed, face up and arms at your sides. Take as long as you need, the first few times you do it, perhaps 10 or 20 minutes. Once you learn what bodily relaxation really feels like, you'll be able to reach a relaxed state in a moment or two, almost anywhere or anytime.

> Relaxation is to the body what meditation is to the mind: a process of turning the attention inward while letting go of the physical tensions that normally inhabit our bodies. We'll learn to use visualization to help us relax, and learn to use relaxation to help us meditate.

The Relaxation Exercise

Make fists with both hands. Really clench your fingers into your palms. Feel the tightness in your wrists, and even up into your forearms. Hold the tension for a few seconds, then relax it. Tense up again, for a similar amount of time, then relax. This time, as you relax your hands, say "warm and heavy, warm and heavy" to yourself, and visualize your hands feeling warm and heavy, just sinking heavily into the softness of the bed. We like to picture our hands being made of mercury, or molten lead, warm and soft and very heavy.

Perform this same process — tensing and relaxing, then tensing and relaxing, and saying "warm and heavy" (with appropriate warm and heavy visualizations) — for each major muscle group of your body. After doing your hands, do your feet, calves, thighs, buttocks, stomach, chest, arms, shoulders, neck, jaw, and eyes. Tense and relax, tense and relax. Warm and heavy, warm and heavy. Try to cultivate as relaxed a feeling as you can, throughout your entire body.

> Try to notice any part of the body that does not seem to "want" to relax. That is probably where you carry a lot of your tension (or even pain). For many of us, it is the jaw or fists that so often clench with anger, or the shoulders that so often hunch up as though to avoid a blow.
>
> If you identify tense body parts, try to focus on them as you continue this exercise. Your goal will be to be able to consciously "drop the tension" from jaw or arms or shoulders at will, as soon as you notice it...

The Relaxation Location

Once you feel really relaxed, imagine yourself in a very peaceful place, a place that you associate with relaxation. Try to develop as clear a mental picture as possible of this place, including the way it feels, sounds, looks, smells, and even tastes. Memorize as many details as you can. You might visualize a lovely tropical beach. Feel the warm sun and the cool breeze, and the sand, as you look up at the waving palm fronds. Hear the waves crash, and smell, almost taste, the salt spray in the air.

The Relaxation Visualization

After you've done this exercise a few times, you'll find yourself able to visualize your relaxation place, and feel relaxed, without needing to do the tensing and relaxing, or at least not needing to do it for so long. With lots of practice, you'll be able to return to your relaxing spot — and a relaxed state — just by thinking of it for a second or two. Whenever you're under stress, you'll be able to take an instant vacation, without even moving!

Chapter Twenty: In a Nutshell...

Like Chapter Nineteen, this short chapter presents another powerful tool for working with thoughts, as well as one for working with physical tension. In the time it would take to read a "review" of this chapter, you could be doing a moment of Progressive Neural Desensitization, or a moment of Relaxation Exercise. So...

Please go for it!

Step Four: All You Need to Know

This step is so short — although important — and the content so simple (though not always easy) that it seems silly to do a full rehash of it. Instead, please skim the boxes, and make sure that you know how to do Visualization, Relaxation, and Progressive Neural Desensitization exercises. And do a few, before going on to *Step Five: Softening Around Pain.*

STEP FIVE:
Softening Around Physical and Mental Pain

In Step One, amongst other things, you saw how neural paths work, and how they trigger the Fight or the Flight Response. You also learned how the Relax and Release Response can be consciously triggered — to short-circuit a Fight or a Flight Response — by focusing attention onto the breath.

In Step Two, you learned how, through a variety of meditation exercises, to build the Mental Muscle™ that allows us (at least sometimes) to stay focused on the breath. You also learned how to use Mental Muscle™ to deal with Dead End Thoughts, and how to split your attention between a painful thought (or person) and the breath.

In Step Three, you learned about various types of neural paths, and how to "map your neural neighborhood" — that is, how to observe your own thoughts and neural paths as though they were objects, as if you were watching a movie.

In Step Four, you leaned Visualization and Progressive Neural Desensitization skills, which will help you — combined with what you learned in previous steps — to tackle the Softening Around Pain exercises and meditations of Part Five.

Chapter Twenty-One: Working with Physical Pain

There are many types of pain. What they all have in common is that softening around them works, if you can do it. Since the basic softening around pain technique is similar, regardless of the type of pain, in Step Five we will alternate descriptive or informational content with the actual exercises, rather than (as in most of the other steps) starting out with the former, and ending with the latter.

We can work with pain on the level of the body (i.e., physical pain) or on the level of the mind (which involves both thoughts that cause mental pain, or thoughts about physical pain). Let's begin with an investigation of physical pain, since we've all experienced it.

About Physical Pain

Physical pain can be as unexpected and acute as a stubbed toe, as predictable as a cold that runs its sniffly course, or as chronic as a bad back. But...

No matter what it's caused by, when we really investigate pain, we find that the *stories* our mind tells us about pain — our self-talk on the subject — is likely to make it worse.

That's because the story, the self-talk, may be what actually triggers the Fight or the Flight Response, *not* the pain itself. Without the self-talk, and *with* sufficient Mental Muscle™ to re-focus attention onto the breath, it may be possible in *some* cases to short-circuit or avoid pain-related Fight or Flight Responses.

The following exercises may help you to work more skillfully with pain, but make sure that you only use them in safe ways. If you may possibly need medical care for a pain — get it! These exercises are only for use with pain that clearly requires no immediate medical attention. We'll begin with intentional ("elective") pain — not because we are sadists, but because it provides an easier way to investigate pain than waiting for the accidental variety to happen.

Acceptance Versus Re-Focusing

In a number of the exercises in Step Two, we've simply asked you to re-focus your attention onto your breath. This works quite well on less difficult or mildly painful issues. But in more serious scenarios, we may not be able to eliminate pain in body or mind by simple re-focusing. In these situations, the acceptance skills — Softening Around Pain (and the Compassion of Step Six — will be more useful. The split attention exercises (as in Progressive Neural Desensitization) from Step Four may also help.

We are sometimes asked the question "When do we try to re-focus, and when do we accept?" As with the question of "What is an appropriate Dead End Thought?" this is a difficult and subtle question. It reminds us of the well-known Serenity Prayer (used by AA members, and often attributed in this wording to theologian Reinhold Niebuhr, although its origin is disputed and may date back two millennia): "God, give us grace to accept with serenity the things that cannot be changed, courage to change the things which should be changed, and the wisdom to distinguish the one from the other."

To this we say, of pain: "…we hope to accept with serenity the pains that cannot be changed, the Mental Muscle™ to re-focus our attention around the pains which can be re-focused around, and the wisdom to distinguish the one from the other. Or if not the wisdom, at least the willingness to experiment and see what happens…"

Pain and Tightening: A Vicious Cycle

In the distant past, when pain was likely to be caused by the bite of a hostile or hungry other, the hard-wired and automatic response of tightening the body in preparation for fight or flight may have been a useful response. In today's world, with a plethora of more subtle and more chronic discomforts, this is often less true. Unfortunately, pain and tightening often form a vicious cycle.

Imagine trying to push away a huge, thorny rosebush. The harder you push, the more its spines impale your hands. Pain often functions in this same "Catch-22" manner, in which the more we resist it, the more we tighten around it, the more it hurts. And the more it hurts, the more we attempt to resist and tighten around it.

Of course it's hard *not* to resist and tighten around pain. Although top-shelf gurus seem impervious to even terminal suffering, it's gonna be a long haul before most of us can refrain from cursing a badly stubbed toe, a missed opportunity, or a tailgating truck driver.

Obviously, some pains require an immediate response — if you lean against a hot stove, the sooner you can move, the better. But for many sources of modern pain, our reaction to the pain only worsens it, as we clench our fists more tightly around its thorny branches.

However, learning to soften around pain, be it physical or mental, is difficult but rewarding. Often discomfort will diminish, or at least become more bearable, when we stop trying to push it away. We may even be able to realize, eventually, how our attempts to avoid pain actually serve to bring it right to us.

Compassion, not Gritting Teeth

Since it's almost impossible not to tighten around severe pain without lots of practice, these exercises work with moderate and self-controlled doses of discomfort. They are not to be performed competitively, with much gritting of teeth, but with gentleness and compassion. If you find yourself trying to "tough 'em out", perhaps you'd better skip to Step Six and work on compassion for a while.

Acceptance Versus Emergency

We often treat the sensation of pain as an emergency — as though "something must be done about this, right away." And as we've pointed out, some pain requires immediate action. But in other cases, it can be instructive to make a conscious decision not to react to pain. Rather, we accept it, and simply experience it, for a moment. These exercises may seem odd, but they will help you to explore this.

The following exercises will be much easier if you have read about, and worked at least a little with, the Progressive Neural Desensitization exercise on page 174 (and don't let the name scare you, it's actually just a version of the split attention work you did back in Step Two). Please make sure that you've practiced the Relaxation Exercise, and especially the "Tense Parts" exercise in the box on page 176.

The Hot Sauce Exercise

Although overuse of hot sauce or chili peppers can be momentarily unpleasant, it is not physically harmful, and an experience of limited duration. So it is a good way to practice softening against pain. However: If you aren't a fan of hot food, be careful. Even one drop of Tabasco™ or other hot condiments may give you more of a reaction than you've bargained for.

So choose your condiment carefully, as a single droplet of "extreme hot" products (whose names, like "Suicide Sauce," or "Insanely Hot," give warning) can be excruciating to non-aficionados.

• Prepare an appropriate amount of your chosen hot sauce in a teaspoon — perhaps half again as much as you'd normally consider eating by itself. If you're used to hot stuff, this will be easy to judge. If not, try a single drop of a mild hot sauce (your local supermarket sells clearly-labeled bottles of this for a dollar or two).

• Spend a moment with your favorite breathing exercise, then take the hot sauce into your mouth (don't just swallow it).

• Notice the sensation of pain, then try to return your attention to the breath.

• If you've administered a proper dosage of hotness, you will want to act — as in an emergency. To rush for a glass of ice water. To be angry at this book ("What a stupid exercise!"), or at yourself ("Why did I try *this*?"). To be filled with angst, and cry ("This is awful. Everything is awful!"). Your shoulders or fists or jaw may tense up.

• Instead of acting, see if you can just notice your thoughts, and try to return your attention to the breath. This may allow you to soften, rather than tighten, around the pain.

• Continue to divide your attention between the breath, the desire to act to reduce the hotness, and the sensations of the hotness themselves, until the sensations subside.

> If you do end up running for the ice water, this exercise can still be a success. Instead of softening around the pain of the hotness, you can simply shift gears and goals, and soften around any pain or self-criticism over not "doing the exercise properly." Then, when your mouth is fully recovered, try it again with a lower dose of hotness!

The Cold Shower Meditation

You can perform a similar meditation while showering. Please ask your doctor about this if you are under a physician's care, and don't burn yourself! Here's how to do it.

• Take a shower. When ready, just make the water a bit colder than you prefer, *while* doing your favorite mind-clearing meditation.

• Notice whatever sensations arise, while staying focused on the breath as much as possible. Does your body think it's an emergency? Does it make you angry, or angst-ridden? Are your "tense parts" tense? Can you consciously relax them, as at the end of Step Four?

As always in pain work, compassion trumps teeth-gritting. This means doing the exercise, and pushing your limits, only to the extent that you can do so without being self-punishing.

Some people like to do this exercise using both slightly hotter-than-normal and slightly colder-than-normal water. Just gradually change the shower setting from a bit too hot to a bit too cold, while meditating and trying not to tighten up, either mentally or physically.

This gently approximates the experience of the Native American sweat-lodge, in which the participants alternate between hovering over steaming rocks in an enclosed shelter, and jumping into an ice cold river. Going back and forth between a bit too hot and a bit too cold can help remind us that we can stay centered within our minds, no matter what is happening on the outside. Too hot now, in the lodge? Soon it'll be too cold, in the river. Then too hot again...

Working with "Uncontrolled" Pain

After you've experimented with these self-controlled pain/tightening meditations, try softening around minor pains that you *cannot* control. It's sometimes possible to use the same techniques that you've been practicing with hot sauce and shower, with headaches and backaches as well, just by consciously softening around the pain they cause. (Of course, if you are really in pain and not absolutely certain that it's "just" a regular headache or backache, call your doctor right away!)

But if you are sure that this is indeed a non-threatening and recurring discomfort, instead of gritting your teeth and tightening your muscles, instead try consciously to relax your stomach, jaw, back, neck. Perhaps you can do a relaxation exercise, as described at the end of Step Four. Maybe even try to do a visualization of sending some love and compassion (perhaps as a sensation of soothing warmth) directly into the place that's hurting.

> If we practice softening rather than tightening around pain, any backache, headache, or cold can become an opportunity to practice, as well as a nuisance. By working mindfully with small pains, we prepare ourselves, if necessary, to work with large ones.

Hit Thumb, Throw Hammer

It's time to talk about *unexpected* pain, as we all suffer from it, on occasion: a stub of the toe, a dropped box on the foot, a banged head on the trunk lid of the car. And we often react with the "Hit Thumb, Throw Hammer Syndrome" — that's the American way of dealing with unexpected pain. Although it's hard to formulate as an exercise, the next time you experience a *mild* but unexpected physical pain, try to soften around it, just as you did in these last exercises. Re-focus attention onto the breath, drop your shoulders, unclench your fists and jaw.

Of course it's harder to do when you're not expecting it — that's the reason for practicing all of our mindfulness techniques in controlled experiments, before trying to use them in real life.   But it's strangely satisfying to soften around the momentary pain of a barked shin or a bumped noggin, even if you can only manage to remember to soften around such a pain once in a while.

You can help yourself prepare for unexpected pain by visualizing yourself stubbing your toe, bumping your head on that low fixture, or some other likely — if unpleasant — scenario. As you've done before with Dead End Thoughts, visualize both the situation, and the pain it causes, as clearly as possible.

Then imagine yourself instantly re-focusing your attention onto the breath, while consciously relaxing shoulder, stomach, jaw, and hand muscles. Do these things (re-focus on the breath, relax the tense parts) as you imagine doing so. Thus reality and visualization come together.

Next time you hit your thumb with the hammer, this may help you react by softening, rather than hardening, around pain. Please note that even if you get mad for a few seconds — even if you curse, and throw the hammer down — belated softening is far better than none.

Chapter Twenty-One: In a Nutshell...

When we learn to take the self-talk out of a pain situation, and practice either re-focusing or splitting attention between pain and the breath, we gain some measure of control over pain.

> Again, in order to do the exercises in this Step with any hope of success, please practice the Progressive Neural Desensitization (just our old attention splitting exercise, with a fancy name) and the Relaxation Exercise of Part Four. And only work with mild pain, so that you can gain skill without undue frustration or discouragement...

If you suffer from ongoing physical pain, or are interested in pursuing this type of meditation in greater depth, Stephen Levine devotes careful attention to working with pain in *Who Dies*. We cannot recommend this book too highly! We have both done meditation workshops with Stephen and Ondrea (his partner in teaching, and wife), and David's first Levine workshop was a turning point in his life. (And teaching Stephen to play the blues harmonica a great privilege!)

Chapter Twenty-Two: Mental Pain

Since the first real life use of mindfulness we suggested at the end of Chapter Four — the Slow Annoying Line Meditation — you have been practicing the work of softening around mental pain (whether you realized it, or not). Now we'll say a few words about specific applications for softening around mental pain in the following sections.

Pain of Unfulfilled Desire

Splitting attention between the breath and an unfulfilled desire is easy to practice on the level of real life. Just take an extra moment or two for a split attention exercise before you head for the fridge or the bathroom, or before you take the credit card from your wallet. To deal with larger or more pressing desires that do not need to be instantly satisfied, use some Progressive Neural Desensitization, and put in a few practice sessions balancing your attention between the breath and the desire before deciding whether to fulfill that particular desire...or not...or not for a while...

Pain of Anger or Angst

These two are also good subjects for Progressive Neural Desensitization. Make sure you start with mildly painful mental objects — low level angst, or annoyance rather than rage. Just follow the general instructions for PND in Step Four, and it will get easier, with practice.

Interpersonal Pain

For many of us, our most acute pains make themselves known in our relationships with others. We gave you some general interpersonal instruction in Step Two, but for now, choose a very specific interpersonal issue that troubles you in your relationship with a particular individual, and use the Progressive Neural Desensitization techniques to work on softening around it.

Begin with a mild interpersonal issue, and work your way up to softening around the more annoying stuff that your colleagues, family members, friends, neighbors, or spouse may present you with. But please: remember the Serenity Prayer on page 181 — these exercises are not intended to help you deny or avoid changing painful interpersonal problems — only to help you soften around the ones which you either cannot change, or choose not to change at the present time.

Pain of the Parents

The fact is that even the most well-meaning and loving parents often manage to forget that even very young children are people, with needs and feelings that matter to that child. So almost all of us have suffered from the pain of loneliness and emptiness that comes from being treated as an object, not as a full-fledged person. It happens first when our needs are not understood ("No, you huge fools! I want a clean *diaper,* not a bottle!").

It happens later when we recognize that our parents have "empty spots" inside themselves that they need us to fill, and begin to believe that we must behave in certain ways to fill those voids and obtain parental love. The fact that our parents did this to us because their parents did it to them may help us to forgive them, but it probably won't help us with the pain that this early "objectification" can cause.

This parental objectification process is probably the genesis of our "shoulds" — the belief that we "should" act or be a certain way, which is the first step to the objectification of ourselves by ourselves. We begin to value ourselves on what we produce, how we look, who we hang out with, rather than on who we are inside. Many therapists believe that this "original pain" is the beginning of much angst or anger in later life. It's a big pain to apply compassion towards and soften around, but recognizing it as an issue (if it is, for you) is a good and necessary start. Once recognized, you can use, as always, split attention to work with it.

Pain of Self-Protection

This conflict between truth and self-protection is an unusually efficient producer of pain in our relationships with others. In his old relationships to family and lovers, David would invariably become angry rather than face even the slightest feelings of rejection (Nina has kindly pointed this fact out to him). Of course, getting mad in the face of real or perceived rejection usually increases the distance between two people (which then results in even more feelings of rejection and thus more anger).

Becoming able to notice thoughts and feelings around rejection, and experience the pain of them, can allow us to either console ourselves with a compassion exercise or share our difficult feelings with the other person. Of course, the ability to do this requires quite a bit of mindfulness, since the painful triggering thought of rejection is apt to produce a Fight or Flight Response if a meditation technique is not skillfully and swiftly applied.

Pain and Self-Image

One of the most important ways that we can "push our limits" in softening around pain is by trying to learn what is *"true"* about ourselves instead of trying to *protect* ourselves from the pain of admitting who we really are. This would probably be considerably easier to do if the truth were always pleasant.

Unfortunately, many truths are painful to acknowledge. Some hurt because they contradict our ideas about what "a good person should be like". Others, whether positive or negative, because they contradict our ideas of what we ourselves are already like.

While growing up, we begin to form a mental picture of who we are, or self-image. This often comes from observing parents, movies, siblings, and friends. For most, this self-image becomes something that has to be maintained at all costs, whether appropriate or not.

In David's life:

"I learned early on that boy children were tough, and never cried. As a young adult, I was then forced (that is, I forced myself) to deny my feelings of fear or sadness, since they just didn't fit in with my self-image. I would either fight when challenged by the local 'hoods,' or more likely experience terrible self-hatred because I had been 'unmanly' and a coward who backed down from a confrontation. I also had to deny my love for and dependence on my first long-term girlfriend, since neither emotion fit my 'tough guy' image.

"As another example, although I'd loved music as a child, when my voice changed during puberty I was ignominiously kicked out of the choir, and told that 'I just couldn't sing.' Rather than face the pain and embarrassment that this caused me, I somehow decided that being 'tone deaf' (like my father thought he was) wasn't so bad. It seemed a tough, masculine, macho, trait.

"I began to cut music class, and make fun of, even look down on, other kids who were members in the school band or orchestra. I absolutely ignored any evidence that I had been, or could be, a musical kind of guy.

"After many years of self-imposed 'tone deaf-ness,' I was able to buy a harmonica to take on a hitch-hiking trip to Alaska. The fact that no one who picked me up knew me made it easier to go against my earlier unmusical self-image (however, a noticeable lack of virtuosity shortened many of my rides!).

"The important part of this story is that for many years I deprived myself of the joys of making music, because I was more interested in maintaining a particular facet of my self-image, than in looking for and learning about what was true."

In Nina's life:

"Being 'a good little girl' felt like the guiding principle of my younger years, and I formed a self-image that felt like a strait-jacket once I realized that my true colors were vivid blues, violets, and reds rather than the 'sweetheart pink' in which I'd always been clothed. Although some who know me now might be surprised, in earlier times I found it frightening to have preferences of my own that might conflict with someone else's. Identifying and allowing myself to let go of a self-image that was based mostly on being-good-all-the-time freed me to be much more real, and more genuine in all aspects of my life."

Pain of Not Being in Control

It's painful to live in a world where any virus or runaway taxi can change, or even end, our lives. We like to feel as though we are in control, while knowing deep inside that we are not. This is one of the most difficult of pains, as it reflects the deep "Existential Pain" that we'll mention at the end of this book. Yet there is a certain satisfaction in being able, once in a while, to admit that we just don't know. Don't know what will come next. Don't know how we'll deal with it. Just don't know…

More Opportunities to Work with Mental Pain

It's not difficult to find creative opportunities to work with mental pain. For example, back when he lived in the Bay Area, exactly at the time that he began to meditate, David would use a neighbor's barking dog for a meditation focus. Before he started meditating, the noise would fill him with anger. Afterwards, although listening to the dog's incessant barking was still annoying, when he could just focus attention onto the sound, the physical sensation, of each bark without thinking, "He shouldn't bark" or, "Why isn't it more quiet" — the noise was not so irritating anymore.

The soundwaves no longer triggered a judgmental story in his mind — "This shouldn't be happening to me!" — and thus didn't produce a Fight or Flight Response. The barking became just another sensory experience, nothing to judge, nothing to react to…

By shifting the focus, the barking dog became David's teacher — along with Stephen Levine and Jack Kornfield — instead of his tormentor.

The "Synecdoche" of Pain

Synecdoche is a poetic device in which one part of something represents the whole, as in "A dozen eyes turned to him." (Actually, six people turned to him. But it sounds more poetic the first way!)

Many of us use a form of synecdoche in a negative way — we let the neighbor's barking dog that wakes us up one morning become the personification, the representative synecdoche of *every* dog that has *ever* frightened or hounded us! A particular rejection brings up the pain of every rejection that you have ever faced, and a single embarrassing episode brings up the pain of every embarrassment you've ever suffered. It's a bit like Over-Generalization ("Embarrassing things *always* happen to me.") Recognizing this common pattern in your life — in advance — will help you to be prepared to soften around the issue and apply lots of compassion, when it arises.

Pain and The Master Skill

In times of mental pain or disappointment, rather than tightening the mind up, and feeling fearful, angry, or somehow blaming yourself, perhaps you can soothe yourself by thinking about The Master Skill in Step Seven. And occasionally you'll still yell, complain, and reach for the aspirin bottle! And you can let that be okay — a healthy dose of awareness and compassion helps us to recognize and accept that we handled the pain as best we could at that moment in our life.

> Of course, the bigger the pain, mental or physical, the more practice and effort it takes to soften around it. That's why it's wise not to wait until you're desperate, to start working on these important skills. As David likes to say, "It's better to learn to swim before the boat starts sinking!"
>
> So please work, as you find opportunities, with appropriately difficult mental pains, using the attention splitting (or the attention re-focusing) techniques that you've read so much about already — and we hope have practiced, as well.

Impermanence: The Greatest Pain

It's a cliche, once again, but true: *Nothing* is permanent except for the fact that everything changes. Everything that you think you know about yourself, your body, your job, your loved ones, your country will alter with the passage of time.

Much of the pain that we experience in our lives comes from the desire to hold on to what must inevitably change. We hurt when our parents grow old and die, and we hurt when our children grow up and move away. We hurt when we lose the strength or beauty of our youth, or the prestige that our work brings us.

Perhaps the deepest level of pain is one which we often deny. This is sometimes called existential pain — the pain of understanding that existence is limited, and that we, and all that we love, must come to an end. Most people try to avoid thinking about this type of pain. Yet this pain is a uniquely human experience, since only humans have enough self-awareness to know that they must die.

If our desire for protection from pain supercedes our desire to face what is true, we are doomed to live lives that attempt to limit or ignore change. And that's sure to hurt. Lots. Of course, facing change will bring pain also. But each meditative step that we take will lessen the amount of pain that we must experience when we face and accept change and impermanence.

Stephen Levine tells a story of a wise man who was given a beautiful and delicate goblet. It was knocked over, and broke, but the wise man only smiled. "Even" he said, "as I held it to the light and admired it, it was already broken in my mind...".

Every sensation we feel, every relationship we have, is made more real and poignant by the advance knowledge of its transitory nature. And how can we fail to develop a sense of compassion and camaraderie towards any being that must exist in this fragile and transient environment that we call life?

The Horn Has Already Honked

The car approaches an intersection, traffic light yellow or red. Instruct your driver not to move the car until just after the car behind you honks its horn (please don't do this under bad driving conditions, in heavy traffic, or on a highway known for road rage).

Relax the muscles of your body, and focus your mind on the inexorability of that honking horn. It's going to honk, a rude, abrupt, noise. There is absolutely nothing that you can do to control the situation, except to accept the inevitable, and possibly by doing so to reduce your own impulse to jump or be startled.

Soften your mind around that impending honk. Witness your own tension, witness your resistance to this exercise. It's a hard one to do, because it goes against everything you've ever been taught. Observe your desire to tighten mind and body against the honk, and watch your desire to make judgments, like "This is a stupid exercise", or "What an impatient jerk the driver behind me is!" And perhaps also look at your own desire to somehow avoid the unavoidable...

The Experiencing Loss Meditation

As you've done with other types of thoughts, bring a thought of something or someone you've lost into your mind, and explore it, as an object in the mind, a movie watched. You may want to begin doing this exercise with an object (a favorite toy or article of clothing that's long gone). Then try it with something that you used to believe in, but have lost faith in (Santa Claus? Socialism? Ronald Reagan's "Morning In America"?). If you feel up to it, experience the thought of having lost a pet, or a friendship.

Do the different losses feel different? How so? Do you feel sad? Lonely? Afraid? If you find yourself getting caught up in the loss thought (and thus losing the ability to observe the original thought), alternate it with a moment of your favorite meditation, to soften around the thought. Or do an attention splitting between the breath and the loss thought, to desensitize yourself a bit.

Don't forget to use this same set of thoughts as the basis for a Meditation Visualization. Beginning with the smaller losses, picture yourself softening around the pain of the loss. When you can do that, go on to the visualization of a more painful loss, and soften around that one. If this exercise seems as though it might be very painful, please read the Step Six, on Compassion, before trying it.

More On Death And Dying

So many changes in life are inevitable. Death, old age, loss. Yet rather than accepting these as a natural part of life, we complain about them, we tighten against them, and we deny their existence.

The death of self or loved ones is perhaps the biggest, yet most inevitable, change. Every person now alive will be dead within ten, fifty, or a hundred years. It's difficult, and excruciatingly painful, to face what we call "The Devil's Contract": that we will all be forced to experience the death of everyone that we love, or else they will be forced to experience ours. There is no alternative, no easy answer.

> Dealing with the knowledge of one's own unavoidable death is the ultimate level of choosing truth over protection of self-image. It is neither a simple nor an easy thing to do. But meditation, and especially compassion, can help.

In David's counseling work with grieving and terminally ill adults and children, he's found all of the meditative techniques described in this book to be valuable, both for him, in his counseling work and life, and for those clients willing to try them. He has written extensively on this subject, and hopes sometime soon to have some of his material online, for those who might be interested in it...

If you must deal with intense grief, we strongly recommend two things: working with a good therapist who has had experience with grief issues, and reading Stephen Levine's *Who Dies*. As the late Dr. Elisabeth Kubler-Ross (another of David's earliest influences) says, "Stephen's work is magic."

Chapter Twenty-Two: In a Nutshell...

As the content of each chapter and step becomes more complex and condensed, we can only ask you to skim the boxes, and read the sections that appeal to you.

> Working with mental pain, in a very real sense, has been the subject of this entire book, as well as the subject of this chapter. We honor your commitment to working with pain in the mind.

Step Five: What You Need to Know

Pain is one of the great challenges of existence, and there are no easy answers. We can only advise you to choose the pains that you would work with, with care, especially in your first attempts.

> And treat yourself as you would treat a young child that you loved, when you are working with pain, mental or physical. That is to say, with deep compassion, a subject that we will approach in the next step...

STEP SIX: Great States — Compassion, Don't Know, and Non-Judging

Step One was mostly about *information:* how the brain and mind work, how experienced meditators think about the world we live in, the types of excuses that many of us use to avoid developing a mindfulness practice (and why those excuses, though convenient, are not really valid).

Steps Two, Three, and Four were largely about *technique:* learning mind-clearing, learning to watch thoughts as though they were movie scenes, learning skills such as Visualization, Progressive Neural Desensitization through split attention, and Relaxation.

> Step Six is about *states of mind* that are useful to cultivate: the mental state of Compassion, the state of "Don't Know," and the state of "Non-Judging." Of the three, Compassion is by far, in our opinion, the most important.

Unlike information, which we can learn by reading words on a page, or techniques, which we can learn and then practice — cultivating important and subtle states of mind can take a lifetime (some would say many lifetimes!). But we'll start simply by reading about them, and doing a few simple exercises.

Chapter Twenty-Three: Compassion

In many ways, compassion lives at the heart of meditation. Because without it, meditation is all too likely to become just another activity that we do "wrong", or "don't do enough" of, or "should be attaining quicker results" from.

It could also easily be argued that the most important meditation we can do — once we've mastered a few of the mind-clearing exercises — is just to spend time with ourselves in a state of compassion and forgiveness. It sounds easy, it even sounds simplistic, but it works. And until we can forgive and feel compassion for ourselves, we can't truly offer it to anyone else.

In this high pressure, performance-oriented society, we often judge ourselves and find ourselves lacking. We're not as beautiful as the movie stars, as rich as the stock speculators, as wise as the scientists that we constantly see in the news.

We monitor, we judge, we boss ourselves mercilessly — as though our mind were an administrator, seeking to constantly improve some personal bottom line. But when compassion becomes our guideline, even for a moment, we learn instead to investigate our own selves as an anthropologist studies a foreign culture. Alert curiosity and Watching the Mind replace disdain or denial, the usual attempts to avoid pain by closing off the heart.

Stepping away from a place of critical judgment, we can seek to find out what is *true*, even if it's not flattering. Then we can bring compassion to these "rough spots". It's easy to love our finer points and nobler qualities, but the unflattering aspects of ourselves — our fears, greeds, angers — are exactly the parts we most need to be compassionate towards before we can work skillfully with them.

Thus, the art of compassion will aid us in those meditations involving both judgment and investigation of the truth. And, as we've said before, an awareness of compassion will prevent us from letting meditation become just another race to lose, just another way to be hard on ourselves.

Four Different Paths

We might say that there are four different paths, and that most people tend to prefer one or two of them over the others. It's a bit on the simplistic side, but not completely inaccurate. Thinking in this way may help us to understand, just a bit more clearly, The Path of Compassion...

Some of us prefer to attribute pain or problems to a hostile world, to blame others for our suffering — we subscribe to a belligerent and vengeful worldview. This, of course, is The Path of Anger — for those whose preferred strategy for dealing with things involves fight over flight.

Others of us blame ourselves for any problem, withdrawing and curling up with an apology — we subscribe to a depressive, guilty worldview — this is The Path of Angst.

Not a few of us go through life in acquisition mode — we are mainly concerned with satisfying appetite, whether it is food, sex, money, or status that is craved — which places us on The Path of Desire.

Most of us embody some combination of these strategies for living in the world — a main course of anger, with a side of appetite. No matter which worldview that we embody, which path we choose, it is reflected in the choice of events and thoughts that trigger our neural paths. It is reflected in the way we self-talk, and reflected in which of the hard-wired paths (fight, flight, need) that are activated. Thus our worldview tends to direct where our neural paths end, with an output of anger, of angst, of desire.

But there is a fourth path — The Path of Compassion. This is the path of the kind and generous neighbor, the path of a Mother Teresa or a Dalai Lama, the path of those who act as their brother's, or sister's, keepers. How is it that some of us face the slings and arrows of life with compassion rather than with anger, acquisitiveness, or angst? How is it that some of us walk, even some of the time, on The Path of Compassion?

What is Compassion?

Compassion might be called a type of love, but it is probably easier to define compassion by what it is not.

Compassion involves self-love, but it is not narcissism (when one is excessively interested in how one appears to others). Narcissistic people often use this interest in appearance to cover a deep, underlying insecurity and lack of love for oneself. The Path of Desire is often their choice, since acquisition of things and attributes (nice abs, a trophy spouse, and a Ferrari) often help them to cover their inner and well-hidden angst.

Compassion is not self-pity, which is often connected to those who tend to follow The Path of Angst. Self-talk of the "Oh, poor me" type often leads to immobilization, since energy is going into feeling sorry for oneself rather than into dealing with the external or internal situations that might be painful or scary. The good news is that those who follow The Path of Angst often find it easier to develop compassion than those who follow The Path of Anger.

A Note on Anger and Compassion

Is your tendency to follow the path of anger more often than the path of angst? Then this chapter's work may be especially difficult for you, since anger and compassion are opposites. If the tendency towards anger exists in you, please read about compassion, and try the exercises. Should they be frustrating, go back to Step Five and work with Softening Around Pain. Come back here eventually, and you will likely find the work on compassion to be more accessible. Please understand that the later steps of this program are more subtle, more difficult, and will take longer to master than the earlier ones, so don't be hard on yourself, just because the work seems hard.

Compassion and Pity

It's important to differentiate compassion from pity, which we try to do by this criteria: in pity, there is an element of fear for oneself. We see the accident victim, and our feelings of empathy are tinged with fear for ourselves ("Gee, that could have happened to me — I'm glad it didn't, and sure hope that it doesn't"). In compassion, there is a wry acceptance of the human condition that we all share, and no attempt to distance the negative events by making them "something that happens to someone else".

Compassion involves love — self-love — for yourself, without self-pity or narcissism, without the need to be perfect. It involves love for others, without eroticism, pity, the hope that they will "make you look good," nor any other expectation of return.

The Path of Compassion is often easier to develop for those who follow The Path of Angst as their primary way of relating to the world, than to those who follow The Path of Desire (often covering inner insecurity) or The Path of Anger. So if these latter two are your main paths, then you will need to work especially carefully with this section, and not allow its difficulty to cause you to be uncompassionate with yourself...

The above are rather fine points, and perhaps will help you to sort out pity/compassion feelings that you experience. The compassion meditations that we find most useful and satisfying will follow. We'll start with easy ones, and lead up to the "real" Compassion Exercise.

The Heartgill Meditation

David came up with this meditation, or at least its central image, one night while he was meditating next to his tropical fish tank:

"I focused my attention on my pet angelfish, "Miss Piggy," and observed her bulging eyes and softly billowing gills. I imagined that my heart was somehow like a "compassion gill", and with each breath in and out, a wave of compassion washed through me, cleaning out pain and self-hating thoughts, and replacing them with compassion."

Although from an analytical perspective it may seem silly, this meditation feels quite satisfying, somehow.

• Just "re-locate" — via visualization — the in and out of your breath from your mouth or nostrils to your heart.

• Visualize a gill slit, like a fish's, right above the heart in your chest, and let the compassion wash through you, like the water washes through the fish with its life-giving oxygen.

As with every other meditation that we've done, when other thoughts arise, simply notice them, and gently return to the image of the heartgill. And please realize that it's easy to create meditations of your own. They don't have to be traditional in any way, or even make sense. They just have to feel right to you...

The Ahhh/Oooh Meditation

This one integrates both awe and pain, by seeing each as necessary to the other. In a world of beauty and splendor, how can there not be awe? But in a world where everyone who is born must die, how can there not be pain? And in a world filled with both pain and awe, how can there not be compassion for those who must live there?

• As you breathe in, say a mental "Ahhh", the "Ahhh" of going outside on a beautiful spring morning, the "Ahhh" of watching the sun set over the ocean.

• As you breathe out, sigh sadly, with a mental "Oooh", the "Oooh" of seeing a war on television, the "Oooh" of seeing homeless people rummage for food in garbage dumpsters.

"Ahhh, Oooh, Ahhh, Oooh". It's painful — living in this strange, lovely, terrible, unfathomable world. It's awesome — living in this strange, lovely, terrible, unfathomable world. The two just can't be separated. How can you not feel compassion for any creature who must exist here, including yourself?

The Forgiveness Meditation

Developing our ability to forgive others can help clear the way for compassion. This exercise, as are so many, is very simple, although not always easy.

• Just picture someone whom you think has hurt or wronged you in some way. It's important, for now, to choose someone at whom you're no longer very angry.

• Visualize them as clearly as you can. And tell them "I forgive you. I forgive you for hurting or wronging me."

• Repeat it a number of times, and try to feel forgiving, try to feel yourself giving up remnants of anger or righteousness towards them.

If you are not sure with whom you're ready to do this exercise, do it with someone whose hurt to you was very minor — a driver who slipped ahead of you on the freeway, or a clerk who overcharged you by a few cents. Eventually, with practice, you'll be able to do this exercise with people who have caused you more serious pain.

> It is crucial to remember that forgiving a person does *not* mean that you condone or accept their behavior. You are forgiving the person, not their behavior.

Letting go of anger, and of feelings of having been wronged, is a very freeing experience. For David, doing this exercise on the publisher who had "appropriated" his harmonica book and title concept (see "Why We Needed To Meditate") allowed him to stop wasting energy on anger and self-hatred, and to get on with his life.

The next exercise is somewhat tied in to this one, and may make developing a sense of forgiveness easier to come by. You can also combine the two, to create a deeper sense of understanding and compassion for the chosen subject of the meditation.

The I-Thou Meditation

Jewish theologian Martin Buber coined the term "I-Thou", to indicate a relationship in which you (the "I") relate to another person with the understanding that the other has as many feelings and needs, fears and desires, as you do, and as much right to pursue them. Buber contrasts this with the "I-It" relationship, in which you act as though the other person is mostly an object, whose principle purpose in life is to help you gain satisfaction.

It's easy to be smug, and to say "I don't do *that*". But how often, especially when you're in a hurry, does a store clerk or a gas-station attendant seem to be a real, complete person with their own history and feelings? When someone cuts ahead of you on line, do you usually perceive them as a person who has problems, fears and needs of their own, just as you do, or are they just some "impolite jerk", getting in between you and the candy counter?

Can you see that the beautiful woman, or "hunky" man walking across the street has a full and complete life of their own, and does not just exist as an object for your visual (or perhaps fantasized sexual) gratification?

Begin by choosing someone, a bus driver, or salesperson, to whom you usually *don't* relate, and try to perceive them as a "thou" instead of an "it". With a bit of practice, you'll be able to do this with a surly waiter, an aggressive panhandler, or a politician not from the party of your choice!

Doing the Shared Breath Meditation from Chapter Fourteen is a great way to enhance this exercise with a friend, a lover, a pet, or anyone else that you are physically near. And the practice of treating the other as a "thou" instead of an "it" so may just help you do the same for yourself, with the next exercises.

How Compassion Feels

A feeling of compassion — the Compassion Response — which we believe is a hard-wired neural path — is often described as a warm, melting, softening, sensation, perhaps accompanied by an "ooooh..." or "awwww..." vocalization. It is triggered in most of us by the sight or thought of a small, appealing, helpless creature. A head and eyes that are large relative to the creature's size — as in a baby — will help to elicit the compassion response.

This sense of selfless love for the "compassion object" — often a human infant of the viewer's family or clan — was clearly an adaptive mechanism to help bring the infant safely through the dangers and needs of childhood. The following exercise will help you to identify this important response, which we need to apply, not just towards babies and large-eyed velvet paintings, but to ourselves.

> The Compassion Response is a part of a neural path that is on the same level, but the opposite of, the Fight or Flight Response. Please read more about it, above. It's important!

The Compassion Response Exercise

This exercise is designed to help you identify the general compassion response, rather than a compassion response directed towards yourself or any particular other.

• Spend a moment with your favorite breathing exercise.

• When you feel relaxed, bring an image that you think may elicit a sense of compassion into your mind. For many people, a beloved childhood pet (especially a kitten or puppy) is a good compassion object.

(It may seem silly, but some people find that the image of the sickly, helpless extraterrestrial "ET" in the movie of the same name is a good compassion object. The design of the alien was clearly chosen to elicit the viewer's compassion, with its large head and oversize eyes, and weak, spindly appendages.)

• Look inside to perceive physical sensations of the compassion response, such as warmth in the center of the body, a "melting" feeling, a silent "awwww" vocalization.

(If your mental image brings up many thoughts or paths other than compassion, you may need to try another image. Or you can simply notice "Ahhh, that's just my mind telling stories again…" and return your attention to the compassion object.)

If the first thought that you attempted to use to trigger the compassion response did not seem to work, just try another one. Perhaps a character from fiction (Tiny Tim, of Dickens' "Christmas Carol," is a classic compassion object) or a scene from a movie might do it. The image of the *Pieta* (a grieving Mary holding the body of her dead son) is often a good compassion object for people of the Christian faith.

> For some of us, especially the "Birds," a visual image — a photo or picture — may make it easier to stimulate the compassion response. Sadly, it's not too hard to find a tragic image of a young child, in these days of war and natural disaster, which just proves how crucial it is to develop compassion.

The Self-Compassion Exercise

This exercise will become easier with practice. If the later portions of the exercise seem more difficult than the earlier ones, just spend some time doing the earlier ones. Or go back and do the Heartgill or the Oooh-Ahhh exercises for a while.

• Picture yourself as a small child at the youngest age that you can remember. Visualize your child-self as clearly as possible, then send feelings of love and compassion to that small child-self.

• Wrap your arms around yourself, or at least place one hand over the other in a loving, compassionate way. In your mind's eye, see yourself hugging your child-self.

(If feelings or thoughts other than love and compassion enter, gently return your mind to thoughts of compassion for your child-self.)

For many of us, compassionate feelings for ourselves at any age do not come easily. Do this exercise with as much loving kindness as you can muster, and try not to be judgmental if it seems difficult. Can you wryly recognize the irony of judging yourself harshly for not being able to do a compassion exercise "perfectly enough"? Just do the best that you can, and recognize that it will become easier with time...

Often, judgmental thoughts such as, "I don't deserve this", or "The kid's gotta be tough" creep in during this exercise. We've gotten lots of practice at noticing them quickly, and learned to use them as a "springboard" to lend renewed vigor to feelings of compassion. Instead of increasing pain, these self-hating thoughts can be used as stepping stones towards increased self-love by saying, "I've been so hard on myself, for so long, that I can scarcely do this exercise at all. It's obvious that I need as much love and compassion as I can allow myself."

• Next, picture yourself as an older child, and do the same thing. Don't forget to hug yourself, at least in your mind.

• Move up to puberty (an age where we all especially need compassion, and hugs) and do it.

• Then continue doing the exercise with your younger selves, in steps of five or ten years until you reach your present age.

• Now do the same thing you've been doing for younger selves — bathe yourself in love and compassion, while hugging yourself. Only this time, do it right now, with your own arms wrapped lovingly around yourself.

If you feel resistant to doing this exercise, examine your resistance. How does it feel? Could you do the "I-Thou" for others, but not be able to do this one for yourself? How does that fact touch you? Perhaps you need to first do the Forgiveness meditation for *yourself*, or for a parent who has taught you to be self-critical rather than compassionate. If you can't seem to do this Compassion Exercise at all, please spend some more time with the mind-clearing and Softening Around Pain exercises, then return to this section when it feels appropriate. If you are working with a counselor or therapist, this could be a very fruitful topic for discussion.

Compassion in Action

As part of your practice of developing compassion, you might visit a nursing home, or a shut-in neighbor. While visiting with them, just follow your breath, or theirs, since the Shared Breath exercise (page 119) is a very powerful compassion evoker. Recognizing the loneliness of another's life can be a great opportunity for compassion, aimed at both oneself and others.

Compassion and Thought Chains

If you've spent any time with the mind-watching exercises of Step Three, you may find it easier to identify places where compassion is lacking, and thus needed. For David, frustration often leads to the path of anger, so when frustration arises (if he is in good meditative shape), he may be prepared and thus able to apply a measure of compassion:

"When business dealings, relationships, or other events don't go the way I want them to, I first feel frustrated, then threatened by my own lack of control. Almost instantaneously the feelings of frustration and fear turn into anger, as my mind attempts to cover up these insecure and painful feelings with more aggressive ones. Acting upon these aggressive feelings, I may then lash out at myself, or at loved ones, without even knowing why.

"But when I can recognize the initial frustration and fearful feelings as they arise, I can meet them with compassion. A moment of Compassion meditation will often interrupt the neural path of frustration-to-fear-to-anger, and allow me to face the frustration and fear directly. It's not easy to face up to my own inability to control people, events and things. But I'd rather directly face these feelings and the pain that they bring, than encounter the far greater pain of the mis-directed anger, with its hostile attack on myself or others.

"Even if I do get angry, I may be able, after a moment, to remember to be compassionate towards myself, both for my pain, and for having gotten mad. All humans feel anger and must somehow learn to deal with this emotion. Feeling compassion for my anger is far more healing in the long run than feeling guilt for my anger, or feeling angry at myself for my anger. Feeling compassion for myself allows me to "watch the movie" in my mind and step outside my old knee-jerk reaction of pain, anger, and self-hate."

Pre-Compassion Exercise

If you just can't seem to locate any shred of compassion in your makeup, try this simple exercise.

• Prepare to do something small but kind for yourself: a warm bath, a favorite food (but not so indulgent that you'll criticize yourself for eating it), an extra hour with a favorite book or movie.

• Begin with a few minutes of breathing exercise, then give yourself the little gift as you'd give it to a treasured friend. Midway during the bath, or treat, or movie, turn your attention onto your breath again.

If this exercise makes you feel sad, it may be that you are realizing the lack of compassion you hold for yourself. If that's the case, please turn back to the first part of the self-compassion exercise (page 207). You are still the child who *needs* and *deserves* love and compassion — as much as any appealing puppy or cuddly kitten — and you have the ability to give it to yourself, right now.

> In many ways, self-compassion is not that different from acting as a friend to yourself. Practice asking yourself — with sincerity and without self-criticism — "How would I treat a dear friend in this situation?", and you may find that the compassion response develops spontaneously.

Chapter Twenty-Three: In a Nutshell...

This chapter has so much in it, and so many exercises, that we are forced to throw up our hands when we think of trying to "nutshell" it! Please read the boxes, and do the exercises. Other than that, we'd just like to say a few words about the seeming contradiction between change and acceptance.

When we want to change ourselves in a positive direction — and no one would either read or write a book like this if they did not — we need compassion to accept ourselves as we are, no matter how much we want or need to change. As with so many things, it's a balancing act. Perhaps a good analogy is that we love a kitten or puppy in spite of its babyish behavior — peeing on the rug, chewing our slippers, digging in the orchid pot. We know that it is a baby animal. We know that with proper training it will grow and change. We want those changes to occur, yet we love the little creature (exasperated though we may sometimes be) during the training process, exactly as it is in the present moment.

Similarly, we must have compassion for where we are and who we are now, understanding that we find ourselves in this place because of many elements in our past. Many of these elements — ranging from the evolutionary biology that provides our hard-wired neural paths, to the parenting we received, to the life experiences that we have had, to the culture that we live in — all of these have been far beyond our individual control.

> The only rational reaction to our current plight — as human beings in a changing, challenging, world — is to accept ourselves with compassion as we are now, while striving diligently to change for the better.

Chapter Twenty-Four: Don't Know

Although it's clear that no one likes a "know-it-all", many of us are often hesitant to admit (a word that expresses our reluctance and resistance) that we "don't know". We usually think that if we don't know the answer, or don't know what's going on, then we'd darned well better be trying to find out!

Yet there can be an openness and a satisfaction to the "don't know" state. There's room for anything in the openness of "don't know"— it leaves us space for every possibility. "Don't know" is at the heart of Zen Buddhism's "beginner's mind", the Jain's "doctrine of maybe" and the Christian injunction to "be as a small child".

Adding compassion to "don't know" gives us a wry acknowledgement of the uncertainty of living in this imperfect and frustrating world. So much of what goes on in our lives is impossible to predict or control. Learning to cultivate a sense of "Don't Know," learning to let this uncertainty be okay, helps us recognize and accept the painful truth — that we are often unable to control what happens in our lives, to ourselves, to our loved ones. Once we accept this fact, we no longer have to waste energy denying it.

At the heart of traditional Japanese Zen Style meditation is the "Koan". A koan is a question with no rational answer. Some favorite traditional koans are:

"What is the sound of one hand clapping?"

"What did your face look like before your mother's birth?"

"Can a dog achieve enlightenment?"

Observe your mind as you focus your attention on one of these questions. Does it strive for an answer? Does it want to reject the exercise by calling it ridiculous?

Try to cultivate a sense of "don't know". It may not feel comfortable, at first. But just let it be okay *not* to know. Look for the empty, spacious feeling of the "don't know" mind. The "don't know" mind has room for absolutely everything!

The standard story used to illustrate the Don't Know tells of the scientist who visited the Buddhist teacher, in order to learn about Buddhism from a "scientific" point of view. Before beginning, the Buddhist suggested having tea. He filled the scientist's teacup to the brim, paused for a second, then poured more tea into the cup. The scientist leaped up as the hot tea cascaded into his lap. "A teacup that is too full", the Buddhist said, "can receive nothing additional. Neither can a mind."

Jesus' statement "Before Abraham was, I Am" (John 8:58) makes a wonderful Christian koan. And since the word that Jesus used for "I am" was also the sacred name for God, it fits in well with some concepts that we'll later present in the "I Am" section of the book.

The "Don't Know" Meditation

After a bit of practice with the above koans:

• Choose a situation from your own life, whose outcome just cannot be predicted. It can be something as innocuous as "Will we win tonight's softball game?" or as serious as "Will I marry?" or "How long will I live?"

• Focus your attention on the question, while trying to maintain a sense of "don't know" in your mind. Notice attempts to make rational predictions, "Our second baseman has the flu, but their best pitcher's arm is sore...", but then gently return to the "don't know".

• Watch your mind as it vacillates between answer-seeking and "don't know".

Try to incorporate more "don't know" into your daily life. Will you catch that bus? Don't know. And that's okay. Will you get that raise? Don't know. And that's okay.

You can continue to strive wholeheartedly to catch the bus or get the raise, even *while* allowing it to be okay that you don't know whether it will happen or not.

> No nutshell for this short chapter. Just one last "Don't Know" question, or perhaps we should say koan: Will you make meditation an ongoing part of your life? Don't know. And that's okay, too...

Chapter Twenty-Five: Non-Judging

Minds just love to judge. Unfortunately, judging is a double-ended sword. And a double-ended sword has no safe place to grip. As you grab it, to swing at a real or imagined enemy, its razor-like handle cuts deeply into the flesh of your own hands.

"Judge not, lest ye be judged" is a statement that applies well to the mind. If we allow our minds to judge other people and events, our minds surely as boomerangs will turn around and judge us too. Quite literally, the sword that cuts both ways.

Learning not to judge so quickly has two great benefits. As we begin to relax the mind's judgment mode, we will judge ourselves less often, and less harshly. So the judging and the compassion exercises complement each other nicely.

> Also. as we try to suspend our judgments of both thoughts and events, we find, as Carlos Castaneda's Don Juan put it, that everything becomes not *either* a blessing if we like it, or a curse if we don't, but a *challenge*.

Our challenge is to try to use every thought, and every event of our life to take us in the direction of increasing awareness and increasing compassion, as we'll describe near the end of this book.

The Thought Judging Meditation

This simple little exercise is rather like the Thought Labeling Exercise, only easier. Instead of watching each thought, and labeling each as to its category:

• Just watch your passing thoughts for a moment.

• Label each thought either as *positive* (you like the content of this thought), *negative* (you don't like the content of this thought), or *neutral* (no particular feelings toward this thought).

• If you find yourself getting *involved* with the specific content of the thought, as in "That's a nice convertible...I really like ragtops...Sure wish I had a Miata...Let's see, what if I traded in the Hyundai..."...

• Just gently note how you feel about getting caught up in content once again, and return to just noting: positive, negative, and neutral.

Noticing the constantly changing likes and dislikes of the mind without getting caught up in the emotions of liking or disliking will also help you to deal with actual events in the outside world as well. Instead of asking yourself "Do I like or dislike this event?", you'll begin to ask "How can I best meet this challenge in a way that will help me to go in whatever life direction that I choose?"

Since we hope that you are beginning to see the satisfaction of a more meditative, calmer, less judgmental way of life, you'll find, more and more often, that you prefer calm acceptance (which does *not* mean resignation) to frenzied struggle, and compassionate understanding to anger. And whenever you "backslide" — and yell or scream, or feel depressed — you'll be able to notice what you're doing, and gently, compassionately, return your mind to the way of the meditator.

The Acceptance Exercise

As you work with cultivating the state of Non-Judging, you'll find that self-acceptance becomes easier. You may wish to read the end of Chapter Twenty-Three (the "In a Nutshell...") again before working with this exercise. This exercise also ties in nicely with the Dead End Thought Strategy that we hope you've been using. Instead of having to treat a thought as a Dead End, you may be able to change your relationship to it, by accepting it.

• Choose something about yourself that you don't particularly like.

(It may be easier to begin with a physical rather than mental quality. Start with a quality that's only mildly annoying — perhaps needing to use reading glasses rather than those extra pounds around your middle.)

• Allow yourself, just for the one to three minutes of this exercise, to accept without judgment that which you don't like. Watch your mind. Is it resistant?

• Most likely it is. Turn your attention to the breath, or do a moment of attention splitting (PND) between the thought of what you don't like, and the breath.

212

- After doing this with a bodily focus, try accepting some unlikable element of your mind. A tendency towards self-righteousness? A reluctance to state your opinions?

- Now try to momentarily bring a feeling of acceptance to some external condition that you dislike.

You might choose a social or political issue, or something about your job or life. Not the worst thing that you can think of, just an annoyance.

- Let it be okay for it to be exactly the way it is, just for right now...

Chapter Twenty-Five: In a Nutshell

Accepting things in yourself, others, or the world without judging them doesn't mean that you won't try to change them in the near or distant future. It merely means that you are allowing them to exist right now, without self-hatred or judgment. Since they *do* exist, you are better off recognizing that and accepting them for right now.

> Every act can be accomplished more effectively when our minds are unobscured by the clouds of judgment. Living with increased acceptance and decreased judgmentalness, we no longer need anger or self-hatred to motivate internal or external changes. We can simply do whatever seems to be most appropriate...

Step Six: What You Need to Know

Cultivating these mental states — Compassion, Don't Know, and Non-Judging — is a difficult and subtle task. It will require:

- The Mental Muscle™ that you've been building up since Step Two.

- The understanding of the obstacles in your own mind that you've been identifying since Step Three.

- The Visualization, Progressive Neural Desensitization, and Relaxation techniques that you've been practicing since Step Four.

- And the Softening Around Pain work you learned in Step Five.

> It's *not* an easy task. It *can* change your life. Be kind to yourself, as you work at it...

STEP SEVEN:
Living in the Now
(and The Master Skill)

There is an effortless and supremely satisfying way to live that those who make mindfulness the top priority in their lives can know. Step Seven describes the two main components of it — Living in the Now, and The Master Skill — and offers exercises that will help you to work with these deeply mindful ways of being-in-the-world.

We, Nina and David, won't pretend that we live in this sublime state — far from it — although we are occasionally blessed with a fleeting visit to bask in its light for a moment. And even these glimpses encourage us, allow us to infer that we are on the right track, if only taking the first few halting steps along it.

And we've only been able to get even that far by practicing what we are here preaching.

To repeat what we said in the very beginning of this book:

"We believe in meditation, even though our first efforts at it were unsuccessful. We believe that it's been good for us, and believe that it will help you too. And that's why we wrote this book."

In this step, we will combine all that we have learned from the ones that came before, to take our mindfulness practice to the next level...

Chapter Twenty-Six:
Past, Future, and NOW

Most of us live most of the time in either the past or the future. Our minds are filled with memories of pain, or triumph, or aggrieved anger, or details of what we've done. Filled with plans for the future, or fears, or desires to be attained. Only rarely is our attention focused on what is happening in the "Right Now."

These thoughts about what we just did, or didn't do, and thoughts about what we should do, or shouldn't do, or might do, continually clutter our minds. Often we use past thoughts in a self-hating way, "I should have done it differently", or "I sure messed that one up". Often we use future thoughts to upset ourselves, such as "What if that happens?" or "It probably won't work out".

Virtually all of our thoughts are either based in the past or the future, and absolutely all of our fears and desires are. Desires are usually remembrances of past pleasures that we plan and hope to re-create in the future. Fears are usually memories of past pain that we plan and hope to avoid in the future.

There is something very satisfying about keeping your mind in the "Now", but it's hard to describe it precisely. All we can say is that the bite of food that you are savoring right *now,* is somehow quite different from the mouthful that you just ate (which you can only remember) or the mouthful that you plan to eat next (which you can only anticipate).

Of course, thinking about either the past or future mouthful does bring it into the "Now" as a *thought* in your mind. But the actual food in your *mouth* is clearly more satisfying than the thought of past or future food which may be in your *mind*. Better to be present with a potato than lost in thoughts of past or future banquets!

> Most people who meditate find that they don't have to do nearly as much "future planning" or "past remembering" as they once thought they did. They learn to trust that they will naturally do what's right, without compulsive planning or second-guessing.

The Nature of the Now

The nature of the Now is somewhat flexible. For Nina, there is more than one definition of the word:

"In my work for Mohonk Mountain House, I'm constantly evaluating what worked in the past and planning outreach efforts that will continue to evolve far into the future. My workplace "Now" involves looking both behind and ahead. But I also have my personal Now, in which I wish to savor the events of the present — smells, tastes, feelings, interactions — without being over-influenced by past or future-related fears and desires. It's a delicate balance, and one that I don't yet clearly understand. But I do know that practicing the "Living In The Now" exercises helps me with this balance..."

Living In The Now

A certain number of memory-thoughts and some planning-thoughts are useful, or at least necessary, for functioning in this culture. But it's important to remember that when we focus our attention on a thought of the past or a thought of the future, we are bringing past or future into our present, thus pushing the actual present, the "Now", out of mind.

When we're thinking of how much work we have to do while our boss is talking to us, or thinking of what we'll say next during a conversation with a friend, we can't be present to listen and to respond meaningfully right now. Similarly, when we're busy filling our fork for the next bite while chewing the present mouthful, or pondering dessert during the main course, we're simply not present to enjoy our eating right now. Even worse, painful thoughts intrude upon pleasant moments, as they did during Nina's walk in the woods.

David began to understand this as he learned to improvise on the blues harmonica: "Worrying about the note I had just played, berating myself for a poorly played riff, or planning ahead for the sequence that I wanted to play next — these all impaired my ability to create improvisations freely. I had to learn to trust myself and let go of a note as soon as I had played it, without thinking about the note to come. Only then did my improvisation begin to improve."

The Living in the Now Exercises

In a way, all of the meditation exercises are "Living In The Now" exercises. When we are Thought Counting or Slow Walking, there just isn't much time to think of the past or the future. In fact, we are not supposed to do so. We learn to let go of such thoughts, as soon as we notice them.

The following exercises, like the ones that came before, are also Living in the Now exercises. However, they are slightly more subtle, and will help us to work at attaining — even though, as we said, it may be only for a few seconds or minutes at a time — the state of Living in the Now.

Walking And Breathing in the NOW

These next two mind clearers involve the focus of attention directly on physical sensations, no counting or labeling — "Barnacles" may find these particularly appealing. They are the mainstays of the "Vipassana" meditative tradition. If they seem hard to concentrate on, alternate them with exercises that you find easier, like the meditations above.

The Walking Now Meditation

Walk slowly, and focus your attention carefully on your feet. What does walking really *feel* like? Which muscles in your calves, ankles, or toes do you use? What is the consistency of the ground — is it hard, or rough, or spongy? Go barefoot, and feel each pebble, twig, or crack in the floor.

You may find it easier to begin this meditation by doing the Walking Breath or the Slow Walk (labeling) meditations from Step Two. After a minute of one of these more structured meditations, stop counting breaths or labeling, and focus only on the sensations of your feet as they interact with the ground. As usual, when thoughts intrude, gently return your attention to your feet.

The Breathing Now Meditation

Breathe normally, and focus your attention on the sensation of breathing. In what part of your body do you feel each inhale most clearly? Some people feel the breath best at the nostrils, right where it flows in and out. Others find it easier to concentrate on the rise and fall of the stomach or chest. Mouth breathers might be very aware of the breath at the back of the throat. Choose one of these areas, and concentrate on it.

Do not try to control your breathing at all, to make it slow, or even, or otherwise meditative. Just let every breath be exactly as it is.

During the meditation, observe *each and every breath* as though it were a strange and unique creature passing in front of you. Is this breath long, or short? Smooth and continuous, or jerky? Feel cool, or hot? Does it go directly from inhale to exhale, or is there a point at which the breath is held immobile? Was there a cough, burp, or hiccup experienced as part of this breath? A sighing or wheezing quality to it? As always, if your attention wanders off, return it diligently but gently to the breath.

Looking And Listening Now Meditations

Two more types of In the Now mind clearing exercises are "for the Birds" (and the "Bats"). Birds, your job is to watch clouds, or the flames of a fire, or the foaming waves at the ocean's shore. Don't try to make sense of what you see. Don't try to look for patterns. Don't judge what you're seeing. Do nothing but see. Just seeing. As soon as you notice a thought creeping into your mind, go back to just seeing.

It's easiest to begin Looking Meditations with natural objects such as those mentioned above, as they are slightly less likely to inspire thoughts in your mind than visual objects like faces or bodies are. But with practice, you will be able to look at anything and "just see". Cars or people passing by, a blank wall, or your own hands can provide visual objects for the focus of your attention.

And the Bats among us can practice *listening* in the same way. No thoughts, no judging, no attempts to make sense. No letting your mind run off stories about what you hear. Just listening. If thoughts intrude, notice that you're thinking, then focus your attention back on the sounds.

Instrumental music is usually the easiest type of meditative listening to begin with, as any music that contains words tends to inspire thought when you hear the lyrics. Then try natural sounds, like bird song, or the rushing water of a stream. With practice, even the rumble of a truck passing by on a street at night can be "grist" for your meditative mill.

The Centering Balance Meditation

Here's a good one that you can do anytime you are "just standin' around." It's not only a good Now meditation, it's also a good metaphor for "staying balanced," as so many of our exercises require us to do — balanced between breath and thought, between our daily angers, fears, and desires, and our need for mindfulness...

• Stand up straight, arms at your sides, with your feet a little bit closer together than you'd usually keep them (but not so close that you feel in danger of falling over).

• Focus your attention on your sense of balance, your sensation of standing upright with your body weight centered over your feet.

• Lean forward an inch or two, and feel the tension as your toes dig deeper into the ground to compensate for the forward incline, as you become a human Tower of Pisa. Lean backwards an inch, until most of your weight is on your heels. Lean slightly left and then right, noting the weight shift from foot to foot.

• Do the forwards, backwards, left, and right leaning motions again, but more subtly, with less movement. See just how little you need to lean in order to feel not quite perfectly upright, not quite perfectly balanced. See how easy it is to over-compensate, in one direction or another. Is there any one position in which you do feel in *complete* equilibrium, when you really focus your attention on it? There may not be one.

You can do this exercise anywhere, without attracting much attention to yourself, if you use the more subtle motions of the second part. Since "feeling balanced" is often used as a metaphor for mental stability, this exercise is a useful one to do anytime you feel off-balance. The few moments' respite that you'll get from the tensions of past and future thoughts will help you to restore both your mental and physical equilibrium!

Driving in the Now

Driving is one of the most hazardous things we do on a daily basis. Yet often, as we drive, our mind is lost in the past or the future, far from a clear focus on the manipulation of tons of iron at high rates of speed. We talk, listen to the radio, eat, drink, make phone calls, or smoke, keeping "half an eye" on the road and other traffic.

In conscious driving, we focus our attention exclusively on the elements important to automotive safety, as intently as though we were Monte Carlo racing drivers, participating in the race of our lives (and our lives, and those of our passengers, *are* at stake, every time we enter an automobile). Like race car drivers (but instead of concentrating maximizing our speed), we pay attention to many factors: the road in front of us, the positions of other cars near us, our speed, driving conditions, and road conditions.

Should any thoughts *not* germane only to safe driving enter, we notice them and gently return our attention to our driving. If this exercise seems, for any reason, to be unsafe, please don't do it. However, we feel that if more people did focus their attention *exclusively* on their driving, the highways would be much safer places.

Your Own Living In The Now Meditations

We can make *any* activity a Living in the Now meditation just by steadily focusing our attention on it. This does not involve doing anything that you don't normally do. Only your attitude will change, as you consciously try to focus your attention on whatever is happening, whether that's brushing your teeth, or washing dishes.

Instead of planning for the day, or wishing that the gravy on the bottom of the pot wasn't burnt on quite so solidly, you will make the brushing, or the washing, into a meditation — just by focusing exclusively on it. No future planning, no past memories: just scrubbing, just rinsing. As we've learned, this conscious focusing of attention is mindfulness. It is the most powerful tool that we possess, a mental spotlight that can illuminate any action or thought!

Try doing this with any repetitive daily task, such as shaving, brushing your teeth (we find that switching hands really forces us to focus on our hand movements, and makes the Toothbrush Meditation quite a challenge).

Just make sure that you are thinking only of the task at hand, and gently return your awareness to it as soon as you notice other thoughts entering the mind.

Nina likes to try to make hand washing into a meditation throughout the day. Instead of using those 30 or 40 seconds to plan, or worry, or daydream, she focuses exclusively on the sensations of warmth, wetness, slipperiness, rinsing, drying. She feels better centered and more relaxed afterwards. Is cleanliness is next to Godliness, after all?

The Zen Buddhist tradition of Japan often utilized this approach. Flower arranging, the Tea Ceremony, Zen Archery, and most of the Japanese martial arts are used as forms of meditation. Their practitioners focus exclusively on the flowers, or tea, or bow, excluding all other thoughts. Sound familiar?

Whenever you keep your attention so strongly focused on something that no other thoughts intrude, that's a form of Living in the Now meditation. Hang-gliding is a meditation for some, harmonica playing for others. These examples are easy to stay focused on, since you would crash, or hit wrong notes, if your awareness wanders.

It's especially valuable — and especially effective for building Mental Muscle™ — to use tasks that do not usually occupy your mind quite so easily. That's why we recommend shaving, brushing the teeth, washing the hands (or the dishes), as excellent subjects for Living in the Now meditation.

A Living in the Now meditation can be *anything* if you focus all of your awareness onto just that one thing, so the usual chatter of the mind is momentarily stilled. No fear or desire thoughts about the future, or "could of, would of, should of" thoughts about the past.

Why is This Important?

Sure, learning to Live in the Now can make you a better athlete (athletes often call this "Playing in the Zone"). Sure, it can make you a better musician (improvisers often call this "Playing straight from the Gut"). It feels wonderful when you are doing it. As one of our favorite philosophers, Sri Nisargadatta, says, "Whatever is perceived blissfully is beautiful." Living in the Now can create a blissful sense of mindfulness wherever you are, whatever you are doing.

But there's even more to it than that. As David puts it:

"Once in a while (usually when I've been diligent about my Three Minute Meditation practice), for a few minutes or occasionally an hour at a time, life seems effortless. Whatever needs to be done gets done without planning or self-criticism. Life seems like a graceful dance or exciting game, not a race or a drudgery."

A healthy, well-cared-for body can be trusted, usually, to react quickly and naturally to the immediate physical requirements of any situation, whether they involve fighting or fleeing, sleeping deeply, or remaining awake and alert.

Likewise, a mind cleared by meditation tends to respond naturally and appropriately to the mental circumstances of the present moment, whatever those circumstances may be.

Memories of what has been done successfully in the past and plans for that next move in the future are just not so necessary when the mind is clear, allowing the meditator to live more fully In the Now.

By combining all that has come before, we can begin to live — although perhaps only for brief moments at a time — in that effortless, almost transcendent state that requires little planning, and little memory. A state in which we act without expectation of reward, and simply do what is right, what is needed. A state we call Living in the Now.

We can also begin to practice...The Master Skill.

Chapter Twenty-Six: In a Nutshell...

After you've practiced a variety of these specific Living in the Now meditations (and made up some of your own, we hope), you may be able to take this to the next level, and practice Living in the Now in a more general way. Or perhaps it's more appropriate and accurate to say that, with great luck and lots of practice, you may be graced with the experience of taking this to the next level.

> When one is able to use a Living in the Now approach to *everything* that happens (a wonderful goal, if difficult to accomplish), life becomes a dance of great and effortless beauty.
>
> It then becomes possible to see and understand the validity of the final exercise of this book, which we call The Master Skill...

Chapter Twenty-Seven: The Master Skill

On Freedom

We generally think of freedom as the ability to do whatever we want. But this type of "freedom" will always be limited, as no one can ever completely control their world. Even kings and rock stars must contend with accidents, disease, aging, pain, and other people — not to mention their own fears and angers and desires.

True freedom lies rather in the ability to allow whatever is happening, moment by changing moment, to be all right. With a state of Non-Judging and Don't Know, so that we are not forced continually to try to predict what will be, impossible as that is to know. With the ability to Soften Around Pain, so that we need not protect ourselves with anger and fear. And with Compassion for both self and others. Using every thought and event as a meditation lesson, a challenge (neither curse nor blessing).

> *We learn to build a road towards Living in the Now out of the very rocks and obstacles that appear to block our way...*

Actions Versus Outcomes

Allowing "whatever happens to be all right" does not imply passivity. We can work with zest and enthusiasm towards any goal that we decide on, or struggle powerfully to oppose that which we believe to be wrong. However, even though we direct all our energy into *actions* aimed at a particular goal, we can try to remain unattached to the eventual *outcome* or *result* of our actions.

Experiment with this. Make dinner from a new recipe. Do so carefully, but without worrying about how it comes out. Using the states of Don't Know and Non-Judging from Step Six will help you to work with this, on the level of the new recipe, or when "frying bigger fish..."

Whenever we make our happiness dependent upon specific results, we inevitably invite pain. Because although we can take responsibility for our actions, the results of our actions, the fruits of our labor, can *never* be controlled.

Recalling the meditator's view of cause and effect (page 58) may help us to realize that actions and outcomes are not as clearly or directly related as we are sometimes tempted to think.

How can we possibly expect to control anything as complex and interrelated as this crazy, mysterious world that we exist in? Thus the cultivation of Don't Know, Non-Judging, and Compassion (for ourselves and others) is far more than a philosophical exercise — it is a necessity for all of us!

The Master Skill

In our busy and status-conscious culture, it's easy to place a great deal of importance on things that happen. We judge ourselves by what we own or don't own, by what we accomplish or don't accomplish. We forget that how we *respond* to whatever happens is more important, in the long run, than the particular event that happens.

Meditation teaches us that how we respond or react to our thoughts or to the events which befall us is more important than the thoughts or events themselves. We learn to watch the process of the mind, instead of getting caught up in the content of each thought that passes through. Similarly, we begin to see that the process of learning to deal skillfully with *whatever* occurs is far more important than attempting (futilely, of course) to control the outcome or content of each particular incident in our lives.

We all possess a variety of skills, to one degree or another. There are verbal skills and athletic skills. Business skills and popularity skills. But there is one skill that's more worth cultivating than all the rest combined.

This Master Skill is the skill of being able to *use* the Three Minute Meditation techniques in all real life situations. It is more important than *any* specific event, no matter how important that particular event may seem.

In a very real way, it is more important to be able to lose the race, or the job, or the relationship *and still be compassionate and aware*, than it would be to win that race, that job, that man or woman. Because eventually there will be a race that we can't win, or a relationship that must end.

If we practice Living in the Now, with awareness of and compassion for our daily fears and desires, we can deal powerfully and effectively with whatever happens in our lives. Even painful thoughts, even unpleasant events, can be *used* to remind us of the meditative work that is our most real and important job on this earth. In this way we can turn *all* that happens, painful or pleasant, into grist for our meditative mill.

Obstacles and The Master Skill

Imagine a downhill skier who sticks to flat terrain, or a whitewater kayaker who stays only on the lake. Sure, the beginning skier starts with the "bunny slopes," and the beginning kayaker practices her basic skills in a pond, or even a swimming pool. But soon, it is the steeper slopes and the whirling rapids that both provide the reason for the sport, and improve the abilities of the athlete.

The Master Skill Visualization

Read the above chapter carefully. Think about it. *Feel* how true it is. Then, using the techniques described in the Meditation Visualization section (page 169), picture yourself involved in a situation in which the outcome is most definitely *not* what you had wished for. You didn't get the raise, or the job, or the trip to Hawaii.

Picture yourself using the skills and knowledge that you are gaining from this book, picture yourself using the specific exercises or techniques — such as Softening Around Pain — that you have learned, to handle the situation with calmness, clarity, and with compassion for yourself.

This is The Master Skill.

Chapter Twenty-Seven: In a Nutshell...

Using the Master Skill Visualization Exercise, just as you've used other visualizations throughout the book, will help you to move in the direction of living a life of mindfulness. It will help you to understand that mindfulness trumps money, trumps sex, trumps power, trumps success of any kind. For without mindfulness, even the most towering triumph is just a precipice from which one must eventually topple.

And when your efforts to be mindful fail — and you are angry, or fearful, or low on faith — *that* is when compassion is most important.

Compassion will allow you to pick yourself up and dust yourself off — as you would pick up and dust off a fallen child whom you love — then resume the most important work towards which a creature with self-awareness can aspire to, the work of mindfulness.

In a nutshell?

Mindfulness is a greater blessing than not getting something that you want is a tragedy.

Realizing this — and using that realization to motivate your mindfulness work — is The Master Skill.

The Three Minute Meditator:
What You Need to Know

In Step One, we learned how the brain and mind work. On a practical level, perhaps the most important thing we learned was how to short-circuit a Fight or a Flight Response that causes anger or fear, simply by re-focusing our attention onto the breath so as to trigger the calming Relax and Release Response. On a philosophical level, we learned how a meditator views the world that we all live in.

In Step Two, we learned a variety of meditation exercises to clear the mind, to give us a respite from fear, from anger, from desire. We learned to deal with Dead End Thoughts and Difficult People, simply by splitting our attention.

In Step Three, we learned how to watch the mind, how to see the thoughts and neural paths that swim through the depths of our mind like strange and exotic fish. By observing when and where they occur, it becomes easier to work with them, often because we can, as David puts it: "See it coming, before it hits the fan."

In Step Four, we learned how to use Visualization, Progressive Neural Desensitization (through attention splitting) and Relaxation. We apply these techniques to the thoughts and neural paths that we have learned to identify using the strategies in Step Three.

In Step Five, we embarked upon the lifelong task of learning how to Soften Around Pain. Physical pain, or mental pain. Acute pain, or chronic pain. When we no longer have to tighten around pain, and resist it, we can explore the reality, the truth of our own minds, our lives, our relationships.

In Step Six, we began to cultivate the mental states of Compassion, Non-Judging, and Don't Know. Without these, even the attempt to practice mindfulness can become just another opportunity for self-hatred, self-criticism, and unfulfilled expectation.

In Step Seven, we embarked upon the road to total freedom, with Living in the Now, and The Master Skill.

> When we learn to use the act of dealing with the obstacles in our life to build Mental Muscle™ — and to practice Softening Around Pain, Compassion, Don't Know, Non-Judging, and Living in the Now — we have spun straw into gold, and turned manure into fertilizer. Even if we can only manage this once in a while, it is truly life-enhancing, and a great and transcendent triumph.

In the Appendices Section that follows, we would like to present a short section on the most explicitly "spiritual" implications of meditation.

We'd also like to offer you a few examples of how the mindfulness techniques in *The Three Minute Meditator* can be applied to specific issues.

Appendix Number One

Further On Down the Road: The Meaning of Life, the Life of Meaning, and the Three Minute Meditation Method

In this first Appendix, we'll take a very quick look at ways of bringing *happiness* and *meaning* into individual life, and then at ways of *transcending* the individual body, brain, or sense of self — and looking at what may lie beyond. These levels have been the subject of perhaps a hundred thousand books: religious, spiritual, and philosophical. But even the minimal content of these few pages may give you a hint on some interesting directions in which to turn your mental attention, in order to explore the human experience in its full depth and glory.

Happiness and Meaning

The two words might not seem to go together, since some people would likely define happiness in a way very separate from meaning in life. Yet increasing amounts of research indicate that the elements — winning the lottery, health, sexual satisfaction — usually thought to increase happiness have little effect on that state. Instead, people who find meaning in their life — from a job, a hobby, a charitable endeavor — tend to rate themselves as happier. A growing body of literature indicates, unsurprisingly, that doing altruistic acts (on the level of five a week) makes people happier. However, the literature also indicates that writing down a few things that make you happy each day can increase your level of happiness.

What You See is What You Get

We believe that this is simply a function of what we've been saying all along — that where you focus your mental attention has a profound effect on every aspect of your life. Write down at least three things a day things that you are grateful for? This gratitude journal forces you to focus mental attention on good things, not complaints or old grudges or the ways in which the world should treat you, but doesn't. And what you focus attention on, you strengthen the neural path to. So if you spend some time each day focusing on good things, you will remember (have stronger neural path connections to) good things, and — you'll be happier.

What Can Be Done?

There is great pain and suffering in our world, and we must not deny its reality. But we can try to maximize our focus on compassionate and responsible actions (and on being grateful when appropriate), while trying to minimize our focus on excessive or un-useful violent stimuli in movies or tv (entertaining and addictive though it may be, violent media gives us little of real benefit). And as with all painful stimuli, understanding and anticipating their presence can help us to soften around them, and perhaps to help ameliorate them through volunteer work and sharing with those who have less.

There are two more things we can do. We can try to encourage benevolent cycles, rather than vicious ones, into our life. And we can try to transcend — even for a moment at a time — the limited body/brain/self that so often seems to be all that we are.

Vicious Cycles, Benevolent Cycles

We've all heard of the vicious cycle, in which two elements interact to simultaneously worsen each other. In the vicious cycle of anger and fear, anger and/or fear contracts awareness — all we can see is anger and fear. And the more tightly awareness is focused on the anger and/or fear, the more angry and/or fearful one becomes.

Fear ➜ Anger ➜ More Fear ➜ More Anger ➜ and so on

In the benevolent cycle of compassion and mindfulness, the more mindful you can be — of yourself, and of others — the easier it is to be compassionate and to soften around pain (including the pain of anger or fear). And the more compassionate you can be, the easier it is to be deeply mindful of yourself and of others.

Awareness ➜ Compassion ➜ More Awareness ➜ More Compassion ➜ Even More Awareness ➜ and so on

The State of Compassionate Awareness

In the state of compassion and understanding — as during a successful compassion breathing exercise — the heart is open, and there is no self-talk. We are conscious and aware, but the mind, for a moment, is not telling stories. There may also be an identification with all living creatures, all of whom must age and die just as we do.

Transcendent States

In the state of compassionate awareness, we move from a focus on specific states of our individual body/selves ("I am hungry, etc.") to a more generalized awareness that we might express as a sense of "I am." Just a sense of...being present, being "here." This is a state similar to that of Living in the Now — for without focus on past or future, and without the story-telling of the mind — we are not particularly identified with our individual body and personal history. We just "are."

Few people take time to think about this deeply philosophical subject — but if you are one of them, and that seems likely as you are reading this part of the appendix — you may wish to do a few Three Minute Meditations whose object is mulling the nature of the "I am" sense. A sense of "am-ness" itself can be identified, and many of us find that recognizing this am-ness provides a feeling of direct communion with God, the universal consciousness, the all-that-is. It becomes clear to us, for a moment at least, that am-ness is what connects all life. So let's consider this sense of "I Am," which seems so connected somehow to the transcendent...

I Am

Many meditators call exercises based on the following concept "the high road without rails". It is probably the most metaphysically sophisticated and least intuitively obvious style of meditation around. So read about it, think about it if you like, try it if you dare. Then, if it seems interesting, get the Sri Nisargadatta book listed in the bibliography. It's one of our two or three favorite books — we've read it a dozen times, and occasionally even think we understand a paragraph or two! Another favorite book to tackle this subject, and an easier read besides, is Stephen Levine's oft-mentioned *Who Dies*.

I Am, Therefore I Think I Am?

Consider the statements "I am happy," or "I am tired" or "I am bored." They are all statements of *temporary* validity. No one is ever permanently happy, or tired, or bored. At other times we can also validly make the negative statement "I am not happy" or "I am not tired" or "I am not bored."

But no one can *ever* truthfully make just the statement "I am not", or "I do not exist." As long as a person exists enough to say or think "I am", they just cannot honestly say, or think, "I am not." So *one* part of each statement — happy or not, bored or not — is permanently true: the *"I am"*.

Although your physical body and your intellectual makeup have probably changed significantly since you were a baby, this basic sense of "I Am" remains remarkably stable. Think back to an early childhood memory. The six-year-old that you were had a clear sense of "I Am". He or she could confidently state, "I *am* a first-grader" or "I *am* a good reader." That child's sense of "I Am" was and is the same as your sense of "I Am" right now, as you think, "I *am* a Three Minute Meditator" or "I *am* hungry."

Yet it's hard to describe the "I am" feeling, although we use it as an expression dozens of times each day. Perhaps it is easiest to identify this sensation when we awaken in the morning. Just exactly as our eyes first open, before we know where, or even who, we are — there is always a sense of (for want of a better word) "am-ness". Someone, or something, some awareness or consciousness, appears to be in the body, looking out. And this "I am" feeling is always present, unless we are in a state of dreamless sleep. In some traditions, this sense of "I am" is called "the witness."

Am-ness

This sense of existing, this sense of "am-ness" that all people possess, is the basis for a series of the most subtle and difficult but important meditations. They are important because the "I am" is, in a very real way, the connection between the small mind of the individual and the big mind of God, or the universal consciousness.

According to the meditator's worldview, the "I am" sense in your individual mind is a very small piece of consciousness that is a part of *all* consciousness, just as a tiny bay is a small, connected, part of the entire ocean. Unfortunately, we usually don't focus our attention on the "I am" feeling clearly enough to realize and perceive the connection. Our minds are too busy with the day-to-day problems and gratifications of the workaday world. We constantly focus on "I am hungry", or "I am a smart person", but never just on the "I am".

An analogy: On a windless summer night the full moon is perfectly mirrored in the still waters of the pond. But agitate the water, and the moon's tiny reflection is jumbled, broken, unrecognizable.

Eventually, as your mind begins to quiet through meditation, the agitations of thought — desires, fears, thoughts of past and future, the "I am hungry" and "I am a good golfer" — become still and quiet for short periods of time. Then, like the moon, a reflection of the universal consciousness of the Meditator's worldview begins to shine in the "I Am" of your clear mental waters. And you don't even have to believe in this, for it to happen. You just have to do it...

The "I Am Happy" — "I Am Sad"

Relax for a moment with a mind clearing meditation, and then choose two contradictory "I Am" statements, like "I am happy" and "I am sad", or "I am tired" and "I am alert".

Take one, and visualize it as clearly as possible. If you chose "I am tired", picture yourself yawning, and feel the sluggishness of your body. Then quickly visualize the other one, "I am alert". Picture yourself brimming with vigor, feeling energetic, eyes bright and watchful. Go back and forth between the two, and try to feel how neither is very "true".

Now just say "I am" to yourself, sink deep into the sense of "I am", and experience how "true" that seems. Try to observe the sensation "I am". What is it like? Is some one or some thing, some awareness, inside you, looking out? Who? Who am I?

234

The "Who Am I?" Meditation

After a moment of mind clearing, ask yourself the question "Who am I?" "Who am I *really*?" Are you your name? Your memory? Your reputation? None of these will probably seem to be you, since you can live perfectly well without any of them.

Are you your body? Perhaps, but your body can continue to exist without a mind in it. If that happened, would your mindless body still be you? You *have* a body, but your body is not you...

Ask yourself "Who asks the question, 'Who am I?'" Or even ask yourself the question "Who asks the question: "Who asks the question, 'Who am I?'"" Hello? Anybody home? Someone must be, to be asking all these questions...

This exercise can function as a koan, a Don't Know meditation. Or perhaps, like many who ask it, you will return to the Meditator's worldview, and conclude that the "I" of "Who am I?" is a piece of "recycled" consciousness, which *animates* the body that it inhabits — the "witness" of so many meditative traditions, a little bit of God.

If you like this exercise, practice it anytime, by asking questions such as "Who desires?" "Who fears?" "Who is angry?" whenever you notice a thought arising. Thinks? Who thinks?

The Life of Meaning and the Meaning of Life

Perhaps the real "meaning of life" is that our current existence on Earth gives us with the opportunity to learn that we are more than our neural paths, our personal history, our brain, our mind, our self as the object that our parents, our culture, our biology has made us.

An essential part of this task might then be to override the animal-based mind with its billion year history, by learning to consciously control our neural pathways.

Another part might be to overcome the existential pain that only humans can know — the pain that makes some close down in a vicious cycle of fear, anger, and contracted awareness — with the goal of seeking a benevolent cycle of wider and deeper compassion and awareness, in spite of all obstacles.

If this is our task, it's clear that we need to be less concerned with "things" and self-image. Rather, we need only to be aware, compassionate, people — not rich, not beautiful, not even well-liked by others — although being sincerely cherished by others is more likely to happen if we are aware and compassionate.

Aware and compassionate humans are also more likely to treat the Earth that bears us with care and respect. More likely to be generous with and protective of the most vulnerable members of our race: the very old and the young. More likely to face the great challenges of our awful and awe-full world with joy and humor rather than with despair and bitterness.

These goals are only possible if we are able to relate to the brain not as a tyrant, but as a wonderful servant, who supports us in our mission, instead of forcing us to waste our precious time, energy and resources on unimportant or counter-productive old pathways, traveled by habit instead of choice.

Appendix Number Two

The Second of Two Secrets About *The Secret*

As we said earlier (on page 171), we appreciate the fact that many readers who might otherwise never have considered the awesome power of thought in our lives have been exposed to that concept by *The Secret*. However, we do have two concerns about this entertaining and enormously popular book.

The first, as we mentioned, is that *The Secret*, while promoting the efficacy of Visualization, does not provide a method by which the reader can build the Mental Muscle™ necessary to achieve a powerful visualization ability.

The second is that, in our opinion, while it is obviously important to take care of oneself and one's needs (starting with the need for mindfulness), *The Secret* tends to emphasize material acquisition of money, homes, cars, careers, or the ideal mate. In these days of individual, national, and planetary disturbance, it might be skillful to consider others along with ourselves. Visualizing world peace, environmental healing, and resources adequate for each individual may be a way to encourage the Universe to provide for all beings.

> We believe that by cultivating mindfulness and compassion, we create a Benevolent Cycle that benefits the Universe. And by doing so, benefits us as well...

More Appendices

We have a great deal of written material detailing ways in which the Three Minute Meditation techniques can be applied to a variety of specific (and usually problematic) issues.

But in the interests of keeping the heft of this book less than that of your average Gutenberg Bible, we are only including a few such issues: Using Mindfulness on Food and Dieting, and short comments on New Parents, Therapists and Clients, and Ageless Aging.

Using Mindfulness on Food And Dieting

Our society gives us many mixed messages about food. We use food to give ourselves love by eating exotic chocolates, tantalizing treats and tempting tidbits.

For some of us, getting "treats" from a parent was one of the few clear and unambiguous signs of love and caring we received. Yet we also punish ourselves and use food and body image to withhold self-approval, with crash diets and lifelong obsessions about those few extra pounds of flab.

We pay lots of attention to what we eat, but little to how we feel while we eat. Often we avoid our feelings entirely while eating, or *by* eating. We do this by eating and conversing in the company of others, and when alone will eat while reading, or in front of the television set.

Or, we may stuff ourselves compulsively without even tasting the food. Standing in front of the fridge and "grazing" is, unfortunately, a classic way to avoid all kinds of feelings and obligations (to oneself, and to others).

The Eating Meditation

A conscious focus of attention on feelings and sensations while eating can be a most powerful experience. Someday, perhaps when eating by yourself, try this "Conscious Eating" meditation.

• Once your food is in front of you, spend a moment with a mind clearing exercise, perhaps one of the breath-based meditations.

• Then, slowly, begin to eat. Focus your attention on each part of the eating process, lifting the fork or spoon, choosing which forkful of food to pick up, lifting the food to your mouth, placing the food into your mouth, lowering the fork, chewing the food and noticing the taste, swallowing the food, and then lifting the fork once again.

• If you like, label each action, as you did in the Slow Walking Meditation: lifting, choosing, lifting, placing, lowering, chewing, tasting and swallowing. If other labels seem more appropriate to you, by all means use your own.

• Perhaps you would prefer to concentrate on how each action feels, rather than labeling them, as you did in the walking and breathing Living in the Now meditations.

• Simply slow down and concentrate on your eating. Some people find that this is easier to do if they hold their fork in the hand that they don't usually use, as this will increase concentration on the hand.

• Notice the sensation of metal against mouth, the muscular actions involved in lifting, chewing, swallowing. Feel each motion of your tongue, your lips, your throat. Concentrate on the texture and taste of each type of food. Be as specific as possible in your investigation. Do the skins of peas taste different from the insides? How close to your mouth is the food before you smell it? What else can you notice? As usual, be aware of thoughts as they arise in the mind, and then return your attention to your food.

David often notices a desire to choose and lift the next forkful before he's done swallowing the one in his mouth. This desire is then usually followed by a guilty thought about greediness. If similar thoughts occur to you, note them, perhaps label them ("aha, there's greed..." or "oh, there's self-criticism about my weight"), then let them pass, and return mindfully to your dinner.

Eating and Compassion

If sad or lonely thoughts (especially around eating alone) come to you, as they may do in the course of this meditation, a moment of Compassion Exercise or Compassion Breath may well be in order.

David realized, over time and with some applied mindfulness, that the reason he usually reads when he is alone and eating is to avoid feelings of loneliness that arise for him when eating alone. He now, when on the road, sometimes consciously eschews book or newspaper at dinner, and simply experiences both his food, and his feelings...

Feed a Friend

An interesting duo exercise for friends or couples is to take turns feeding each other, while silently focusing on physical or mental sensations. For some, this brings up compassionate feelings for the feeder, and vulnerable or infantile feelings for the one being fed.

Meditations on Hunger

For many of us, food is more than sustenance or simple nutrition. It can be a companion, friend, painkiller, or enemy. For women, especially, the act of eating may be an experience that goes beyond hunger, into the realm of desires, needs, and fears. And of course meditation is the most effective method of dealing with such feelings.

After a long day at work, when she needs to feel self-nurtured, Nina can find herself mistaking the sensation of fatigue for the sensation of hunger. Instead of going to bed, or to a hot relaxing bath, she eats.

The following exercises deal with hunger and food — and can be very effective in understanding what is *really* going on inside.

The Hunger Scan

Have you ever found yourself eating when you weren't really hungry? Eating to avoid work? To stuff down feelings? Out of boredom, or tiredness perhaps? If so, this meditation may help you to better understand why you eat, when you eat.

We'll start by doing a "body scan" meditation. Try doing this meditation while you're eating to help get you in touch with sensations of hunger and fullness, or satiation.

To do this exercise, choose a snack or meal during which you won't feel rushed. And, at least for the first time, we suggest you try this when eating alone or with a friend who'll also try it, or who will at least respect your need to focus within.

• Before you begin, spend a moment or two with your favorite mind clearing meditation, and relax your body.

• Then focus on the sensation of hunger, asking yourself "How hungry do I feel right now?"

• Explore your hunger, by labeling it. Do you feel "just a little hungry?" Not hungry at all? Moderately hungry? Ravenously hungry?

• After you've begun to eat, continue to check your sensation of hunger every one or two minutes. Does it change during the course of the meal? How full are you? Comfortably full? Very full? Absolutely stuffed? How does that feel?

Doing this mini-meditation for even a few seconds at the beginning, middle and towards the end of a meal will help focus your consciousness on your degree of satiation, help you realize when you're hungry, and when you're full. It's also interesting and important to realize how much of our food may be ingested out of "greed", avoidance, sociability, or for other reasons, and not out of "need," not out of real hunger.

It can be useful to study the continuum between totally empty and totally full, between "Ravenously Hungry " and "Absolutely Stuffed." Think about these levels of hunger when you are neither eating nor hungry: can you recreate, visualize, how each of them feel? Doing this may help you to access these labels while you're eating.

Once you've begun to be more aware of your level of fullness or emptiness, you may find it easier to avoid extremes of undereating or overeating, by making time to eat before you are Ravenously Hungry, and stopping before you become Absolutely Stuffed.

Labeling Types Of Hunger

If we can become more aware of our sensations around hunger, and at the same time watch our thoughts, we'll notice that there are many types of hunger. Sometimes hunger seems to be at a "panic" level — we feel we have to eat or we'll starve! Hunger sometimes feels "picky" — we're not really hungry, but we'll happily graze if the food smells/looks/tastes appealing.

Hunger may also be "compulsive" — when we start eating to avoid certain feelings, thoughts or activities but are not really hungry, or perhaps when we start but just can't seem to stop. "Cued" hunger occurs after we've just seen an advertisement or some other cue that "reminds" us to be hungry — in other words, a trigger event has started a neural chain that ends in…eating. Occasionally, we may even find ourselves eating out of "normal" hunger — simply eating to gain energy and ready to dig in and really enjoy the food.

Hunger And Compassion

If you do this exercise, and find yourself unwilling to stop eating even though it feels "compulsive," you may feel self-hate beginning to creep in. If so, just return to the Compassion exercise (page 205) or one of the Compassion Breaths (pages 200 and 201) and remember to be gentle with yourself.

As we've said so many times, the Master Skill of being able to use meditative techniques skillfully in difficult times is far more valuable than having things go the way you want them to go. Better to apply compassion when you're gorging, than to be svelte and self-hating…

There's Dieting…

Nowhere is this more true than as concerns dieting. Treat yourself with loving acceptance and compassion, whether or not your figure or your eating behavior meets the standards that you set for yourself (or the standards set by Madison Avenue). If it seems to be hard to allow yourself to be compassionate, just remember: Compassion will get you through the absence of slimness better than slimness will get you through the absence of compassion. Because without loving self-acceptance and compassion, you can *never* be slim enough. Or rich enough. Or famous enough…

Our culture's relentless focus on women's bodies and thinness makes it difficult to stay in touch with a realistic body image. Many women diet on and off throughout their lives, sometimes compulsively, with greater or lesser degrees of "success."

We feel the pain of denying our body sense, ignoring our hunger. Unfortunately, the more hunger is denied, the more it attempts to creep in around the edges.

Compulsive little nibbles...eating past satiety...lusting after the forbidden foods… are all signs that a relationship to food is out-of-whack. The above meditations helped Nina get back in touch with her body's ability to know what it needs in terms of food. But even more important than eating "correctly" is the ability to apply compassion to feelings about food and eating.

Dietary "success" can more skillfully be defined in terms of health and self-acceptance than in terms of conforming to unrealistic (and perhaps misogynistic) advertising images. If Nina starts to feel compulsive around food and ends up making eating choices that she regrets the next day, she's now more able to notice and clear away that old self-hating mental chatter, replace it with compassion, and start anew in the Now. That's worth a lifetime of dieting. And as David points out, if people like or don't like you for your body, that's more a reflection on their lack of depth and brainwashing by the media, than on your clothing size!

And There's "Never Diet Again"...!

Understanding why we eat will help us work with our eating patterns. Applying mindfulness to our eating behavior and the thoughts that surround it can break through a lifetime of pain, restriction, and control around food.

> Nina's program, Never Diet Again: Welcoming Weight Loss and Wellness, offers tools and techniques that *real* people can apply in their *real* lives to make *real* changes. (Please note that www.mohonk.com/spa has more information on this program.)

New Parents

Children can provide a delightful and challenging focus for your attention. The Shared Breath meditation is an easy way to use your child as an object of meditation, and older kids will enjoy returning the favor (simply ask them to watch closely, and breathe with you). A great variety of just listening or just looking meditations can be fun, too.

Meditative Listening can be a great way to hear what a child is really saying, and the sections on Acceptance, "Don't Know", and Softening Around Pain have obvious applications (especially for parents of teens and pre-teens).

Infants can really help us to focus on the present, as they always live in the Now. They can be perfectly happy and content one moment (or even one second), and then crying piteously the next, or vice versa, all for reasons entirely obscure to you. So if you want to relate to them, you just have to meet their moods instant by instant.

When they are crying and miserable, you can't let the fact that they were completely ecstatic only a minute ago affect your response to their condition now (rather like the sweat lodge is too hot, then the river too cold, in the Cold Shower Softening Around Pain Meditation)! And you impair your own ability to enjoy them if you let the crankiness of a few seconds past interfere with your reaction to their blindingly joyful now.

And consider this: the times that they are most acutely miserable are exactly the times when they need compassion the most — and (especially at 3 AM) exactly the times that compassion may be least available to us.

Perhaps we can learn from this to provide compassion to ourselves also during those very times when it is most needed, and all too often least available.

Therapists and Those In Therapy

An increasing number of therapists are incorporating meditation into their work with clients. Some of them are using *The Three Minute Meditator,* and similar books, and obviously David's combination of meditation and cognitive behavioral science — in the form of Neural Path Therapy — is a prime example of this complementary trend.

There are two main ways in which mindfulness can be used to facilitate therapy. The therapists themselves can meditate, and the clients can meditate in order to "supercharge" their therapy.

We believe that a meditation practice can increase a therapist's efficacy by helping to keep their attention focused on the client and by developing a non-judgmental attitude. It may be that the cultivation of compassion (an essential meditation skill) has the most impact on the relationship between client and therapist; many genres of psychotherapy are based exactly on this unconditional regard and "transference" between the two.

And interestingly enough, the father of modern psychotherapy (like it or not), Sigmund Freud, recommended for the therapist a mental state that he referred to as "evenly suspended attention". As he put it, "(the therapist) should simply listen, and not bother about whether he is keeping anything in mind."

In the past, when David worked with clients, he often found himself planning what he was going to say to a client while they were talking. Although he mostly now works with groups ranging from a few dozen to a few thousand, in his *pro bono* hospice work meditation has helped him to become more present while with a client, because he can "just listen" (with or without a breath focus).

At first, he used to worry that if he didn't think while the client was speaking, he wouldn't have "anything helpful to offer" when it was his turn to speak. Now he's realize that not only are his insights and suggestions clearer when less time is spent planning responses (as in a Living in the Now state), but that the entire idea of "fixing things" for clients is erroneous. The goal is to create a space in which an "I-Thou" relationship can blossom, and not to "help" clients, but to help them to help themselves.

The benefits of meditation for the client are equally clearcut. Mind-clearing meditations help to allow previously unconscious material to rise towards the surface while Softening Around Pain techniques minimize the denial that can block the process, and the pain which it often brings at first. The ability to understand motivation and defense mechanisms is facilitated by working with the thought watching exercises, and, of course, by learning to look at them in terms of neural paths.

Lastly, the progressive investment in the meditative worldview can provide a context for softening the estrangement and isolation that many of us feel.

A Few Words on...Ageless Aging

In a culture which trumpets that "60 is the new 40," it's hard to feel good about aging. While years of life experience bring valuable insight, they also bring wrinkles and the need to slow down a little... and many baby boomers are determined not to give in to either!

However, change is a certainty in life (one of the only things that is!) and being able to handle change skillfully is an ability that is age-less.

Remember the years from age 10 to age 20? It was a ten-year span in which you changed dramatically, from child to young adult. The years from 30 to 40, or from 40 to 50 show much less visible signs of change. Yet, the process of maturing continues, for better or worse.

Becoming able to Watch the Mind as change occurs and feel compassion for any fear or anger, sense of loss or sadness that may ensue — is truly part of the Master Skill.

Softening around change by using Compassion meditations and opening to the Don't Know aspects of Living in the Now can create a space in which we continue to gain insight.

Living joy-fully and lovingly one moment at a time is not contingent upon age or energy or looks or body size. Being dynamic, vital, interested, and alive is an age-less opportunity. It's simply the *choice* to be mindfully present and to use skills that are available to clear the mind, watch the mind, and be compassionate with the mind — one moment at a time.

About the Authors

Nina Smiley, Ph.D.

If you knew there were something you could do that would enhance your life significantly and would take only minutes at a time — you'd probably be interested. Most likely, very interested! The practice of mindfulness and *The Three Minute Meditator* techniques do exactly that. And Nina delights in sharing these concepts and techniques with others!

Working at Mohonk Mountain House, a remarkable Victorian castle resort in the Hudson Valley (only 90 miles north of NYC), Nina directs mindfulness programming and offers private one-on-one sessions in person and by phone — coaching individuals in how to apply simple and effective mindfulness techniques to real life issues and interactions. From improving family and workplace relationships to reducing stress and creating healthful new habits, applied mindfulness works to change lives one moment at a time.

Nina's work on mindfulness, along with its effective application to food, weight, and diet issues (Never Diet Again: Welcoming Weight Loss and Wellness) has been seen in *O, The Oprah Magazine, Real Simple, Martha Stewart Living, Marie Claire,* and *Shape* magazines and on the *Discovery Health Channel.* Her Never Diet Again program was named by *thetravelchannel.com* as one of their "life changing trips."

Nina received her undergraduate degree from Vassar College and a Ph.D. in psychology from Princeton University. She was Associate Director of Research at Porter/Novelli, a marketing and public relations firm in Washington, DC, before bringing her skills to Mohonk Mountain House — a resort which has been in the Smiley family since 1869 — where she serves as Director of Marketing. Offering visitors the opportunity to experience "recreation and renewal of body, mind, and spirit in a beautiful natural setting" has been the long-standing mission of Mohonk Mountain House and Nina embraces this vision wholeheartedly.

Understanding the stressors endemic in this fast-paced world, Nina recognizes the importance of actively seeking wellness in everyday life. She works with the award-winning Spa at Mohonk Mountain House (www.mohonk.com — ranked the Number One Spa in the United States by readers of *Condé Nast Traveler* magazine) to put forth *Solutions for Modern Living*. These spa treatments have been designed specifically to relax and relieve tension and to enhance wellness with treatments aimed directly at real-life woes, including Attainable Sleep, The Texting Tension Tamer, Breathe Deep and Be Well, and more.

REDUCE STRESS. CONTROL FEAR. DIMINISH ANGER.
IN ALMOST NO TIME AT ALL. ANYWHERE. ANYTIME.

The Three Minute
MEDITATOR

New
Audio CD!

BY NINA SMILEY, Ph.D. AND DAVID HARP, M.A.
CO-AUTHORS OF THE THREE MINUTE MEDITATOR
AS FEATURED IN THE SPA AT MOHONK MOUNTAIN HOUSE

Nina is co-author, with her beloved twin brother David Harp, of two books on meditation and mindfulness (*MetaPhysical Fitness*, minds i press, 1989; *The Three Minute Meditator,* minds i press, 2007). She is also the main force behind *The Three Minute Meditator's* companion CD.

David Harp, M.A.

As you may have guessed from comments interspersed throughout this book, much of David's work involves speaking to a wide variety of

corporate, non-profit, governmental, medical, hospice, mindfulness, and yoga groups. Since a near-death-out-of-body experience while an undergrad at Wesleyan University, he's been fascinated by that amorphous intersection between brain, body, mind, and soul.

Although David's academic experience began with experimental social psychology and continued, in graduate school, with applied cognitive behavioral science, he soon began to integrate two additional disciplines into his psycho-therapeutic interests.

The first of these disciplines was mindfulness. During a time of great personal turmoil, he "fell into" a ten day meditation retreat — something he'd never even considered trying — led by Stephen Levine and Jack Kornfield. On the fifth day of the mostly silent retreat, David suddenly realized the nature of his own mind (and it was *not* a pretty sight!). From that moment his mission became to further explore "that mysterious and mutinous entity known as the human mind." He had the great good fortune to be accepted after the retreat by Dr. Kornfield as a private client, and his work began.

If David's mission involved the mind, his passion was for the blues harmonica. Starting out in college as the world's worst player ("other

musicians would run and hide if they saw me coming"), he has become, in addition to his speaking career and writing close to two dozen books, America's best-known harmonica teacher, with over one million students to his credit, and the holder of the undisputed world's record for "Most People Taught to Play Blues Harmonica at One Time" (2,569 participants — but he'd "like to do a big one soon").

David's Presentations

Combining his mission and his passion, he now uses the humble blues harmonica as a tool for teaching mindfulness, stress reduction, team-building, communication, creativity and change management to groups  including Kraft Foods, Ben & Jerry's, the FBI, Merck, the Red Cross, Blue Cross, Easter Seals, and ComCast, and has worked with many more groups in the US, Canada, Europe, South America, and Australia. David also teaches his Harmonica-Based Mindfulness™ and HarmonicaYoga™ programs at The Kripalu Center in MA, and the New York Open Center.

While teaching mindfulness — quite literally — through the harmonica might sound strange to those who have not read this book, the use of breath focus to short-circuit the fight or flight response has been a theme throughout these pages. And there is no easier or more entertaining way to introduce a group to the benefits of breathing meditation than teaching them a great sounding blues/rock solo — which David guarantees he can do for any group, of any size, *within three minutes* (yes, he does like that "three minute timeframe")!

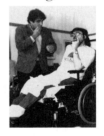

David also does one-on-one coaching and training, and small group work by phone and Skype™ on mindfulness, working with issues of grief and illness, and, naturally, harmonica.

David's volunteer work is mostly for hospice, and he lives in rural Vermont with his wife, children, and pets. His writing and group presentations help to subsidize his *pro bono* endeavors. So if you'd like to learn more about David's work, please visit his websites:

DavidHarp.com for general information.

HarmonicaBasedStressReduction.com for corporate/group events.

HarmonicaBasedMindfulness.com and **HarmonicaYoga.com**
    For, well, just what you'd expect…

BluesHarp.com for David's music instruction methods, and

AdaptiveMusic.net for his work with people with disabilities.

250

Bibliography: Recommended Reading

Benson, Herbert. *The Relaxation Response* (Morrow, 1975)

Becker, Ernest. *The Denial of Death* (Simon & Schuster, 1973)

Borysenko, Joan. *Minding the Body, Mending the Mind* (Bantam, 1988)

Borysenko, Joan. *Guilt Is the Teacher, Love Is the Lesson* (Warner, 1990)

Buber, Martin. *I and Thou* (Touchstone, 1970)

Chödrön, Pema. *When Things Fall Apart* (Shambhala, 1997)

Csikszentmihalyi, Mihaly. *Flow* (Harper, 1990)

Eccles, John C. *Evolution of the Brain* (Routledge, 1996)

Garfield, Charles. *Peak Performance* (Tarcher, 1984)

Goleman, Daniel. *Emotional Intelligence* (Bantam, 1995)

Hanh, Thich Nhat. *The Miracle of Mindfulness* (Beacon Press 1976)

Hanh, Thich Nhat. *Being Peace* (Parallax Press, 1987)

Harp, David, and McKay, Matthew. *Neural Path Therapy:*
   How to Change Your Brain's Response to Anger, Fear, Pain, and Desire
   (New Harbinger, 2005)

Harp, David. *Three Minutes to Blues, Rock, & Folk Harmonica, 3rd Edition*
   (musical i press, 2007)

Harp, David. *Mindfulness To Go: How to Meditate While You're On The Move*
   (New Harbinger, 2011)

Johnston, William (Edited by). *The Cloud of Unknowing* (Image Book, 1976)

Jack Kornfeld, and Goldstein, Joseph. *Seeking the Heart of Wisdom:*
   The Path of Insight Meditation (Shambhala, 1987)

Kornfield, Jack. *A Path with Heart* (Bantam Books, 1993)

Kornfield, Jack. *After The Ecstasy, The Laundry* (Random House, 2001)

Levine, Stephen. *A Gradual Awakening* (Anchor/Doubleday, 1979)

Levine, Stephen and Ondrea. *Who Dies* (Anchor/Doubleday, 1982)

Levine, Stephen and Ondrea. *A Year to Live* (Bell Tower, 1997)

Mitchell, Stephen. *Tao Te Ching* (Harper and Row, 1988)

Moore, Thomas. *Care of the Soul* (HarperCollins, 1992)

Pelletier, Kenneth. *Mind as Healer, Mind as Slayer* (Delta/Lawrence, 1977)

Ram, Dass. *The Only Dance There Is* (Anchor, 1974)

Selye, Hans. *Stress Without Distress* (Lippincott, 1974)

Siegel, Bernie. *Love, Medicine and Miracles* (Harper and Row, 1986)

Smiley, Nina, and Harp, David. Illustrations: Robert Crumb.
   MetaPhysical Fitness (mind's i press, 1989)

Sri Nisargadatta, and Maurice Frydman. *I Am That* (Acorn Press, 1973).

Suzuki, Shunryu. *Zen Mind, Beginner's Mind* (Weatherhill, 1970)

Trungpa, Chögyam. *Shambhala: Sacred Path of the Warrior* (Shambhala, 1984)

Watts, Alan. *The Way of Zen* (Vintage/Pantheon, 1957)

The Three Minute
MEDITATOR

REDUCE STRESS. CONTROL FEAR. DIMINISH ANGER.
IN ALMOST NO TIME AT ALL. ANYWHERE. ANYTIME.

DAVID HARP AND NINA SMILEY, Ph.D.

Please visit us at
our websites!

To see where Nina Lives and Works:
www.mohonk.com

For information on David's Work:

www.davidharp.com

And... www.thethreeminutemeditator.com